CRAGS, EDDIES & RIPRAP

The
Sound Country
Memoir of

Wolf Bauer

CRAGS, EDDIES & RIPRAP

The Sound Country Memoir of
Wolf Bauer

Wolf Bauer and Lynn Hyde

NORTHWEST PASSAGE PRESS

Seattle

PUBLISHED BY
Northwest Passage Press
Seattle, Washington

DESIGNED AND PRODUCED BY
Boulder Bookworks LLC, Boulder, Colorado USA
www.boulderbookworks.com

PHOTOGRAPHIC IMAGES
All photos are couresy of Wolf Bauer, unless otherwise noted.
We acknowledge the contribution of photos from the Spring Trail Trust, www.springtrailtrust.org.

COVER IMAGE
Wolf Bauer, 1934, models the latest in climbing attire.
PHOTO BY OTHELLO PHIL DICKERT.

First Edition

ISBN: 978-0-615-33353-3

Printed in the United States of America

"Be ashamed to die until you have won some victory for humanity."

HORACE MANN

CONTENTS

INTRODUCTION

O N SUNDAY, SEPTEMBER 13, 1927, a German boy of fifteen clambered into his family's sailing dinghy in Kirkland, Washington, and set a solo course westward across the gray-blue waters of Lake Washington. His mother, a third generation descendant of Seattle's pioneer Epler family, waved him off with little reason for concern. He was the son of a captain in Kaiser Wilhelm's Navy—the man who first charted the world's ocean tides. Hubert Bauer had equipped the skiff with a deliberately small sail to keep his eldest child from straying too far, but on that day, for a reason long forgotten, Wolf chose to row the entire way. His mother felt little fear at the boy's departure.

In 1917, during World War I, when Wolf was five, his father had hoped to smuggle him aboard the German minesweeper under his command in the North Sea. But his mother had a last-minute premonition that forestalled the outing and kept him home. Her instinct proved true: Wolf's father and three other men were the only survivors of that excursion. The vessel hit a friendly mine and the ship sank in a matter of minutes, drowning most of the crew.

Yet on that day in 1927, untroubled by foreboding, Wolf's mother watched her son leave on his own youthful mission: to watch Charles "Lucky" Lindbergh land the *Spirit of St. Louis* at Sand Point Naval Air Station in Seattle.

Up until his arrival in the United States in 1925, young Wolf Bauer's hero had been (as for many Bavarian boys of his generation) Andreas Hofer, a Tyrolean freedom fighter resisting the forces of Napoleon in 1810. Legend holds that when Hofer was about to be executed by a French firing squad, he refused a blindfold; he wished to see his mountains and his people to the last. He opened his shirt to expose a better target, and insisted upon giving the command to fire himself. Not killed instantly, his last words were, "How poorly you shoot...."[1]

It is a jaded soul who does not appreciate the cinematic impact of that scene. But there is likewise a happy resonance in the image of the fair-haired, blue-eyed Wolf Bauer, at the helm of his own ship, steering towards history-in-the-making, to see his new *living* hero, the first man to fly solo nonstop across the Atlantic Ocean.

Everyone knew that Lindbergh would land at Sand Point and then embark on the yacht *Alarwee*, docked at the airfield, which would take him on to speeches and parades in Husky Stadium and downtown Seattle. So Wolf strategically guided his skiff to the very same dock and watched breathlessly as the plane approached. Because of the large fuel tank on the front of the plane, Lucky Lindy had to circle the field twice and sideslip onto the airstrip.

"I watched the whole thing," Wolf would beam nearly eighty years later, with traces of accent still in his speech. "He was such a great pilot, you know. And when he came to get on the yacht, he walked *right by me*. I bragged to the kids in school the next day, 'I could have reached out and *touched* him!'" And the devilish grin he wears in telling the story is undoubtedly unchanged from that happy day in 1927. There is something in Wolfgang Bauer that has simply refused to age.

But as Wolf tells the story, there is no sense that there are five thousand people at the field waiting in relentless rain. Nor that the waters around the site are teeming with boats, and that the Coast Guard is enforcing nautical crowd control, keeping the boats at bay. Conspicuous by its absence is the sail-less strategy that enabled the boy to slip unnoticed through the blockade. Wolf fails to mention that the crowd faced south in anticipation of Lucky's arrival, but that the flyer snuck up behind from the north, giving rise to an orchestra of sirens and cheers. There is no mention, as the Seattle Post-Intelligencer reporter made, that Lindbergh looked tired, was quiet, and offered no smiles for the camera.[2]

Wolf was focused on something else, something more mythological: a spark, a flash, a dot-dot-dash of whatever vision and drive made Lindbergh great. It was a moment for the boy and the aviator. Everyone else was just background static.

Wolf Bauer may not have achieved the world renown of Hofer or Lindbergh, but in his own quiet way, he *has* become a hero for legions of outdoorsmen and conservationists in the Pacific Northwest. Anyone who has strapped on a pair of downhill skis, rappelled down the face of a mountain or fastened a spray skirt over a kayak in this part of the country owes a debt of gratitude to Wolf. Anyone who walks today because of the Seattle Mountain Rescue Council owes thanks to Wolf. And anyone who frequents public beaches, or values the glorious undammed and undeveloped beauty of the Green River Gorge in western Washington, can place a blessing on the head of Wolf Bauer. A pioneering outdoorsman and shoreline ecologist, Wolf's legacy touches everyone who lives in the Northwest, whether they recognize his name or not.

—⟨⟨⟨⟨⟨∫⟩⟩⟩⟩⟩—

I FIRST STARTED HEARING WOLF BAUER'S NAME bandied around at the turn of the current century. As a member of The Mountaineers, Washington State's oldest and largest outdoors and conservation club, I kept hearing Wolf's name connected to disparate arenas. There was the Wolf Bauer whose ski racing team set the course record for the grueling and famous Ski Patrol Race of the 1930s. There was the Wolf Bauer who made the first summit of Mount Rainier from the north side, up Ptarmigan Ridge. There was the Wolf Bauer who founded the club's pivotal climbing program and taught world-renowned mountaineers Jim and Lou Whittaker how to climb. A certain Wolf Bauer introduced "foldboating" and started up what was to become the Washington Kayak Club. Then there was that Bauer guy who helped start the Mountain Rescue Council, one of the first organized mountain rescue groups in the United States. Were these Wolf Bauers really all the same guy?

Well, yes, they were. But that was just Wolf having fun. When the clock was ticking, he had another life. As an engineer in a kayak, Wolf began to study river hydrology and shoreline ecology from the water. For fun, he charted all the rivers in western Washington for recreational navigability. By the time he was done, he was on the way to developing standards of shoreline management that revolutionized local governments, both stateside and in British Columbia. His then-revolutionary ideas were the basis for Washington State's

Shoreline Management Act of 1972. More visible to the public are the thirty-plus "Bauer Beaches"—public parks designed and restored by Wolf to better accommodate both man and wildlife.

When future Governor Dixy Lee Ray wanted to put the Seattle Aquarium at the recreational hot spot Golden Gardens, somebody had to show her it was better to restore the wetlands and waterfront habitat and put the attraction somewhere else. Wolf took on Dixy Lee. When he wasn't able to save Dunn Canyon on the Cowlitz River from being inundated by a dam, he set his sights on saving the glorious sandstone Green River Gorge from development. And to put the icing on the cake, Wolf wrote lyrical poetry about life in the outdoors. All this packed into a five-foot-nine-inch son of a sea captain, half his blood running straight and true from Seattle's earliest pioneers, and half of it running from loyal sons of the Kaiser, laced liberally with Bavarian snowmelt. Wolf is, indeed, our Yankee Strudel Dandy.

Wolf has spent his near-century of life as a conduit, as a bridge—bringing European ideas about safety and the enjoyment of the outdoors to the American Northwest. He regales us, across generations, with tales of times long gone by. In listening to his stories, we can find the treasured time capsules of a different life, as well as an inspiration to hold on to the best natural and social legacies of our past.

Being an engineer, Wolf tells his stories in neat units, dispensing lessons with unflagging humor. Modest, yet aware his yarns are good ones, he has agreed to let me present his memories to posterity. But I would never dream of narrating Wolf's life. His wonderful and unique voice is strong and engaging; you will "hear" the twinkle in his eye without any help from me. When he speaks, imagine you are listening as I did—not sitting in a chair for hours with a tape recorder, but trying to keep up with him on the wooded trails around Anacortes, Washington. He tells his stories on the fly, powering up the hills, passing uninitiated dawdlers, pointing out the beauty of every vista as well as its geologic history. If pressed, he will confess to a touch of arthritis in one hip, but you will work to keep up anyway. He will engage every pedestrian, cyclist and canine he encounters, but you will still be back in time for the Early Bird Special.

As the co-writer of his biography, I will try to craft those tales into a larger single story, sharing insights about how Wolf came to be Wolf—insights that might require the perspective of distance, angles that might surprise even Wolf himself. I will endeavor to offer you a look at the forest, while Wolf tackles the business of describing his trees. Together, we hope you will find a marvelous landscape.

It has been a privilege to listen to and learn from Wolf Bauer, and it is an honor to help him bring his story to light. On behalf of the people of the Northwest, thanks, Wolf!

LYNN HYDE
Seattle, Washington
March 2009

PREFACE

A COUPLE OF YEARS AGO I was encouraged by members of The Mountaineers' History Committee to write about my life experiences, especially in terms of historic activities dear to the club. I suddenly realized that they had pegged me—*oh, no!*—as the guy with the longest club membership—eighty years.

Giving me that task with tongue-in-cheek, they nevertheless, on second thought, appointed a co-author who would keep me "in line," and would look at my life story from a fresh perspective. Thus Lynn Hyde, an enthusiastic member involved in numerous club activities, took me under her wing. Not only did she breathe new life and enthusiasm into my writing, but she also made me realize the importance of judging life situations through the eyes of other generations. This story can have a dual role— explaining the past in order to plan and guide the future.

As I literally "took pen in hand," jotting down enough memories to fill a book, I soon realized that I have a personal life and also a public life. While the former would be of interest to family members and friends, my public contributions would serve a much wider readership in terms of background and historic value. As one gets older and more philosophical about life, one also has to reluctantly admit to periods of selfishness. It is all very complimentary to be tagged a pioneer in the development of some outdoor sports in our Pacific Northwest, but in the final analysis, those activities allowed me to continue boyhood pastimes observed and learned in the Alps. Introducing and developing the kayaking sport in a landscape of ideal river and island-studded waters became, for me, a consuming discovery. That it eventually led to a second career in the new environmental field certainly proved to be a surprise and a challenge. My scholastic emphasis in engineering and geology now offered belated opportunities. It was an opportune time to develop environment-friendly solutions to river and coastal flooding and erosion problems that would be accepted by the general public and involved governmental agencies. I had found an exciting and rewarding career that allowed me to contribute to the common good. While my bread and butter first came from a demanding engineering career, environmental spearheading became a final love affair. How lucky can you get?

WOLF BAUER
Anacortes, Washington
March 2009

PART I

Germany

ONE

The Bauers of Bavaria

W HEN WOLF BAUER TELLS THE STORIES of his boyhood in
Germany, it is easy to forget that World War I had broken out
when he was two years old, and that the war and its aftermath set
the stage for the troubles of every adult around him. His father was
drawn fully into the war effort soon after its inception, and the post-
war depression ultimately drove the family in search of better
prospects outside of Germany. But there is little trace of the negative fallout of those times in his reminiscences. As a boy, and
throughout his life, there was adventure and learning to be had
everywhere he turned. If the dark shadows of fear and uncertainty
hung over the family in those times, Wolf neatly filtered them out
of his memories. Optimism is one of his defining characteristics. He
is even optimistic about the past.

Wolf was born in 1912, the eldest of five children of Hubert and
Elsbeth Bauer. Over the next twelve years he would be followed by
sister Mabel ("Friedl"), brothers Hubert ("Hugh") and Dietrich
("Dick"), and eventually sister Brigitta ("Gita"). Wolf's father,
Hubert, was the youngest of thirteen children in a comfortable
German family. Their father was a successful attorney. Hubert was a
brilliant man, who spoke seven languages and, as Wolf recounts,
was "crackerjack in math," a mixed blessing when it came to helping Wolf with difficult homework. A highly educated adventurer,

his academic specialty was economic geography. After university, Hubert enrolled in a three-year merchant marine program, during which time the mariner was once shipwrecked off of Cape Horn in a three-masted schooner. Undaunted, he became a second officer for the North German Lloyd Line, a position that led to his automatic conscription into the Navy during World War I. Years later, in 1930, he would become the first person to earn a doctorate in economic geography from the University of Washington, and he would become the first man to map the world's tidal currents.[3]

Though once a Catholic altar boy, Hubert became, like many scientists, a "private skeptic of all forms of the supernatural," as Wolf puts it. On principle, he wanted to let his children decide questions of faith for themselves, but he could not help remarking that any belief system that coerced adherence with threats of eternal damnation was little more than an extortion racket.

"Enthusiastic as hell," according to his son, Hubert enjoyed life fully. An accomplished photographer, he taught Wolf how to develop photographs and how to enlarge, dodge, and burn them. Wolf's boyhood friend in Bavaria, Richard May, recounted eighty years later that all the children loved Hubert. Unlike the other more serious fathers, Hubert loved to tell his own improvised stories, play games and horse around with them. He even made his five children their own puppet theater. "Unlike most Germans, my father had a good sense of humor. You know, the word 'kidding' doesn't exist in the German language," Wolf explains, adding unequivocally, "He couldn't have been a better father."

Wolf's mother played a less conspicuous role in her son's life, but as he would reveal, he ultimately was much closer to her than to his high-profile father. Elsbeth was born in the upper crust First Hill neighborhood of Seattle, to the English pioneer Epler family, in 1894. The family's early Northwest pedigree was apparent in the tales that Wolf's beautiful American grandmother, Mabel Epler, told of her youth, when Duwamish Indians still lived along Seattle's waterfront. But Elsbeth's position in her family was compromised, through no fault of her own. She was born illegitimate, the result of an indiscretion committed by young Mabel while traveling in Germany. To escape the scorn and embarrassment of her "respectable" family, Mabel raised Elsbeth in Germany, and as a result, Elsbeth's father, who would become a general in the German Army, was not unknown to her or to his grandchildren. Mabel maintained that he had taken advantage of her, and though he had wanted to marry her, she would never consent, and in fact never did marry. When Elsbeth was ready for secondary education, Mabel sent her to school in England, and Mabel returned to Seattle.

Commensurate with her class, Elsbeth was educated well, compelled to study classical piano, and continued traditional summer vacations with her mother in the Alps. She was completely bilingual, with no accent in either language. It was as a student in England that she became close to one of her teachers, a woman with a younger brother named Hubert Bauer. Five years older than her, Hubert was dynamic and engaging. She married him when she was seventeen, and began a family right away. Still virtual newlyweds when Wolf was born, they lived well in Munich. Elsbeth never needed to work outside the home, and as Wolf recalls, they were very accustomed to a classed society. There were always two women servants in the home, and after children were born, nannies were added to the staff.

But, as world events would dictate, such comforts would ultimately become rare in Germany. By the time Wolf was five years old, the outbreak of war had set the family in motion. Hubert was conscripted into the Navy, being assigned commander of a fleet of minesweepers in the North Sea, and the family relocated to the Wilhelmshafen Naval Base to be closer to him. Improbable though it may seem, Wolf can remember those early years of nearly a century ago. His memories of those days are happy ones, and he recalls them with pleasure.

Family History in a Nutshell

WHEN I WAS OLD ENOUGH TO LEARN and understand adult situations, or at least when my father thought so, I learned that my mother was born out of wedlock. Her mother was Mabel Epler, member of an old Seattle pioneer English family. We children called our grandmother Tante (Aunt, in German) for obvious reasons. Mother's father was a general in the German Army, and

Grandmother Maria Bauer with Wolf at three months old, June 1912.

I remember him as Uncle Hartmann. I still can recall him leading a mounted military parade in Munich, just after the outbreak of World War I. He later took me to the famous Rathskeller restaurant for my first sip of beer.

Father's side of the family, on the other hand, provided us with a grand-mother who was as typical as one can be, with her brush of white hair, rosy cheeks and smiling animated presence, and with many uncles and aunts, of which our father was the youngest. A grandfather from that side of the family died before our time.

My mother, Elsbeth Hasbrouk (she borrowed her surname from her married sister to keep up respectable appearances), was educated in England, which also included private lessons in classical piano. She and my father, Hubert Bauer, met as teens when she and her mother vacationed in the Bavarian Alps. They were married in the years just before World War I broke out. Mother died of a brain tumor at sixty-three. Dad returned to

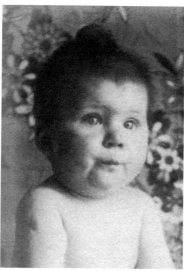

Wolf Bauer at eleven months, January 1913.

Germany after World War II, leaving Mother and the rest of us in the United States, and died at ninety-two.

Legacy of a German Boyhood

WHEN, IN RETROSPECT, one traces the direction of one's life past all the many junctions and crossroads, those paths taken were chosen either by oneself or by others, i.e., by intent or by circumstances. One might say that parental, social and environmental childhood experiences affect early likes and dislikes, since many often carry through into later life. In my case, at least, those first thirteen years did establish an early bond with mountains, rivers and coasts that continued on through life.

The Early Years in Munich

IN MY OWN MIND, I really never considered myself a "child," because I could lord it over my younger sister from the start. Painfully, I was later reminded by my mother that I made my sister cry when I tried to make her eat my molded sand cookie in our sandbox. My affinity for research in later life was, according to my parents, expressed as early as two years of age—

Wolf prepares to force-feed his sister Mabel sand cookies.

I invariably put anything strange into my mouth first, including freshly dropped "horse-apples" after the parked vegetable wagon left the curb in front of our Munich apartment.

Trips to the zoo were, of course, major highlights. None was more vividly recalled than the time mother gave me some bread for feeding the caged monkeys. Sitting at a park table, she suddenly saw me come running and yelling bloody murder. I had evidently been teasing one monkey with my bread offers to the point where he reached through the bars and tweaked my nose in a bloody warning. At that point, I learned what my sister should have taught me in the sandbox!

Scary situations are often easily recalled from early childhood. Every child has them. One still sticks with me. I was riding on the streetcar with my parents. Unbeknownst to both of them, I got off the streetcar a stop ahead of their departure. After a half hour of utter panic, and having attracted a crowd, we were tearfully reunited. I don't know who suffered more—I or they.

Son of a sea captain, Wolf at age two, May 1914.

"Deckhand" in the Kaiser's Navy

WORLD WAR I HAD BROKEN OUT, and father's extensive career as an officer in the Merchant Marine automatically brought him into the German Navy in 1917. He became commander of a flotilla of converted minesweepers based at Wilhelmshafen on the North Sea. It was his responsibility to keep the German shipping lanes free of drift-mines, both German and British, extending up the Danish Coast and to Norway.

The family moved to Wilhelmshafen, where Dad could join us during regular port-visits. So it was in the last year of the war that he hatched an audacious plan to smuggle me on board for an unprecedented boyhood experience in the face of certain court martial, if discovered.

On the morning of my departure, and with my clothes already on board, Mother, at the last minute, objected to the scheme. She had had nightmares, and told my father it was just too risky. He left, deeply

Wolf, age five, stows away on the minesweeper under his
father's command, July 1917.

Wolf, and his father, Captain
Hubert Bauer, on the bridge.

The crew instructs Wolf on proper fish handling.

disappointed. Three days later, two naval officers came to the door advising my mother of the fact that Dad's boat had sunk, and there was no news yet of any survivors. Two days later came the good tidings that he survived, but with only three members of his crew.

Thankful that I hadn't been on board, my father later related how he was on night watch on the bridge when the boat shuddered. One of their own mines had evidently broken loose from its anchor and drifted into the shipping lane. Most of the crew members were asleep under the deck, where the blast had torn out the ship's bottom, sinking the boat in minutes. Dad said he had only enough time to blow air into his life vest and jump free of the ship's suction. He and the three night-shift sailors finally got onto one of the free-floating life rafts, and were picked up the next morning by the rest of the fleet. Had I been on board, he figured that probably we both would have drowned in his effort to bring me on deck.

Call it premonition, or just good sense; mother was a practical and down-to-earth woman. She proved that when, a few months later, Dad did take me to sea as originally planned, and without her objections. The rationale evidently was that it surely couldn't happen twice!

The accompanying photos are proof of my stint in the Kaiser's Navy. I instantly became the crew's mascot. Sworn to utter secrecy, they nevertheless seemed anxious to make a sailor and crew member out of me—letting me lead-paint rust spots and help measure questionable depths of the shallow North Sea with a line-probe, checking my courage holding onto live fish, and even fixing me a swing off the wheelhouse bridge. Not all was fun, for I also became seasick, and they stuffed me with rice, for whatever reason. There also occurred a ticklish situation when an inspecting high officer came on board, and Dad had to hide me during his visit. Being told to stay under his bed covers without a sound, I was additionally warned that, if found, I would probably be thrown overboard. I became nearly asphyxiated in my panic to remain unseen. It still seems like yesterday.

Even war stories sound like fun when Wolf tells them. His stint in the Kaiser's Navy sounds simply like a great adventure. But he would later qualify the memory of the mine explosion incident. "At pre-Kindergarten age, kids only knew that in war you had to defend yourself. Mother's two days of crying was my main psychological impact, which was happily followed by reunion, relief and celebration." One has to actively seek such footnotes to his tales, though. In all my conversations with Wolf, the only hints that the war affected him negatively were remarks he made about diet. Being the shortest of the Bauer men, at five-foot-nine, he blames his height on food shortages and poor nutrition at a formative age. His younger brothers, being born later, fared better and grew taller.

After the War was over, the Bauers tried to return to a normal family life. They moved to Misdroy on the Baltic Sea for three years, before moving more permanently to Wasserburg. The eight-hundred-year-old town of Wasserburg became the focus of family life for the remainder of their time in Germany, prior to their emigration in 1925. But for more than three of those years, from 1919 to 1922,

Wolf (left) with friend Richard May (right front) and his older brother Heinz May in Kreuth, 1920.

Wolf was separated from his family. Wolf was suffering from asthma (an affliction that happily did not follow him into adulthood), so his family sought a healthier situation for him. Hubert's sister Maria was tutor and nanny for a doctor's family near the Austrian border. Dr. May, from a long line of Bavarian doctors, ran a clinic or "sanitarium" in Kreuth, a small town near Tegernsee in the Alps. Because it was deemed that the mountain air would be good for Wolf's asthma, and because Dr. May had a young son, Richard, who was just about Wolf's age, it was arranged that Wolf should take a cure with the May family and be tutored, along with their children, by his beloved Tante Maria.

Thus began a period in Wolf's life that laid the most formative foundation for all of his later accomplishments. Despite being separated completely from his family for three years—seeing his father only once and his mother and siblings not at all—Wolf still considers the mountains and rivers of Kreuth to be his own Garden of Eden. He only remarks how much he missed his mother when asked point blank, as the images conjured of those days are not of longing, but of joy. It was in Kreuth that his love affair with nature truly began, and it was there that the seeds of his true "religion" were sown. The beauty of nature, commingled with all the wonderful ways to enjoy it, endowed him with the perspective that would cross an ocean and a continent and take root in the Pacific Northwest.

Misdroy Ice and Sea Races

THE YEAR 1919 IS REMEMBERED IN GERMANY not only for the war's aftermath—the shock and misery of defeat, but for the exceptionally cold winter to boot. Our family had moved from the North Sea to the Baltic, which, because of its low salinity, had formed a frozen rim of seawater extending out hundreds of feet. At the outer edges of the freeze, a small seawall or ice-ridge had formed from wave action. With the happy coincidence of a high sand dune behind the beach, it didn't take long for some of us boys to cash in on this unique combination of nature. Pulling our sleds up the dune, we sledded down to the beach, where we had gained enough momentum to coast across the ice to the frozen seawall, which, when climbed, provided a return slide to the beach. That year, the weather gods had us boys in mind.

Wolf (right) and Richard May with their first peak, the Leonhardstein, in the distance, 1920.

Wolf (right) and Richard May pose on skis while an unidentified friend engages the photographer, 1920. This is the earliest image of Wolf on skis.

Young Richard May (left) and Wolf pose by a tree in the May family yard, 1920.

The same boys pose (in the same order) by the same tree eighty years later, 2000.

As the weather got warmer, the sea continued to provide entertainment. Our Baltic location was on an island served by competing commuter ferries from adjacent docks. Although their schedules were slightly different, there were times when their departures coincided, and then the trip took on the aspect of a race. While some competitive ego may have played a role in how much steam pressure the boilers could be trusted with, it was, according to my father, a matter of wind and wave action. One ferry was a side-wheeler and could beat the propeller boat only in calm seas. It was an early lesson learned by this future engineer, but a most exciting competition and experience at the time.

Wolf was a born engineer. It can, of course, be argued that all little boys have a bit of engineer in them: constructing and deconstructing are their trademark activities. But the desire to figure out how things work in nature—and how to turn physics or natural processes into a way to have fun—came in spades in this particular boy. The man who would one day teach himself (and then others) how to safely surf whitewater in a kayak started out on frozen seawater, riding the world's first "terrain-park half-pipe" on a sled. The man who would one day teach other engineers the mechanics of wave and wind action on fragile coastal shorelines got his start watching the effects of wave and wind action on an impromptu ferryboat race in Germany. Wolf's relationship with the forces of nature was never an adversarial one; it was always collaborative. In this, he evolved very differently from many others in the profession of engineering.

This may be attributable to his Bavarian years. In the Germany of Wolf's past, the Alps were a place of extraordinary beauty, inhabited by people who had lived in harmony with nature for centuries. In Bavaria, in particular, that still rings true. Comparing an aerial photograph of the Bavarian Alps with one of the Washington Cascades would illustrate an important point. The devastating and rapacious forestry practices of the American Northwest have spread what looks like a virulent mange across the wilderness, marking the mountains as a place of rampant consumption, not habitation.

In contrast, the human presence in the Alps is seen in ancient farms and towns nestled into the valleys and couloirs in such a natural way as to improve their appearance. Monks were building churches and shrines atop high peaks in the Alps eight hundred years ago, understanding that God lives in his sanctified mountains, too. The relationship of the Bavarian people to the mountains and rivers is loving, not voracious, because they have been sustained in those same places for well over a thousand years. They evolved in the mountains long before they had the capability to destroy them. The land has nourished them; they have not devoured it. In contrast, the American legacy of seemingly limitless wilderness resources has, in our short history, engendered a careless feeling of entitlement that must puzzle a more mature culture.

For Wolf, transplanted to America at the age of thirteen, the puzzlement has never ceased. From the beginning, he was astonished that all of Seattle looked at the north face of Mount Rainier every day (cloud cover allowing), yet no one had ever climbed that side. Visually, he established a relationship with the north face of Mount Rainier, and thus he would have to be the first to climb it—not to conquer it, but to deepen the bond. Bonding to mountains is what Bavarians do.

Today, contemplating the glacial pace of environmental progress, Wolf continues to be amazed at our painfully distant relationship to the land that sustains and inspires us. Nature is still primarily a place we *visit*, as we would a theme park, grown children who return home only to raid the fridge, borrow twenty dollars we won't return, and disappear again for the season. Luckily for us, thirteen years were enough for Wolf Bauer to bond with Bavarian mountains and streams, a bond he had no trouble transferring to the wild Cascade Mountains and Puget Lowlands of Washington.

Wolf's favorite recollections of his years in Kreuth demonstrate his love for the life he left behind.

Butter vs. Knife

THE YEARS IMMEDIATELY FOLLOWING WORLD WAR I posed tough problems for most people in defeated Germany, not the least of which was obtaining an adequate supply of food. Farmers were obviously better off than city folks. Despite great losses, the local war veterans put on their annual parade and festivities for children, including an archery competition for boys. After winning third place, I was directed to a long table to pick up my prize, a shiny pocketknife. At eight years of age, that was indeed a treasure! But further down the long table I spied a lower prize in the form of a half-pound loaf of butter, which the surprised judges let me exchange my knife for. During the war, only the military had access to such a luxury. Suffice it to recount that the butter lasted me well into its rancid stage; even then it was a bargaining chip at our dinner table.

Forbidden Climb

RICHARD MAY, who, like his brother and father, also became a medical doctor, was my constant sidekick in all our boyhood adventures. The doctor-house, where we lived, was situated on a glacial bench above the village, backed by the landmark Leonhardstein mountain peak behind us. Climbing it was, of course, forbidden to us little boys. Hero-worship comes early in boys, and mountain guides in our Alps were a natural target—we even went to the point of mimicking elderly guides by walking with bent knees. So there was our forbidden peak, looking down on us every day. One early summer day, we sneaked away, ostensibly to pick wild strawberries in the

The May family home at the base of the Leonhardstein in Kreuth.

meadows below the peak. While the climb was no big deal on the well-marked route, failing to find even one strawberry to justify our long absence later became embarrassing. I don't recall any dire consequences resulting from the episode. I enjoyed retracing the route eighty years later during a reunion visit to Richard in the 1990s.

Strangely, after all these years, we both can recall certain adventures vividly, and others not at all. Richard, who has climbed Leonhardstein a number of times, seemed to have scant memory of our first ascent. I similarly didn't recall that we released a restaurant's penned trout into the river, with consequent punishments.

In 2005, I made a pilgrimage to Kreuth to see the May home where Wolf had spent these formative years, and to meet his old friend Richard and his family. Though also in his nineties, Dr. Richard May proved nearly as spry as his former playmate. Owing to his facility in English, which far surpassed my rusty old college German, we were able to spend a lovely evening discussing the old days and visiting the sites of Wolf's stories. Except for his time as a doctor in Hitler's Army on the Russian Front, Dr. May spent most of his life in Kreuth, just as the generations before and after him did. But these are no country bumpkins. Richard, his wife Gertrudis and his daughter Christiane, also a physician, proved to be more than just educated. They are progressive and cosmopolitan in their political and philosophical ideas.

Most striking about the visit was the unchanged and peaceful nature of the town. The May house still stands with as much seeming permanence as the 4,757 foot Leonhardstein peak the boys surreptitiously climbed. The slow and comforting tinkle of cowbells still echoes around the hills as the cattle lazily graze. In Tegernsee, the St. Quirinus monastery/brewery/elementary school (yes, that's right) still serves up beer and Weisswurst the way it did when Wolf lived there. There are no industrial campuses, no strip malls, no franchised chains. The people here have made a commitment to preserving the best of who they are in a fast-changing world.

I arrived in May, when there was a religious holiday being celebrated that required traditional music and dress in every hamlet I passed through on the way to Kreuth. Such holidays are common, I was told, though it was a beautiful day in the beginning of tourist season, so it was easy to be skeptical. In Oberammergau, the streets outside the town square were nearly vacant, yet the square itself was teeming. Sausages on the grills, kegs frothing, traditional music blasting and a freestanding climbing wall monopolized the attentions of the townspeople. If this was a show for the tourists, it was remarkable for its lack of people out of costume, cameras dangling conspicuously. I began to feel conspicuous wielding one myself. I was hard pressed to find anyone who would rather speak English than listen to me butcher German and misunderstand their Bavarian dialect. The truth is, in Bavaria the residents' knowledge of English is not a given wherever one goes, as it is in many other parts of Germany. But my awkwardness was always softened by the welcome smiles of the shopkeepers, encouraging my cacophonous efforts to communicate. Wherever I stopped, the people were, to a man and woman, very gracious and welcoming.

The comfort that comes to a people who embrace their past and their culture is something for an American to witness, particularly a western one living far from New England, where American history is still widely celebrated. In the town square of Oberammergau, I came across a large table of young men, perhaps in their late teens or early twenties. With spiky hair and Dirty Harry shades, they were smoking, pounding beers and laughing it up, just as their American counterparts would. But there they were—a tribe of tough young rockers that otherwise could have been from Anywhere, U.S.A.—all clad in lederhosen, knee-high socks and felt Tyrolean hats. They exhibited an astonishing comfort with who they are. Aside from the singular rites-of-passage of donning a tuxedo for the senior prom or a cap and gown for graduation, most modern American teenagers could never—would never—be cajoled to dress publicly in anything but their uniform of what's-cool-now.

Perhaps there is a correlation between Americans' restlessness and Americans' disconnection from their land and their past. Perhaps that comfort inside his natural habitat—his acceptance of his time and place—were part of Wolf Bauer's energy and his successes in his life's work. What he was doing in so many of his recreational and environmental campaigns was acting on the traditional values of his Bavarian childhood, on the bedrock of a thousand-year history of living with the land.

WHEN WOLF HAD OVERCOME HIS ASTHMA and his family had tired of his absence, he rejoined them in Wasserburg, a Bavarian town located half way along the chalkline between Munich, Germany and Salzburg, Austria. The Inn River flows through the town, weaving through the ancient churches and narrow streets in the foothills of the Alps. Here, they lived on a farm owned by Hubert's brother Viktor, with plenty of room to roam, and a place for Hubert to keep his bees. With about five acres to raise hay, vegetables and some livestock, the family was able to produce enough food to feed themselves.

Wolf's parents, Hubert and Elsbeth, with the family dog, Sascha.

Reunited with his family, Wolf graduated from Tante Maria's tutelage and enrolled in school. In traditional grade school, Wolf found a much more disciplined environment. Classes were held Monday through Saturday. It was not uncommon for teachers to paddle their students. The teachers were all men, and only a third of his classmates were girls. Rote memorization was highly valued as an exercise in intellectual discipline, but luckily for Wolf, he was good at it, just as he was at Gymnastics. He studied Latin and French, and by the time he immigrated to the United States, he was academically a full year ahead of his new fellow eighth graders.

His exposure to religious ideas was also broadened, as school included weekly visits from both a Catholic priest (most of Bavaria being Catholic), and from a Lutheran minister (for the minority Protestant students). Hubert was a non-practicing Catholic, and Elsbeth was a non-practicing Protestant, so Wolf was free to choose whose session he attended. He chose the Lutheran minister for his amiable accessibility, and his lively telling of the story of Martin Luther. He remembers visiting Wartburg Castle, where Luther stayed for a number of months in 1521-1522, hiding out and writing his German translation of the New Testament. "What a brave guy!" Wolf would later exclaim about Luther. "You know, the Devil visited him there and Luther threw his inkwell at him. You can still see the ink stain on the wall! Isn't that something?" The charm of the tale is not lost, even on a lifelong skeptic like Wolf.

Religion

WHILE MANY PARENTS INSTILL A GOD-FEARING ATTITUDE in their children from early childhood on, this was not the case with either of my parents, or when I raised my own family. Dad was raised in Catholic Bavaria, the youngest of twelve children, and early on served as an altar boy in his family's church. By the time he graduated from university, however, his studies and readings in earth and life sciences had freed him from religious dogma, that, he felt, had to depend on fear of eternal punishment to sustain itself.

My grade school in the Bavarian town of Wasserburg was visited once a week by a Catholic priest for an hour's Bible study. We Protestant minority students were excused to visit with our minister at another time. Earlier, I had sat in on one or two Catholic masses, which were very formal and strict, as compared to those of the younger Lutheran minister, who made us laugh with his allegories. It was to Dad's credit that, without pushing, he simultaneously introduced me to his extensive library of textbooks and photos of the obvious natural worlds of botany, zoology and geology.

In a family headed by a practical and reasoning academic, it was probably inevitable that Wolf would journey down a path of disbelief. His strong sense of moral values came from a secular fount. In all our discussions, Wolf always demonstrated a commitment to personal integrity and an egalitarian humanitarianism. He lived by these principles without fear of divine retribution.

—◁▦◟▦▷—

WOLF'S YEARS IN WASSERBURG were spent making friends, like lifelong pal Alois Kreckl, getting into mischief, and living the good life in the Bavarian countryside with his own family. Having a classroom full of playmates was a great change. The boys had all read *The Last of the Mohicans* in German translation, so they played Indians, became "blood brothers" and put manure in improvised "peace pipes." Most of the stories Wolf is eager to share come from his idyllic days in Wasserburg. To listen to the tales—history to most of us, yet clearly only yesterday to Wolf—is to understand how close we all are to the past.

Mistaken Identity

MY DAILY WAY TO SCHOOL led across a short railroad tunnel under the highway. On occasion, the local train, pulled by a little steam locomotive ('that could'), passed through it at a time when my school chum Alois and I walked over it. Obviously, that presented snow-pelting opportunities. One day we realized what an inviting target the big smokestack would make for a rolled up snow-lump.

The long-awaited day of opportunity found us poised over the tunnel with our snow bomb at the ready as the train approached. "Bombs away!"

we cried. It was a perfect hit, shutting off the belching smoke as the engine entered the portal and emerged on the other side, apparently unperturbed. With secret satisfaction, we continued on to school.

That afternoon, our teacher got a note from the office, asking Alois Kreckl and Wolfgang Bauer to report to the principal's office at once. "Uh-oh," we thought as we looked at each other. Somebody must have seen us. Trembling, we lined up in front of our would-be accuser, ready to confess, when he charged that we had been seen throwing rocks from the train tunnel exit portal and cracking a cab window of the locomotive. In disbelief, and then relief, we tried to convince him that we did not throw rock-filled snowballs, nor were we at the tunnel's exit portal. It turned out that, unbeknownst to us, another boy had a similar urge to pelt the train—his father eventually had to pay for the damage. When we came clean with our fathers, their admonitions were long remembered.

Years later, after World War II, Alois and I spent some reunion time together in the Austrian Alps, and learned to our surprise that we had both vividly remembered this boyhood incident under very different circumstances. Alois was reminded when, as a tank commander in Rommel's North African army, he witnessed the "decapitation" of a Moroccan locomotive. Meanwhile, I recalled the incident in a more benign situation in the Cascades. A skier and I were on a winter bivouac and had built a small cooking fire under a large storm-protective fir. It was when the heat melted a huge weight of snow on a branch above, and the resulting dump completely buried both of us, that this old prank instantly came to mind.

Skating Interludes

ALTHOUGH SKIING WAS OUR FAVORITE WINTER SPORT ON THE FARM, there also were unique ice skating opportunities. The Inn River that almost encircled our ancient town had an island with a shallow backwater that froze over early to become a safe skating rink. The only problem for us kids occurred when the ice reached a thickness of about four to six inches, at which time adjacent farmers came with their saws and started to cut ice chunks, to be stored for summer use in an adjacent earth barn.

The sawing started near one end of the island, slowly crowding us skaters into an ever-shrinking skating rink. If the cold weather held, we would gingerly test the ice support of the sawed and re-freezing end where, if we skated fast enough, the slightly bending and complaining ice upheld our impatient and fleeting weight. Luckily, the water depth was never more than a couple of feet, and a break-through was, according to us, no big deal. That attitude was not shared by my mother when we came home with wet pants and shoes and blue feet.

Winter "Trapping"

ANOTHER WINTER EPISODE vivid in my mind centered on trying to catch a wild rabbit. My trap consisted of a large square box with a chicken-wire bottom. A stick propped it up at a forty-five-degree angle so that the rabbit could see and get at the dried corn kernels underneath. A long string fastened to the prop-up stick led up to my bedroom window where, as I envisioned, I would pull the string and collapse the trap. After a long night vigil at my window, I dimly saw some movement at the tilted box below, and eagerly pulled on my trigger-string. I heard some commotion, and then silence. I was hard-put to wait until daylight to look at my catch. Imagine my surprise when my rabbit prisoner turned out to be a grouse! It was too skinny for a family dinner, so the proud trapper was persuaded to set it free.

Turning the Table

WHILE WE CHILDREN HAD OUR OWN FARM ANIMAL PETS that couldn't be tabbed for dinner, such as rabbits and fowl we personally raised, our year's provision of meat, fat and sausages came from butchering a pig. This was a special occasion that engaged a traveling butcher at our farm for a few days. This resulted in an amusing incidence of applied psychology I have never forgotten.

The men were trying to guide and shove the chosen porker out of the pen and the barn. The harder they shoved and pulled, the stronger the pig resisted and backed up. Mother had been watching the contest and, noting the growing frustration of the men, coolly said, "Why don't you turn him around and try to push him back into the pen?" Was it a case of stubborn man versus stubborn pig versus stubborn woman's intuition? Taking her advice proved that the pig had no sense of premonition, as it backed out of the barn faster than they could hold on to it.

The Road Hog

SPEAKING OF PIGS, I remember one that was truly the proverbial "road hog."

My Uncle Viktor, the local country doctor, often passed our house on his way to out-of-town farm patients. Knowing when he usually would pass by in the afternoon, I would look for him in case he had room to take me along. In this instance, he stopped to let me sit in the sidecar of his motorcycle—obviously more thrilling than his horse-drawn sleds or gigs, or the old Opel two-seater.

Getting close to the patient's farm, we were rounding a narrow dirt road when, too late, Uncle tried to avert collision with a dozing pig stretched across the road. While the cycle just missed the hulk, my sidecar wheel went over the pig and tipped us halfway over and brought us to a complete stop. I was thrown in a wide arc out of the sidecar into the road ditch, while Uncle was pinned with one leg under the machine, which was still noisily kicking.

Picking myself up, still in one piece, I was able to shut off the engine and help pry my uncle's leg out from under it. The pig, in the meantime, was leaving unfazed, with irritable grunting. I've always felt that our uncle-nephew bond had anything but suffered from that shared close call.

Autos

IN A TOWN THAT, aside from one public bus and an occasional truck, could only muster two or three passenger cars, one of them was Uncle's two-seater Opel. The four-speed gearshift stick, like the hand brake, was outside the cab. Constant shifting with a wet arm in the rain was a drawback. The occasions when we got stuck in the farm muck, and Uncle put me behind the wheel to steer while he pushed were boyhood highlights. One time it took an ox to pull us out. These were still the years when the horn was activated by squeezing a big rubber bulb, and when, at dusk, you stopped the car, got out, and lit the carbide (plus water) chemical headlamps. I'm sure no one, in those days, could go to sleep at the wheel.

Learning to Swim

WHEN WE WERE STILL LIVING ON THE BALTIC COAST IN 1919, summer activities centered on the sandy beaches and warm seawater. Father was anxious to get me to swim, but he sure used the wrong technique. He would let me ride on his back, but then would dive under the water. He was doing it for fun, but it left me gasping for air and making for shore in holy terror. Instead of gaining confidence, I became scared of deep water and Dad gave up in disgust.

It wasn't until several years later in Wasserburg that I secretly taught myself to swim in a nearby pond. Not having access to a swim-vest, I made my own by wrapping hollow water weeds into a floating bundle that I could lie on, and thus float. Using the froglike breast-stroke, I slowly pulled more and more stalks out of the bundle, sinking ever deeper until I was truly swimming on my own. Dad was the first to congratulate me, and a painful episode for both of us was erased.

Recitation Angst

LOW AND HIGH POINTS often come in quick succession when anxieties end in unexpected relief. Thus it was we had been given an assignment to memorize a six-verse poem, which we were to recite one week later. Our no-nonsense teacher (who later became a Nazi general) became ever more disgusted and mad. As one student after another couldn't get past the second or third verse, he abruptly halted the dismal display of our class laziness. To show us his ability to read character, he announced that he could pick a student that did his homework, purely by means of psychology.

He slowly walked down the rows of benches, looking each of us straight in the eye, then he returned to his desk. "Will Wolfgang Bauer please stand up and show the class what this assignment was all about?" he said. "Uh-oh," I thought. I was hoping he would pick one of the girls, and I wasn't sure that under this stress I could recite all six verses. As I started to slow down somewhat by the end of the fourth verse, and tentatively began the fifth, he suddenly stopped me, announcing that was enough to show the class he could read us like a book. Obviously, he had saved us both.

Persuasion Tricks

OUR FRENCH TEACHER WAS A PORTLY OLDER GENTLEMAN who liked his beer, often to our distinct advantage, when we perceived the remaining after-effects. On such occasions, we were often able, as a class, to argue him out of a heavy homework assignment. There were also times, on sunny spring days, when we would "entice" him to hold class outdoors on the school meadow. By keeping classroom doors and windows tightly closed, and taking turns blowing on the thermometer just before he entered the room, we would convince him that it was too warm to stay indoors.

Despite Wolf's idyllic recollections of his golden days in Wasserburg, the years were very difficult for Wolf's parents. The seaman, forced into retirement from the sea by the economic disaster of post-war Germany, scrounged for work. Though the family farmed Uncle Viktor's land, and received subsidies from "Tante" (Elsbeth's mother) in Seattle, times were still very difficult. Hubert had been a company photographer for North German Lloyd, and he had also taken many photographs while in the Navy. One of his resourceful means of earning money was making photographic slide presentations of marine vessels, especially military U-boats. His black-and-white glass slides, both of his own photographs and those of other German naval officers, attracted people in many towns.

But Hubert was restless, and remembering the stunning landscape of New Zealand from his merchant marine days, he decided to pack up the family and journey halfway around the world to start life over. After a short stop planned in the Pacific Northwest to visit Elsbeth's family and earn some money, they would be off to settle in the South Pacific. The family saw this as a great adventure. Elsbeth was looking forward to being reunited with her mother in Seattle, and the children rejoiced in such novelties as a trip to Munich to obtain store-bought shoes and clothing. Wolf's sister Friedl recalls that up until that time seamstresses, tailors, and cobblers would come to the house to custom-make the family's clothing. To go to the big city to be outfitted in the fine stores of Munich was as exciting as a trip to Disneyland.

Wolf remembers that the very worst part of leaving Germany was leaving their German Shepherd, Sascha, behind. "The day we left, she knew something terrible was happening. You can see in the pictures that her ears were down. It was heartbreaking." But unlike dogs, one can write letters to friends. He would correspond with Alois, and his Tante Maria would help him stay in touch with Richard May in Kreuth. So, going to America was an anticipated event—finally they would accompany their father on one of his exotic world expeditions. The future was exciting and bright.

PART II

Coming of Age
in America

TWO

The Transplant Takes Root

MOST AMERICANS CAN CONJURE UP IMAGES of the old black-and-white newsreels: ships full of European immigrants waving from the deck as the vessel passes the Statue of Liberty en route to Ellis Island. In 1925, such images were instrumental to American myth-building, and it might be tempting to try to place the uprooted Bauer family on one of those decks. But Hubert Bauer had once been the second officer on the very ship they arrived on—the North German Lloyd steamship *Bremen*. New York had been a turn-around port for him while he was a seaman, and though he was impressed with the city, he didn't particularly like it. Thus the magic of its novelty was reserved for the children. Unaware that the passage into New York Harbor was to become culturally iconic, Wolf took no particular notice of his first glimpse of the Statue of Liberty, primarily because the family was neither desperately tired nor hungry nor part of the huddled masses yearning to breathe free. Their journey had more to do with maintaining their accustomed quality of life than with a last-chance bid for basic survival. As for Ellis Island, the thirteen-year-old Wolf only retained the impression that it was a bureaucratic bore. "That's not what I was interested in," he said. "We just had to talk to lots of people. That's all."

Hubert Bauer, born in the days of European empire building and romantic sentimentalism about nature, was most certainly a product of his generation. The late nineteenth and early twentieth centuries were a time of great exploration around the globe. Technology and nationalism fostered a race for imperialistic conquest in uncharted territories. Germany took part in the colonization of the African continent, along with the other European powers, during the great Scramble for Africa of the late 1800s. The Arctic and Antarctic Poles in particular saw Britain, Norway, and the United States vying for dominion through exploration. Germany also participated, albeit less successfully, in the competition. These competitive expeditions were universally deemed a test of national character as well as a bid for imagined and real territorial resources.

The explorer himself was seen as a paragon of self-reliance, independence, and masculinity; exploration was a lofty culmination of science, athleticism, and military strategy. The German explorer, though, had a slightly different perspective on his mission. The typical adventurer in any country was from the educated middle class and was highly nationalistic, but the German explorer had a deeper focus on the scientific value of his endeavors. Civilian scientists led the way rather than military men, as was typical in other countries, and the German explorer often viewed his more celebrated competitors as mere glory-seekers, showing off rather than furthering the aims of science and knowledge. And so, German explorers might not have acquired the fame of Shackleton, Peary, and Amundsen, but their acquisition of scientific data during their campaigns was prodigious. As such, many developed a sensitivity to the impact of exploration on the wildlife they encountered. David Thomas Murphy writes in *German Exploration of the Polar World: A History, 1870-1940* that "an emerging awareness of the global environment as something more than the object of political or economic acquisition might be seen in the occasional protests raised by German observers against the wanton slaughter of polar life."[4] This seed of environmentalism was the function of a particularly German ethic.

Wolf's father was clearly influenced by this cultural marriage of science and adventure. Having sailed the Seven Seas with the German Merchant Marine at the turn of the twentieth century, the future professor of Geography was not a man to be reduced to scratching out a living on his brother's farm in the desperation of post-war Germany. His business ventures had failed, but he still had worlds to explore and understand, and thus he set his future course towards the exotic destination of New Zealand, a port he had visited in his earlier journeys. The stunning landscapes in the United States may have appealed to him, but he was never won over by America. The Bauer tenure in the Pacific Northwest was supposed to be a time for family reunions and some economic refueling before moving on. But circumstances intervened, and his stopover in the United States became permanent for the family. Hubert returned to Germany alone after World War II, but the rest of the family would remain Americans for the rest of their days. Happily, much of the German attitude towards exploration and the environment that Wolf had picked up from his father and his homeland was transplanted to America along with him.

Atlantic Crossing

FOR FATHER, CROSSING THE ATLANTIC IN 1925 on the old steamship "Bremen" of the North German Lloyd Line was a nostalgic voyage, recalling his pre-war trips as second officer. While three days of heavy storm seas kept most of the queasy family below deck, Dad and I, as "old sea dogs," obviously had no such weaknesses, and enjoyed the experience.

New York Impressions

AFTER THE IMMIGRATION HASSLES AT ELLIS ISLAND, we were finally ready to be introduced to our new land. Dad's familiarity with New York provided three unforgettable days of sightseeing, starting with the climb up the Statue of Liberty. To me, of course, the fast, traffic-dodging taxi ride to the hotel was a special thrill. Then there was the view of Manhattan from the top of a skyscraper. Dad's sense of adventure and history also had the family walking the Brooklyn Bridge, across and back, with us three boys ceremoniously spitting down into the East River. Dad seemed to be less impressed by our even greater enthusiasm for the latest automat, which dispensed complete sandwiches for a quarter's coin drop.

Universal Language

FOR US KIDS, of course, all these new experiences were somewhat diminished by our lack of ability to read, understand, and speak the language. This, however, was not altogether true for my little two-year-old sister Gita. We were now on the three-day cross-country trip to Seattle, and the train had stopped in the middle of nowhere to replenish the steam locomotive's water supply. The conductor announced that we could disembark and stretch our legs on the open platform. While the family was breathing in the pastoral atmosphere, little Gita suddenly came running to Mother and excitedly cried, "Mommy, the cow speaks German; it just said 'Moo!'" She became comfortable with her new country that easily.

Scenic Train to Washington

CONTINUING ON TO CHICAGO, we changed to the Chicago, Milwaukee, St. Paul and Pacific Railroad to Seattle, marveling at the vast prairies and lands without habitation. In Washington State, the train stopped at Wenatchee to hitch on an open observation car for the scenic crossing of the Cascades over Snoqualmie Pass. Our train was now hitched to an electric locomotive that would allow us to ride in the open observation car, and go through tunnels without smoke in our eyes. Little did I realize that, just four years later, I would be riding this train to ski at my club's Snoqualmie Pass ski lodge.

Hello, Seattle

AFTER WE GOT ACQUAINTED WITH OUR AMERICAN RELATIVES, grandmother Mabel Epler took us sight-seeing through Seattle's high points, which, like today, included the Woodland Park Zoo (which was smaller then, and had caged animals), the Chittenden Locks in Ballard, the then-famous Smith Tower, and the Public Market. She took us to the dockside waterfront, where two green, sharp-bowed steamships, the "Emma Alexander" and the "H.F. Alexander," were waiting impatiently for their dash down the coast to 'Frisco, and where Indians were selling woven bark hats and baskets. It was only later in life that I learned to appreciate the time she took us down to the original Rhodes Department Store. Pointing to the hosiery counter near the entrance, she explained that "about here, were some big wild rose bushes, and out here at the building's corner came a trail up from the smelly shoreline."

"Tante" Mabel Epler, Wolf's maternal grandmother from Seattle.

Mabel's family was made up of well-to-do pioneer people (the Eplers and Abts), who lived on First Hill before the Great Seattle Fire of 1889. One of her girlhood recollections included riding on horseback through old-growth timber to reach Lake Washington for a picnic.

"Tante" Mabel Epler welcomed the family to Seattle, renting a house for them in the "U District" near the University of Washington. The first night in their new home a cook arrived to provide their first meal. When afterwards she left for home, the Bauers got their first reality check. Hired for one night only, the cook was not the regular servant they were accustomed to. Shocked and disappointed, Elsbeth and the girls had to learn how to run a household by themselves for the first time.

Still, Tante continued her efforts to ease their transition. Well connected through her long-established pioneer pedigree, she helped Hubert acquire his first job at Lummi Island, as a bookkeeper at a cannery. Lummi Island, the closest of the San Juan Islands to the American mainland, is twenty miles south of the Canadian border, and slightly northeast of Victoria. Before European contact, it was a seasonal camp for harvesting berries and shellfish, too exposed and vulnerable to raiding northern tribes to be a permanent village. Though the island was called Skallaham by the Lummi tribe, the U.S. government named the island in 1853 for the Lummi themselves, whose reservation on the mainland contains the ferry terminal at Gooseberry Point. Just west of Bellingham across Bellingham Bay, the island is, even today, far less trammeled than the trendier destination San Juan Islands. Its population is a little more than six hundred, many of whom are artists and craftsmen. Devoid of RV parks and campsites, the rocky nine-mile-long, two-mile-wide island is still accessed primarily by a small ferry called the *Whatcom Chief*, which carries up to twenty cars and a hundred passengers from Gooseberry Point to the island in six minutes. In the 1920s, however, the island was even more remote from civilization, and its main industry was fish canning.

The Bauer brothers—(left to right) Hugh, Dick and Wolf—on Lummi Island, 1925.

For a cosmopolitan European like Hubert, the rural seclusion of life in the San Juan Islands archipelago must have been a jarring change and a humbling demotion. But for a thirteen-year old German boy, who spoke no English and whose only conception of Native Americans was from *The Last of the Mohicans*, the family's mercifully short tenure on this island was a much greater challenge than for his multi-lingual, peripatetic father.

First American School

AFTER OUR FIRST SEATTLE IMPRESSIONS AND ADVENTURES in the summer of 1925, we moved to Lummi Island that fall, where father was to start his first American earnings as bookkeeper for the local salmon cannery, and my sister and I experienced our first American classes in a one-room island schoolhouse. My first letter to school chums in Bavaria related with excitement the fact that I was sitting next to a "real Indian boy," as well as a Japanese girl. Big deal? You bet! These were, however, often difficult and embarrassing days, when the room of children broke out in loud laughter at my attempts to speak the language. About all I could readily accomplish was arithmetic and drawing, where I was well ahead of these first to sixth grade students. Slowly that Fall, however, I gained confidence, and almost weekly moved up the grade ladder. My language skills were also greatly improved, because of the happy fact that the young teacher wanted to improve his German. Thus, there developed a unique after-school relationship and sessions that served both our needs.

Catching up to the seventh grade students and attaining language fluency by the end of the school year, Wolf looked forward to moving closer to civilization. The family briefly stayed in Bellingham, where Wolf's father had to put up with the lowliest job of his life—nightshift labor in another cannery. From there, fortune batted them to West Seattle, briefly, and finally to Kirkland, on the eastern shore of Lake Washington, within striking distance of Seattle. The family spent a year there before a return to urban life could be attained. Herbert continued to struggle to become established, picking up work wherever he could. Wolf recalls that no opportunity was missed for the family to make a little money, including family trips to Puyallup to pick raspberries for fifty cents a flat. Still, the memories of his time on the lake were characteristically positive.

The Lindbergh Encounter

IN THE CASE OF CHARLES LINDBERGH, teenage boys were, of course, not the only ones that succumbed to the spell of hero-worship. Not unlike Nathan Hale for Americans and Andreas Hofer for Germans and Austrians, Lindbergh became the newest world hero.

In 1927, he came to Seattle on his "victory tour" around the country, landing the "Spirit of St. Louis" at Sand Point Naval Air Station. Living at the time in Kirkland, across the lake from Sand Point, I realized that I had a great opportunity to see him up close by rowing across and parking myself alongside a narrow walkway dock that he would have to use in order to reach the yacht that would take him to Seattle.

The day of his landing saw me expectantly parked alongside the dock, and from there I watched his unique landing maneuver. With his cross-Atlantic extra gas tank still in place and blocking his forward view, he carefully sideslipped his Ryan monoplane toward the landing apron before straightening out for touchdown. Soon thereafter, sure enough, there he came, walking with the welcoming dignitaries just above me, in my boat. The next day, in my eighth grade class, I recounted my adventure with an awestruck "I could have touched him!" Such is hero-worship.

My Own First Flight

IN THE 1920S, Juanita Beach was, and perhaps still is, the best shallow sand beach facing south on Lake Washington. Three separately operated public beaches were situated next to each other, named Shady Beach, Sandy Beach and Juanita Beach. The latter was the main attraction to us boys, because of the high trestle amusement ride. It was like a ski jump: sleds on rollers would gain you the speed to plane over the water below.

In those years, Boeing had built a so-called "flying boat" biplane that, for a short time, carried mail between Seattle and Victoria. Pilot Huber would earn a little extra cash on weekends by picking up a few passengers off the beach for short scenic rides. Some of us boys helped him turn the plane around in the shallow water, while passengers got on and off. He evidently appreciated our help (or recalled his own boyhood times), promising to take us up after his last paying flight. By the time the three of us climbed into the open cockpit, we were already shivering cold. After our fifteen-minute flight of a lifetime, we landed again, and he told us to hurry and jump off, but the three of us couldn't move. The open cockpit and air blast must have coagulated our blood, for he had to carry us individually to shore. What a "blamage" (disgrace), as they say in Germany. That was obviously a detail not recounted to friends the next day.

Treasure Diving

BEFORE THE LAKE WASHINGTON FLOATING BRIDGES, Kirkland was intimately connected to Seattle via a combination streetcar and Madison Park ferry system, primarily used by daily commuters. Summer weekends also saw outsiders and vacationers use the ferry, crowding around the upper deck to view the landing. That was our moment of truth, as we boys dove into the water alongside, yelling "penny-nickel-dime!" to entice the tourists to throw change into the water for us. But if anyone threw a heavy quarter, the near-drowning scramble seldom recovered the treasure in the sandy bottom. Remember, for us, this was B.S. (Before Scuba—not what you thought).

At long last, the Bauer family's banishment from city life ended after Wolf graduated from eighth grade and they moved to Seattle's Wallingford neighborhood. Enrolling at the old Lincoln High School near the north end of Lake Union, Wolf began to make the community connections that he would enjoy his whole life. Here he met neighbor Harry Higman, who was to become like a second father to him. Mr. Higman was a Boy Scout leader, and at one time was the president of the Audubon Society. He not only recruited Wolf into the Scouts, he also initiated him into the joys of river exploration, putting him into a foldboat for the first time. Channeling his passion for the outdoors, Wolf instantly took to life in Troop 145. Before long, he became a senior patrol leader, and as he put it, one of the "den mothers" for forty Cub Scouts.

Meeting in the empty concrete basement of the Latona School, Wolf created fake "campfires" around which his Cubs would tell stories, simulating future outings. The echo chamber of the basement became a deafening, cacophonous riot, which drove the adults nearly insane. "It would take your ears off," he laughs. But like a snake charmer, he devised a way to control the unruly Cubs with a special signal system. Rewarding dens for coming to the speediest military attention at a given signal, Wolf's efficient system of Cub-control made him the fair-haired boy of the Scouting adults. Though still only in tenth grade himself, this hinted at the knack for efficient leadership he would cultivate in the coming years.

Among Wolf's happiest recollections of his high school years in Seattle are simple vignettes of times long gone and impossible to duplicate. Due to changes in climate, technology, landscape and social norms, those golden moments can only be lived in the imagination of the listener now.

The Higman Factor

AFTER A RAPID SUCCESSION of meeting new people in new environments, as the family shifted around from Seattle, to Lummi Island, to Bellingham, to Kirkland, and back to Seattle from 1925 to 1927, a more stable period followed in the Wallingford district. This was apparently where the "Gods-that-be" decided it was high time to introduce me to people that would influence my life thenceforth.

Enrolled as a Freshman at Lincoln High School in the Fall of 1927, I joined the local Boy Scout Troop 145, one that met weekly in the basement of nearby Latona Elementary School. The Scoutmaster, Mr. Harry Higman, soon became a counselor and father-figure to me, often taking us boys on nature hikes and bird-study outings, such as to the Tacoma Prairie. The old saying "All for One and One for All" has never been truer than it was for us one Saturday when our Scout Troop arrived at Crystal Pool, the popular public downtown natatorium (indoor swimming pool). As we all filed past the ticket booth, something stopped the procession. The attendant would not allow one of our Scouts into the building. Scoutmaster Harry Higman, with his arm around the shoulder of the boy, who was of Japanese descent, explained to the attendant that Scouting is a worldwide brotherhood, but

Wolf on his first hike in the North Cascades, at age sixteen, with Scoutmaster Harry Higman, 1928.

to no avail. All of us who are still alive must recall that incident, when Mr. Higman returned the tickets, had us all, in unison, recite the Scout Oath and Scout laws to the ticket man, and then led us to the streetcar for the Woodland Park Zoo—to lessen our disappointment. That this small incident would presage the massive internments of both U.S. and Japanese-born citizens during World War II would have been hard to believe at the time.

It was sheer coincidence that Mr. Higman's young nephew, Bob Higman, lived two houses from me, and we became longtime close friends, organizing and leading a Seattle Cub Scout pack, and adventuring in climbing and skiing. Even before we enrolled in Engineering at the University of

Washington, we both had surreptitiously rigged up a secret wire through the neighbor's backyard that connected our bedrooms, so we could communicate with each other using Morse Code.

Harry Higman's son Chet also became a longtime friend with whom I grew up, participating in the skiing fraternity, where we both competed. I recall most vividly the eighteen-mile cross-country Patrol Race, patterned after the Italian winter troops' competition. The Mountaineers laid out a course between their lodges at Snoqualmie and Stampede Passes, to be followed by three-man patrols. Chet Higman and I, along with a third member, Bill Miller, won with a time of four hours and 37 minutes, never again equaled.

The most important happening of the Higman saga, however, was the introduction of my future wife, Harriet Woodward, into my life story. It was Mr. Higman who "dared" me to meet her, telling me tales of this young lady's hiking prowess.

Unbelievably, there would appear a fourth Higman to add to this epic, long after Harry, Bob and Chet had passed to their happy hunting grounds. It was in early 2007 that I had a phone call from a man who claimed to know all about me from his father, Chet Higman. His name was Perry Higman, and he was anxious to meet me. He told me that he, too, was writing his family's memoirs, and that I had played an important role in their lives. What do you know? Bob Higman was a close neighbor in Seattle, and now Perry Higman was in my Anacortes neighborhood, eighty years later. I'm not the first one to claim it's a small world.

Green Lake Ice Capade

THE WINTER OF 1927 witnessed a fleeting and impromptu ice carnival, reminiscent of a New England winter scene. Several weeks of unusually cold weather allowed thin ice sheets to grow out from Green Lake's shores, initiating strict police surveillance in an effort to prevent children from straying onto thin ice. When the city finally pronounced the ice safe for public use, only a few days remained before warmer weather started melting the frozen surface. This was also the year that the brand new Field House was completed at Green Lake Park, from which colored searchlights would illuminate a frolicking public in the evenings on the frozen lake.

On about the last day of the week-long "ice-o-mania" on the lake, a young man appeared with a home-made ice-sailer that he had hurriedly built before the ice could melt, and which he now triumphantly put to the test on that breezy afternoon. When he finally got the hang of his sail-sled, his speed and tacking maneuvers soon caught the attention of the two city policemen who, riding their motorcycles with attached sidecars, patrolled the frolicking crowd. Having decided that this sailor's actions constituted a public menace, they went after him. Little did they realize that they were setting the stage for that afternoon's high-comedy theater—better than anything the Green Lake Aqua Theater, built decades later, could ever offer.

Each time the two cops thought they had the young sailor cornered, he sharply tacked, leaving the three-wheeled motorcycles spinning helplessly toward shore. When the crowd began to realize what was going on, we all cheered and gave him room to maneuver. Realizing that the jig was up, our sailor played the game as long as he could, until police reinforcement ended the chase. It was great free theater, although the actor probably had to pay some fine in the end. Too bad we couldn't all chip in for viewing his show.

Streetcars

ONE OF THE GREAT SEATTLE ATTRACTIONS FOR US KIDS was the Luna Park saltwater natatorium at Alki in West Seattle. Its main attraction, for us, was the high slide from which, in either a sitting or supine position, you ended up surfing or planing across the pool. To get there, you had to take the No. 1 Alki streetcar from First Avenue, which continued south over the tidal flats on a series of high wooden trestles. My fascination with streetcar operation usually found me sitting as close behind the driver as possible, learning all the controls and maneuvers—which I then re-hashed many times in daydreams. This run, in particular, was exciting, because we coasted down and back up from the ground-level stops. The direct-current motor speed was controlled by one hand on the rheostat crank, while the other hand moved the air-brake lever, and one foot sounded the traffic bell. What could be simpler? You didn't even have to steer. "I could immediately take over if anything should happen to the operator," I thought, somewhat darkly. I was ready, and right behind him.

Cable Cars

IN THOSE DAYS, Seattle's cable-car system had three lines that I often rode on, operating up First Hill and Yesler Terrace, along Madison, Yesler and James Streets.[5] Some cars had only two long benches located directly across from each other. The cable-grip was sudden on a steep incline, so it was hard to keep from sliding against your downhill neighbor, which could be an inconvenience or an opportunity. One time, I was sitting half a bench-length up from the downhill bench corner, which was occupied by a pretty girl. When the car started up with a jerk onto the steep uphill section, I grasped the edges of the bench to keep from sliding. But—you guessed it— I "lost" my grip and slid down into the girl's lap with, of course, profuse "apologies." Such were the innocent years.

Those years, in many ways, do seem innocent by modern standards, but at the same time, a young man of his era was given tremendous latitude and independence to prove himself. Young men might have been innocent, but they were far readier for adult responsibilities than many of their modern teenage counterparts. Wolf's story about his solitary walk-about after his junior year at Roosevelt High School, at the age of seventeen, shows the confidence a young man of Wolf's era could enjoy, both in himself and from his fearless parents.

Motorcycle Adventure

THE FALL OF 1928 FOUND ME AT THE SEATTLE PUBLIC LIBRARY, going through any and all books on motorcycles until I found some technical information on the British Excelsior machine I had picked up for ten dollars at a junkyard. Dad said that I could keep it and use it the next summer, provided I could put it into proper operating condition. He wisely figured it would give me a basic education in gas engines and work ethic. He wasn't kidding! That winter's spare time was entirely devoted to scrounging for foreign parts, and cajoling shops to make do with those that weren't a perfect fit. By the time school was out in June, I had convinced Dad I was ready to roll.

My destination was the lower Wenatchee River Valley, with its many fruit orchards. With my sleeping bag and spare clothes strapped on behind me, I negotiated gravel Snoqualmie Pass without a hitch. What a feeling—finally on my own, with the resolve to at least earn my expenses, and prove I could be trusted. Putt-putting along past the reservoir lakes, I got onto a heavily graveled road section that the trucks had deeply grooved. Approaching the Cle Elum River Bridge, I had to swerve suddenly to get out of my gravel groove so as not to be sideswiped by an oncoming truck. Going into a skid with my narrow high-pressure tires, I went across the curb and over the bank, landing just short of a dunk in the river (this brought to mind the pig episode with my uncle). Well, my spirit wasn't broken, and my cycle was OK, except for a smashed headlamp. Somewhat shaken up, I nevertheless went on to the top of Blewett Pass via the old and steep winding road, gladly stopping for a cold drink at the summit roadhouse.

In view of the long downhill stretch ahead, I decided to save some gas and just coast as long as possible before starting the engine. When I finally tried to start the motor, the kick-starter wouldn't budge. The air-cooled cylinder had shrunk against the piston, and it took me over half an hour of oiling and kicking before I could get under way again. It was almost dusk, and without a headlamp now, I was anxious to find a place to wash off the road dust, eat a meal, and find a roadside camp in which to sleep. I was fatigued, and had swollen wrists from the gravel road vibration, when there suddenly appeared alongside me a young buck on a brand-new four-cylinder Indian motorcycle, shouting, "Wanna race?" 'Nough said! Anyhow, I stayed that night at the Wenatchee River hamlet of Monitor, and the next morning, I found my first job there thinning apples at a nearby orchard, at forty cents per hour wages.

The job consisted of climbing up a large stepladder, and, with thumb and forefinger pinching off any of the little green apples that were touching each other. This, I found out, was a job most locals avoided, especially as you would be coated with itchy lime-sulfur spray deposits coming off the leaves. Jumping into the adjacent Wenatchee River for a cooling rinse after work was something to look forward to.

I was expected to take a half hour off for lunch, which I had regularly done. One very hot day, I leaned back in the shade of the tree after lunch for a few minutes' rest, but dozed off. When I woke up, there, above me, stood the boss, with my check already made out. He didn't need to tell me it wasn't pay day. After three weeks of diligent labor I was being "encouraged" to try something else. Innocent though it was, that has always been a haunting memory.

With mixed feelings, I cranked up my cycle, and took off toward Wenatchee. My first-ever check in my pocket calmed my conscience, and I soon earned more pocket money picking cherries and other fruit. By August, the old motorcycle wasn't doing too well, and it was about time to head home. A local boy in Wenatchee offered me fifteen dollars for my pride and joy, and I was happy to jump on a bus for Seattle. Dressed in a new straw hat and shirt, with more money than when I left, I greeted my folks, who were obviously relieved to see me, and who shared my pride in my demonstrated self-sufficiency. In retrospect, I realize luck played a major role.

Throughout these years at the onset of the Great Depression, it was not uncommon for young sons to exert their independence and to relieve their families of the obligation to support them. Since leaving the cannery on Lummi Island, Hubert had been struggling to bring in money any way he could. He continued to make his slide presentations of naval vessels but was unhappily still dependent on Elsbeth's family for aid. During the years in Kirkland and in Wallingford, he had pursued his doctorate in geography at the University of Washington, and by the time Wolf was ready to commence his senior year of high school, Hubert had landed his first full-time regular job in academia. Unfortunately, it meant moving the family all the way across the continent to the Appalachian Mountains. With characteristic aplomb, Wolf does not recall his senior year in Montgomery, West Virginia with disappointment, but with an amused fondness for a classic American experience.

West Virginia, the Mountain State, was originally part of Virginia and lies mostly below the Mason-Dixon Line. But it distinguished itself and seceded from its parent state, and from the Confederacy, mid-way through the Civil War, making it the only state to secede from South to North. Its odd shape may add somewhat to its hybrid identity, as its limbs squirm in between its other surrounding states of Pennsylvania and Ohio in the North, and Maryland and Kentucky in the South. The long legacy of this split on the people

From a high ledge, the young transplant Wolf overlooks the Kanawah River in West Virginia, 1930.

of West Virginia certainly must have presented a great cultural change from both the Northwest United States and Bavaria. But Wolf had already demonstrated cultural adaptability and rose to meet the challenge.

Montgomery lies just southwest of the center of the state, straddling Fayette and Kanawha counties, along the Kanawha River. Its population in 2000 was calculated at 1,942; the town has lost about 150 residents since Wolf graduated from high school there in 1931. At approximately 636 feet in elevation, it sits nestled amidst the folds and corduroy of the ancient Appalachians. Though the highest peaks of the closest mountains lie below 3,500 feet, the charm of the region's river valley vistas and waterfalls cannot be overstated. Geologically, the Appalachians are unique here, having a three hundred million year history that laid diverse layers of sediments. Sandstone, limestone, shale, and some of the world's most extensive bituminous coal beds, all rest here—fascinating for a future geologist, but problematic. Rooted in the heart of mining country, Montgomery labored in the late 1800s under the lyrical moniker of Coal Valley City.

When Wolf moved there, he was struck by the beauty of the West Virginia landscape ablaze in fall colors. With most of the mines hidden underground, the only negative aspect of the pre-dominant industry that he noticed was the endless parade of long coal trains. The hills were certainly a beautiful place to engage in his beloved scrambling, but it was not until he attended university that he would understand and appreciate the geologists' mecca he no longer inhabited.

This rural eastern town, having little in common with the western city he had adopted, might have proved too sleepy for Wolf, but he does not feel a need to say so. Rather, it is with a wink and a smile he ribs, "They called the hills there 'the American Alps,' so of course I felt right at home."

The Studebaker That Could

FATHER WAS OFFERED A POSITION as president of a junior college in the coal mining town of Montgomery, West Virginia. It was to be our last move as a complete family of seven. We all looked forward to an exciting cross-country "expedition" in our old Studebaker sedan. Whether it liked it or not, the old chariot had to not only carry seven people, plus baggage stacked to its ceiling, but, to add insult to injury, it had to pull a two-wheel trailer as well. We children were to keep watch that the trailer stayed hitched at all times.

Everything went according to plan (a very loose statement, considering the seven flats and blowouts suffered on the dusty Highway 20 northern route prior to reaching a paved Nebraska.) It was not until we were driving down a winding grade in Ohio that mother excitedly pointed to her window and said to Dad, "Look! There is a car wheel rolling alongside us near the curb." Dad couldn't believe his eyes when he recognized it as our wood-spoked wheel. With a loud and stern voice he commanded, "Everybody move and lean toward the left side of the car!" while he cautiously applied the remaining one-wheel brake for the three-wheeled stop. After chasing and retrieving the escaped wheel, we cautiously limped to the next repair shop. Only then could the wheel be reattached with new nuts. It was a new caution that now made us regularly check all wheel nuts from here on. After another long day on the road, we finally pulled into Montgomery—trailer, wheel, and all—ready for more adventures in our new surroundings. The old Studi had gotten us here after all!

Football Memoirs

IN MANY OF THE SMALL COAL-MINING TOWNS tucked away in the West Virginia hills, high school football was the entertainment and all-year talk of sports-oriented folks. I was in my last year of high school, and figured this would be my last and only chance to experience this sport, so I decided to join the team. Most of the boys on the team had already come through three years of play, and while I was in good physical condition, I had to learn the game in a hurry.

As the most untrained player on the squad, I was to be substitute guard in a line of boys that averaged more than thirty pounds heavier than me. The oversize pieces of uniform I was issued were evidence of the weight difference. With two experienced guards ahead of me, the chance of getting into an actual game looked slim. Then came the season's first game with the neighboring up-river school. The first half ended without a touchdown for either side, but with several injuries and position switches that, unbelievably, put me into the game. The start of the second half saw me standing in the far corner of our end zone with our best runners awaiting the kickoff ahead of me. Uh-oh—the ball came directly at me. The onlookers must have wondered, "Who is this boy in the sloppy uniform scooting along the sideline nearly the length of the field, only to stumble short of the goal line?" The team's next play was our first touchdown. It was pure luck, but the coach got me a fitting uniform, and soon put me into the backfield.

The last game of the season was a frosty Thanksgiving Day on our home field, with light snow falling during the first half. It became increasingly difficult to hold onto the ball. Coach made a smart move when he sent a boy into town during the half to buy up all the available canvas gloves for our team, to the chagrin of the visiting coach and team. Sportsmanship was obviously not part of our coach's philosophy in such a case. The game ended with surrounding parked cars directing their headlights onto the field. A futile last-ditch effort by the other team throwing high, hard-to-see passes above the headlight beams ended in a hilarious car-honking victory for our team, and a treasured memory of small-town America.

The Abe Lincoln Factor

THE CLASSES AT THE LOCAL MONTGOMERY HIGH SCHOOL were quite limited, compared to the Seattle schools, and Dad, as head of the local junior college, arranged for me to take an additional calculus class on campus. That class turned out to be an important factor the following year at the University of Washington. It enabled me to enroll in engineering classes as a freshman.

My high school English teacher in Montgomery was a pretty young lady who encouraged me to enter a state oratory competition at the University of West Virginia in Charleston. The winner would be given free tuition there for four years. Participants had the choice of working on some famous speech or picking their own subject matter. I decided on the latter, and chose the subject "world peace."

Young Wolf, probably a high school portrait.

The teacher helped me with context and delivery, and after many after-school sessions, she finally pronounced me ready, while I had definitely acquired a secret crush. Taking the train together to Charleston, the next day found us sitting in the University auditorium, listening to the other aspiring students perform. When, after my orations, I returned to my seat, she said I had done well, and had a good chance to win. Then onto the stage came a tall, gangly student with a beard and a dark suit, announcing his speech to be Lincoln's "Gettysburg Address," which he delivered in a deep, stentorian voice. What the heck! Who would find fault with that performance, even though it was not his own composition? In a way, I was actually relieved, for I couldn't wait to get back to my beloved Pacific Northwest. And it also eased the final parting from my unsuspecting secret love.

Native adaptability aside, Wolf was homesick for Seattle, and thus counts his defeat in the oratory competition as a gift of fate. A scholarship to the University of West Virginia would have been flattering and economical, but it was the University of Washington he aspired to. Setting off on his own once and for all, Wolf packed up his belongings, kidnapped a West Virginia football buddy for the summer, and set his compass for the West.

Montana "Ranchhands"

GRADUATING FROM HIGH SCHOOL was, of course, a major step in lifestyle. I was confident that, with minimum help, I could work my way through college, despite the Great Depression. Trading West Virginia for Washington, and high school for university, were dreams come true. Jim, a buddy from our high school football team, wanted to come along for the adventure, and so off we went in my 1929 Ford Coupe (with rumble seat) that Dad helped me buy, which would last me for the next nine years. The immediate object was to find a summer job en route. But it was not until we reached Montana during that summer of 1931 that the opportunity presented itself on a large cattle ranch near Poplar on Highway 2.

We hired on as "hands" to do whatever basic work assignments were given for the summer months. The ranch was situated alongside what was locally called the "Missouri Bottoms," with rich alfalfa fields near the river,

Wolf bales hay at the Frye Ranch in Montana, 1931.

and beef cattle ranges in the adjacent prairies. The dried alfalfa hay was baled, and then stacked for winter cattle feed, and oats were raised and milled for the workhorses and riding horses.

We soon got used to the hot but dry climate and were allowed to sleep in one of the cool underground potato cellars. There were nights when we would not only hear coyotes howl, but also the long and steady drumbeats coming from the nearby burial ground of the Assiniboine Indian Reservation. Almost weekly we were shifted around to different jobs and locations, and not always together. One of our coolest activities was operating a fan mill, in which the rotating blades removed contaminating thistles and hulls from the thrashed oats. We were allowed to do this work during cool morning and evening periods, as long as we put in our eight daily hours. There was work in the alfalfa hayfields, where we first had to catch our horses in their fenced pastures, and harness them before the breakfast bell at 6 a.m. I was also allowed to ride on the last day of the cattle drive.

The toughest job, however, was when we were assigned to the branding corral. As greenhorns, we, of course, were given the lowliest job—maybe to test our mettle or provide some good laughs. A cowhand on horseback would lasso the rear leg of a bawling yearling calf, which was my signal to grab and partly lift and dump it, kicking, to the ground. Holding it down while they tied up its legs, the little victim was ready to be mutilated. In rapid order, they tagged one of its ears, punched in a vaccination needle,

During his summer job in Montana, Wolf attempts to bring a calf down for branding...

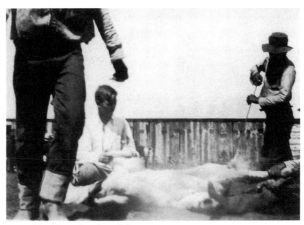

...and is ultimately successful.

castrated it with large tongs if it was a bull calf, and seared its hide with the "Frye" brand. When the little bugger staggered up to its feet, it really didn't know what was what until it was reunited with its anxious mother. Working six hours a day in foot-deep corral dust, those were probably the longest weeks we spent on the ranch. An ample but quick lunch at the accompanying chuck wagon was the major attraction during that period.

Tough as nails by summer's end, and with some hard-earned money in our pockets, Jim and I finally parted; he caught a bus back to West Virginia, while Lizzy (my beloved Ford) and I started rolling toward the cool Puget Sound country. "U-Dub," here I come!

Career Decisions

BY THE TIME I GRADUATED FROM HIGH SCHOOL, I had narrowed career choices pretty much to Geology, Engineering or Forestry. It seems that, subconsciously, I was leaning toward an outdoor-type calling which would not necessarily tie me to an office chair and routine. My various contacts with Forest Rangers, however, left me with mixed signals as to their opportunities. (Foresters, trail crew members, lookouts and managers had all left me with the impression that professional advance, more often than not, depended on who was retiring.) Despite the high standing of the University of Washington's Department of Forestry, I chose the School of Engineering, for its broader applications and opportunities.

As incoming freshmen in 1931, we were exposed to the curricula and job opportunities by professors and deans from each engineering department, including electrical, civic, mechanical, mining, metallurgical, and ceramic engineering (later called non-metallic minerals engineering). Because this was in the early Depression years, it wasn't easy for the schools to make their case for great opportunities. However, when I heard from the professor of ceramic engineering that only three students had graduated from his department the previous year, I pricked up my ears. I was hearing about a relatively new profession in the engineering field. The term "ceramic" was historically associated with pottery and art, but this new engineering field specialized in the high temperature treatment and production of calcined lime and gypsum products, Portland cement, glass, building brick and tile, refractory materials, expanded lightweight aggregates, and specialty fire-treated minerals for science.

It was an opportune profession choice. Not only would I be entering a relatively new engineering field, but with only one other engineering student signing up, we could look forward to what would amount to four years of private instruction from an outstanding professor who wrote the textbook for the discipline. I've never regretted that decision, as it eventually led to a worldwide consulting practice that I ran over a thirty-year period.

University Years

IN RETROSPECT, my five years at the University of Washington from 1931 to 1936 were probably among the more exciting in my life, especially since they also included adventurous summer jobs that helped make that education possible.

The freshman and sophomore standard engineering courses were nip-and-tuck, making me feel lucky to pass at all. This was, perhaps, partly due to the very limited curriculum I was exposed to during my senior year in the West Virginia coal-mining backcountry. However, during my junior and senior years at the "U," I had some choices of elective courses, and my grades and interest began to climb. This led to advanced studies, and paved the way for a Bureau of Mines fifth year fellowship grant for summer research in 1935. A lucky break!

School and studies occupied most of my time during my college years, but there remain, nevertheless, vivid memories of recreation, sports and people. While I did not turn out for any team activities, I learned and competed in both boxing and wrestling for self-defense, while also taking up gymnastics and tennis during school sessions. But when soul-searching decisions had to be made on weekends, when homework or tests competed with "important" skiing and climbing events, the latter often won out. This would invariably result in hasty textbook studying on ski trains and in lodges, and/or staying up late into the night after such outings. As I write about this now in my mid-nineties, I feel like a braggart, but at the time it was no big deal, especially when you consider the lot of so many Depression-era students who worked their way through school with night-shift schedules.

Timber!

WITH MY FRESHMAN ENGINEERING YEAR BEHIND ME, it was time to line up a summer job to fund continued education. Ideally, from that point on, work would be associated with one's chosen engineering field. This was wishful thinking for many of us who were in college during the Depression years.

Hans Grage, one of my skiing friends from The Mountaineers club, a husky young fellow who was also of German extraction, asked me if I would be interested in cutting "pulpwood" with him. I said, "You've got a deal!" He showed me a stand of second-growth timber near Stanwood where we would selectively cut hemlock for a pulp mill contract at four dollars per cord.

Hans was not only a happy-go-lucky optimist, but also a rare jack-of-all-trades, who could invent his own unique solutions to problems. A nearby primitive shack in the woods was to be our abode. Our contact with the outside world would be in a weekly pulp mill truck run to load up our output of cut and peeled cordwood, and a trip to Stanwood for a week's groceries.

We had much to learn in order to finally make wages, but in a couple of weeks we had worked out a system that we could live with. The product had to be four-foot logs within a certain diameter range, peeled of all bark, and stacked alongside a narrow forest road for easy truck pick-up. (Remember, for us this was B.C.—Before Chainsaws.) Each day we became more proficient and also more competitive in timesaving techniques. For example:

- We learned to fell a tree across a previous one on the ground in order to de-limb and saw it up above the dirt. We soon got so good at felling that we could hit a tin can on a nearby stump with the falling tree.

- We learned that we had to remove the bark from the sawed logs the same day the tree was cut; it would become too difficult, a day or two later, to get the bark to part from the wood.

- We invented our own rapid two-man debarking technique that in a pulp mill would be carried out in a large revolving drum. Using a heavy-duty garden spade with a sharpened edge, one of us would slice and peel the bark, like a paring knife peeling an apple, while the other would whack an axe into the log's end, using it as a crank handle to rotate the log for the peeler. Smart, eh?

- We soon found out that in order to produce one or more daily peeled and stacked cords, we not only had to replenish our worn bodies with food each day, but also had to rejuvenate our work saws and axes with files and saw sets. Democratically, we alternated doing those chores each evening.

Being alone and out of the earshot of the public all day, we often made the woods reverberate with our Alpine yodeling practice sessions that would, later that winter in "professional" form, be foisted on our fellow mountain skiers.

Alaska Fisheries

THE OUTLOOK FOR STUDENT SUMMER JOBS had not improved over the next academic year. The break in 1933, however, came about through a friend of my grandmother Epler, a Mr. Jack Gilbert, who was the head of an Alaska fisheries operation. He thought I could be useful in a number of jobs at his salmon cannery in Port Althorp, on Chichagof Island, Alaska. My duties ranged from counting fish to maintaining equipment; from manning a floating fish trap to helping to put the cannery back into its winter storage mode at the end of the season. This was not exactly in my engineering field, but was my first monthly salary, and it put me further through school.

Much of cannery work is hard labor, and because of the sporadic fish runs, the work level ranged from lots of leisure time to more than twelve-hour days for the crews. Common labor was performed by a crew of Filipinos under the jurisdiction of their "China boss," who was, in fact, an educated man from China. Other common labor, primarily final fish cleaning, was traditionally done along a conveyor belt by native island women who set up a temporary summer camp in makeshift cabins on the hillside above the cannery, known as "Hoonah Heights." As you can imagine, there was a well-worn path between the Filipino bunkhouse and Hoonah Heights.

During the early weeks, waiting for the first fish runs, I became well acquainted with some of the boys who were friendly and athletic, and who taught me many of their skills in gymnastics and boxing, up in the "webloft"—the net-drying room. The season finally got under way. The "seiners" out in the Straits unloaded or "brailed" their nets onto the cannery "tender," which, when loaded to the gunwale, just short of swamping, staggered to the cannery. My first job was to identify and count fish coming up the conveyor, which delivered the fish to the noisy "Iron Chink." This offensively named device decapitated the salmon before the "sliming gang" (the native women) cleaned out the guts and trimmed the remaining fins.

Later in the season, I was assigned to an anchored offshore fish trap, in the form of a log frame, enclosing a submerged pocket net with a flared entry-trap, and oriented in the direction of known salmon runs. A tiny shack on the raft was my abode, along with a 22-caliber rifle to dispose of any sea lions that got caught in the net, and, as was explained with a smirky smile, to defend the trap against any fish robbers trying to get at my catch. Was I again being tested, as in the branding corral? Happily, I never had to use it.

Most of the actual daily work consisted of constantly removing floating kelp from the nets. I also had a seaworthy dory that one day came in handy when I had to seek refuge from storm waves around a nearby promontory. The cannery tenders supplied me with food and water. This lonesome stint lasted for only a few weeks, because of the skimpy catches the occasional cannery tender brailed out. I was glad to get back on land. Floating fish traps were soon phased out, making this a unique experience, in retrospect.

A memorable, but not exactly pleasurable, incident took place during my return trip to Seattle at the season's end. The first port-of-call was Prince Rupert in British Columbia, where the boat landed close to midnight. Prohibition was in the process of being repealed that summer in the States, and the cannery crew could hardly wait to get their hands on some hard liquor. They rousted the proprietor of the local liquor store out of bed and practically bought out the store. I still remember having to leave my under-deck bunk in disgust and sleep for the rest of the trip in my sleeping bag up on the open deck to get fresh air. Some of the men had become too drunk to find the head! 'Nough said.

I arrived in Seattle not only with my check intact, but happily lugging a big sack of choice king salmon I had personally canned, with some tomato ketchup added before sealing and "retorting" in the last cannery cooking operation. The fish made appreciated Christmas presents later.

While I didn't gain any field experience in my chosen engineering profession doing these odd jobs, they were, in a way, blessings in disguise. My forty years in the engineering field was followed by thirty years devoted to environmental issues, which touched on critical farming, forestry and fishing problems. Thus, the time spent learning about Montana ranching, Washington logging and Alaska fishing were not entirely wasted in the long run.

Boy Scout Summer

THE SUMMER OF 1934 was the first since graduating from high school in the Depression years that I failed to land a steady paying job. What money I earned came from helping Frank Henderson, a former Boy Scout executive, build and run a summer camp for boys at Westcott Bay on San Juan Island. It was, in fact, the boys camp located on Roche Harbor Lime Company land that, in 1936, led to my first professional engineering position in the lime burning industry. In the last month of the summer vacation in 1934, I acted as a climbing guide and instructor for two gentlemen from the east coast, spending three weeks in the North Cascades.

Skagit Interludes

WITH THE GREAT DEPRESSION BEGINNING TO SHOW SIGNS of a slight weakening, it nevertheless was an unfortunate time to graduate, with few employment opportunities. Having made Geology my second major and earned a Sigma-Xi Science Honorary on graduation, I asked the local office of the U.S. Bureau of Mines to consider me for a graduate fellowship that would assist me in a fifth year of university studies. This was granted, and I was assigned to make a geologic as well as a product-development study for an operating soapstone and talc mine located in the upper Skagit River Valley, downstream from the lower Seattle City Light dam at Newhalem. After all my non-technical summer jobs, I was finally getting into something practical and related to my engineering and geology curricula.

The technical part of my position at the mine was to determine the extent and quality of the deposit from surface outcrop sample analyses, to be followed with high-temperature ceramic testing and product development at the University and Bureau of Mines station. This field and lab work was also to serve as the subject for my Master's Degree thesis at the school. (For better or worse, my career would preclude me ever finishing my Master's Degree.)

Mining and processing was rather unique at this location in that the two operations were done almost simultaneously underground. A room was sawed out of the relatively soft soapstone in the form of benches that could, in turn, be further sawed into bricks that would withstand the high temperatures and chemical attacks of pulp mill soda-recovery furnaces.

Local Inspectors

TO REACH THE MINE IN THE SKAGIT RIVER VALLEY, you crossed the river on a small wood bridge located about halfway between Marblemount and Newhalem. On some hot summer nights, I exchanged my bed in the crowded bunkhouse for a cool gravel bar on the river. When the workmen found out, the kidding started, and I was regaled with lurid tales of stalking cougars. I have to admit to getting a little apprehensive, and that evening I gathered a pile of dry wood and placed it next to my sleeping bag, with the intention of keeping a small fire going by replenishing it now and then during the night. I soon went to sleep, and awakened only once to tend the fire. When I woke up the next morning with some relief, noting that there was still a little smoke curling up from the fire pit, there were—to my amazement—unmistakable large paw prints around my sleeping spot. I had been investigated! Whether it was the smoldering fire that kept the curious cat at bay, I'll never know, but Forest Rangers told me later they were not surprised. The bunkhouse, however, saw my bunk occupied thereafter.

Other Locals

DURING THE DEPRESSION, the West Coast saw an influx of people from Oklahoma settling in California and other areas, including the Skagit Valley. Some of the "Oakies" were employed at the mine. One Saturday evening I was invited out to one of their family gatherings, and was asked to be sure to bring along my little concertina accordion. It was a memorable get-together of twenty or more inter-related friends, family members and kids. After an evening meal of meat and vegetables from their own farms, they gathered for what I thought would be a few songs. That, however, turned out to be a marathon of one ballad after another, recounting either unrequited love, or the demise of scoundrels. The repetitious melodies soon wore out my accordion finger on my right hand, but I carried on to the bitter end, with two fingers working the left-hand bass notes to provide the endless rhythm. It was a touching family-fest of "Americana," at its old-time best.

Spit and Polish

ONE SUNDAY EVENING, I had gone to Marblemount for a Coke and ice cream, as well as to tank up Lizzy and give her a wash and a polish. On my way back to the mine, I picked up an old grizzled prospector, thumbing for a ride. He got in, and grumpily muttered that he was headed "up the Skagit," which could be anywhere.

Without any further conversations, he sat next to me chewing his tobacco, then turned his head and spat out his juice at what he thought was an open window. Without embarrassment or excuse, he continued to just sit there in silence, until I gladly let him out before turning off to the mine. It was getting late, and I decided to clean the brown-spattered window the next day. A big mistake. Whatever chemistry was involved, the mess had hardened to the point where soap and water and scratching could not rid Lizzy of this ignominy. It was not until a week later, after several tries, that a shop found a solvent that would remove the mess without marring the window. The expression "spit and polish" took on a new meaning for this frustrated driver.

The Girl

IT WAS IN MY FOURTH YEAR AT THE UNIVERSITY that I fell in love with Harriet Woodward, an outdoor-type girl who, a few years earlier, my scoutmaster had introduced me to with the hint that she could out-hike any boy that he knew. Harry Higman probably figured he could get to me with an implied challenge. Suffice it to say that Harriet and I became good friends during our University years, when she was studying art and I was studying Engineering and Geology. In those days, the art students interested in ceramics came to the engineering labs—which we called "Lower Slobovia"—to fire their work. There were only two ceramic engineering students, and not too many women in any engineering department, so, naturally, we loved it.

Despite our shared interest in the outdoors, there nevertheless grew in me, with time, the realization that her Christian Science upbringing and beliefs would surely bring us into conflict if we eventually married, especially if we had children. According to the founder of the Christian Science movement, Mary Baker Eddy, all so-called sicknesses are only of the mind, and can be healed by "holding a good thought" while reading or being read to from her book by "Science Practitioners." When I went to the Seattle Public Library to read up on the history of this so-called science, I found out that the books were not in the regular stacks, but for some rea-

Harriet Woodward in high school.

son had to be requested from a locked-up special case. I found, therein, books on the history of that so-called religion, and the lawsuits and deaths resulting from its practice.

There came a day when, after an absence of several weeks, Harriet greeted me on campus with hand-gestures, as she had lost her voice due to a severe case of tonsillitis. She had diligently visited her Christian Science "Reader," but obviously without success. I challenged her to be fair, and give equal time to the medical profession. She agreed, although she had never been to a doctor. That afternoon, we visited one of the interns at the university infirmary, explaining the situation. Taking me aside, after he had swabbed out her tonsils with a healing disinfectant, he told me that she was in the last stage of tonsillitis. The next morning, she called me and said that she was able, already, to eat breakfast. Our future children would have proper medical care! As for me, I was long at odds with the gods who, despite all prayers, entreaties and religious commitments, could ignore the unbelievable tortures of disease and starvation that befall millions of children every year. Modern psychology frowns on the use of scare-tactics in child education, yet Christian religion still hints at hellish consequences.

Always attributing his good fortune strictly to luck, Wolf doesn't take credit for any of the serendipitous opportunities that came his way during tough economic times. But even if unconsciously, he truly did have a knack for making things happen to his advantage. He may have lamented that his summer jobs did not further his engineering career, but as he became more and more involved in environmental advocacy, it was those jobs in farming, forestry and fishing that enabled him to hold productive dialogues with various stakeholders in environmental policy. Maybe it was luck, but none of those jobs could have been done by just anyone. It took someone completely at home in nature's isolation, and who saw backbreaking and often mind-numbing labor as an adventure. Wolf was up for anything, and so anything came his way.

As busy as one can imagine Wolf was during those university years, he had an entirely separate life going on outside (literally) of his university studies. In 1929, prior to his departure to West Virginia, The Mountaineers, a Seattle-based outdoor recreation club, awarded memberships to three worthy Boy Scouts in the Seattle area. Nominated by his Scout leader, Harry Higman, Wolf was one of the three lucky recipients. Claiming it was only because he could ski, and The Mountaineers wanted him to share his expertise, he nonetheless happily joined. The opportunities for skiing and mountain climbing in Washington's Cascades were opening up to him with his recruitment into this great club. Matriculation in the University of Washington and matriculation in The Mountaineers were both commenced with equal vigor, and it was during these years that Wolf began to put himself on the map of the cultural landscape.

THREE

Wolf the Fox

S KIING WAS ALREADY AN ANCIENT MODE OF TRANSPORTATION in 1206 when Norwegian heroes Torstein Skevla and Skjervald Skrukka used skis during the Norwegian Civil War to spirit the two-year-old future King Häkon Häkonsson to safety in Trondheim. Thanks to the wondrous preservation possible in subarctic peat bogs, skis have been found throughout Scandinavia and in Russia that some historians believe date back to the Mesolithic era. A ski found in a peat bog near Lake Sindor in Russia has been carbon dated to between 6300 and 5000 BC. Other bogs in Sweden, Norway and Finland have offered up skis and ski fragments that date from 4700 BC to 1000 AD, and petroglyphs of men on skis in Norway are dated at five thousand years old. Evidence even exists to show the Chinese skiing by the seventh century AD and the Japanese using skis with bindings by the end of the first millennium AD. But this history of skiing is one of practical transportation; Nordic skiing was primarily an aid to hunting and warfare. The development of alpine or downhill skiing strictly as recreation is a modern phenomenon, and can be traced to the late 1800s in the German and Austrian Alps, where Bavaria and Tyrol share the spine of the mountains. Here, free of the tradition of skiing as a utilitarian activity, Alpine *skipioniere* created a new sport.

Though individuals in isolated places in Central Europe were beginning to reconceive the use of the hardwood slats, Austrian

Mathias Zdarsky is credited with the original vision of the sport and the design of the first specialized alpine bindings. But the real revolution came with a young man from the village of Stuben am Arlberg in the Austrian Tyrol. His name was Hannes Schneider, and his gift was not just for developing better techniques; it was for marketing the unknown pastime.

In 1898, catching sight of one of his elders strapping on slats purely for the pleasure of speed, the eight-year-old Hannes was possessed by a transforming passion. His destiny as a cheese maker was forever averted. For him, it was all about the speed attained on a downhill run—the approximation of flight. The radical theories of turning and maneuvering that became his legacy were designed purely to keep him on the knife's edge between velocity and mortality. Father of the Arlberg Technique, Schneider succeeded in combining maximum speed with control and safety. (This teaching method centered on the "stem christie" turn, in which the skier begins each turn in a wedge stance, and gradually pulls one ski in until the skis are parallel. Ultimately, increased skill and practice would lead to a wedge-less parallel turn, which allowed both speed and control.) His trademark method of teaching turned the resort at St. Anton in Austria, where he ran his ski school, into a Mecca for the wealthy in search of thrills in the mountains.

In 1924, when the first Winter Olympics were held in Chamonix, France, the ski events were strictly cross-country (or Nordic) skiing and ski-jumping. Predictably, the events were ruled by the descendants of the likes of Häkon Häkonsson's rescuers—Norwegians, Swedes and Finns. By 1936, when the first downhill or alpine ski events were held in Garmisch-Partenkirchen, Germany, they were dominated by the home team. Trading in the equipment and the Telemark turns of Scandinavia for alpine bindings and stem christies, the Austrians and Germans had made the new sport their own.

Meanwhile, world famous by 1920 for his competitive victories and his successful ski school, Hannes Schneider caught the eye of filmmaker Dr. Arnold Fanck, who knew good visual drama when he saw it. On the cutting edge of adventure filming, he enlisted Schneider for a series of films that showcased the excitement and beauty of this new sport in the Alps. Mountain films were to become to German cinema and popular culture what Westerns would become in the United States, and Fanck's films were at the forefront. The third film of his collaboration with Schneider, *A Fox Chase in the Engadine*, was released in 1922 and sent a shock wave throughout every country it premiered in. People flocked to Schneider's school from all over the world, disseminating ski fever upon their return home. It was a worldwide sporting epidemic.

Wolf Bauer saw the fabled film under the German title, *Eine Fuchsjagd auf Skiern durchs Engadin,* at the age of eleven, and like every other young boy who shared the love of the Alps, he wanted a piece of that adventure. Moving to the American Northwest may have removed him from the forefront of the world revolution in alpine skiing, but the Cascade Mountains were more than ripe for a cultural transplant. He was just in time to ride that later wave.

He recounted his experiences in the 1963 *Mountaineer Annual.*[6] Following are excerpts:

"Telemarks, Sitzmarks and Other Early Impressions"

AT THE RISK OF OFFENDING MY OLD SKIING COMPANIONS with important omissions while boring our younger schussboomers and schneehaserl, let me ramble a bit about our ski-doings as seen from the happy-go-lucky eyes of a Bavarian teenager experiencing the excitement of ski explosions twice in two successive decades on two separate continents.

Certainly we kids in the Bavarian Alps who started skiing in 1919 after the war were quite aware that graduating from oak sleds to skis opened up a new world to us. It had many practical advantages as well. No longer was it always necessary to walk along the road to school, for instance, as the buoyant skis allowed straight shortcuts across the fields, and many a flapping stocking yarn or bit of leather from our shorts marked the path of our efforts to beat the school bell over and through barbed-wire fences. Only when the horse-drawn snowplow had to open the drifted road officially and belatedly did we dutifully walk or tie our sleds behind the plow, cherishing the slow laborious pace.

Many embarrassing situations were to tag my skiing days to come. But no more auspicious start could be asked for than that innocent morning on the farm when, as was our custom, my dog Sascha and I sailed across the wind-crusted fields in pursuit of imaginary rabbits. This was skijoring[7] at its best, with me hanging on to his collar as we swept along at full tilt in futile chase. Negotiating a wire fence—almost—I found myself upside down, unable to reach my bindings for release, while a rabbit, a real one this time, upheld Sascha's faltering faith in the true purpose of this skijoring sport. Only this time, with me in the ditch, he had, at last, a sporting chance. It seemed an eternity before he returned and his barking attracted rescue help.

Our skis were heavy and long, an economical way for parents to address the growth situation. Flat toe irons were simply passed through burned-out slots made in the sides of the skis, and bent up to suit the shape of our shoes. These Schuster-type bindings consisted of a leather strap with clamp threaded through the slot behind the toe-iron. While at first we used our stout summer boots with soles and heels shaved to fit this harness, village shoemakers and those who traveled from farm to farm soon produced acceptable ski boots. Poles were usually of hazelnut wood and rather long. While the use of two ski poles was actually normal practice, many of our teenage set disdained such crutches from the beginning, and stems, Telemarks, and even small jumps were made with the single pole held cross-wise in front of the body. (How much closer to impalement can you get?) All this soon changed, however, for the movement toward controlled high-speed downhill skiing was well under way in the regions around us. Mass skiing, as far as Europe was concerned, had arrived, with the impetus and inspiration engendered by that incomparable film "Fox Chase in the Engadine," in which our new hero, Hannes Schneider, laid down the new fundamentals of the Arlberg technique. The new stem Christiania turn was now adopted with a vengeance, and the Telemark began to return to its old trade-mark status as the landing form of the Scandinavian jumper. It was during this transition period that I emigrated from Bavaria in 1925 to Seattle, home of my pioneer grandparents. I had already looked forward with great anticipation to skiing with Seattle youngsters, but the mild Puget Sound climate and lack of winter road access to the mountains soon made me realize that I would probably have to forget my beloved sport for some time to come.

When The Mountaineers offered young Wolf membership in the club, he suspected it was because he knew how to ski, but that

Wolf, the lodge entertainer, poses with his accordion, 1930.

didn't hurt his pride. After several years away from good schussing, he was eager to share his wisdom to obtain companionship on the slopes. The Mountaineers, like the ski clubs in the Alps, had its own ski huts, at Snoqualmie and Stampede passes. The familiar alpine tradition of riding the train to the mountains and sharing the hut with friends and fellow skiers was happily re-created here only fifty miles from home, and Wolf's recollections of the times spent at Snoqualmie Lodge are amongst his happiest.

When the Snoqualmie Lodge fraternity found out Wolf could play the accordion, he became even more popular, and there was always a ready invitation for him to come along and bring his concertina with him. So hospitable were his fellow lodge dwellers that they volunteered to carry his instrument up the grueling one-and-a-quarter mile ascent from the Denny Creek train station to the lodge. But once he fell for their guileful hospitality, he was a marked

Wolf enjoys ice skating on Lodge Lake at Snoqualmie Pass during an early season freeze in 1929.
Heavy snow pack usually precludes opportunities to skate in the Cascades.

man. Always obliged to provide the evening's music, Wolf rarely
had an opportunity to dance himself, a regret that seems to have
dogged him ever since. Yet the photo that remains of him skating
on the nearby Lodge Lake in front of a gramophone at three thousand feet gives testimony to an occasional day off; so does the photo
of an empty-handed Wolf and his future wife belting out a tune
inside the lodge, no instrument in sight. The yodeling theater alone
was ample compensation for his trouble.

Even before Wolf's arrival, The Mountaineers were carving out a
ski culture based on the fragmentary transmissions from the ski
front in Europe. Accessible 14,410 foot Mount Rainier had been
declared a National Park in 1899. With an average of six hundred
inches of snow annually, and wide, treeless snowfields, Rainier was
a superior nursery for the fledgling sport. Tacoma Mountaineers
were skiing its Paradise Valley by 1915. Ski tournaments began there
in 1917, which included spectacular jumping and attracted thousands of people to the park. But the alpine events of downhill and
slalom were still to come.

In the early 1930s, Wolf was still a young student at the University of Washington, but his weekends were full of the mountains.

Wolf belts out a yodel to Harriet Woodward's enjoyment, 1929.

He and fellow Mountaineers of German and Austrian descent were leading the charge of the new ski culture. Hans Otto Giese, ten years older than Wolf, had been born in Frankfurt, and was a formidable cross-country champion as well as an alpine skier. He had been an extra in Hannes Schneider's *A Fox Chase in the Engadine* and was well schooled in the Arlberg technique. Wolf's former lumberjack partner, Hans Grage, a first-born German-American skier, was likewise a competitor to be reckoned with on both kinds of skis. In the very first downhill and slalom races in 1930 at the Mountaineers' Meany Ski Hut near Stampede Pass—the first formal alpine races in Washington State—the top three finishers were Grage-Giese-Bauer in the downhill and Bauer-Giese-Grage in the slalom. This seeming monopoly caused Dr. Edmond Meany, club president, to complain about the "Teutonic Gang-Up." Other Bauer slalom and downhill victories would follow in 1932, 1933 and 1936, the 1933 victory at Meany being the most noteworthy. Because the skiers all began the race together and were allowed to seek their own course from top to bottom, Wolf pushed out the envelope of skiing creativity by jump-

Hans Grage, climber, skier and
Wolf's fellow lumberjack.

Hans Otto Giese shows top ski form.

Wolf jumps the snow cornice to win the 1933 downhill race at The Mountaineers' Meany Lodge.

ing a snow cornice to victory, prompting a dramatic photograph for the record books in the process.

Two premier annual events, the Silver Skis downhill race and the cross-country Ski Patrol Race, put the Northwest skiing arena on the world map, dominating winter sports in Washington throughout the 1930s. The more famous was the Silver Skis race, an all-out ski-for-all, staged from 1934 to 1942. Purportedly initiated at the suggestion of Hans Otto Giese to legendary Seattle Post-Intelligencer sports editor, Royal Brougham, as a way to promote alpine skiing, it was organized by a consortium of clubs that included the Seattle Ski Council, Commonwealth Ski Club, the YMCA, the University of Washington Ski Club, the Washington Athletic Club, and the sponsor, The Seattle Post-Intelligencer. The first year of this event was the only year the race began with its mass or "geschmozzle" start, which set it up to become a suicide stampede only possible in an era before litigation

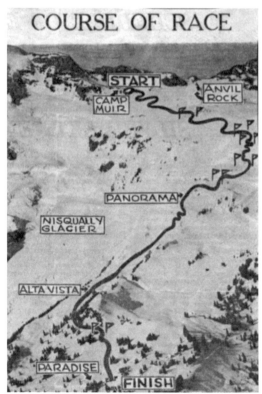

Map of the Silver Skis Race course on Mount Rainier, 1934.

became rampant. Brougham called the participating immortals "the daring riders of the hickory staves."[8] Besides navigating the 4,600 foot drop in elevation over the 3.9-mile course, competitors had to climb the 4,500 feet to the Camp Muir start point prior to the race, in itself a two-and-a-half to three-hour ordeal.

Conditions varied considerably and unpredictably from start to finish. Of the infamous ice washboard wind-slab, participant Bud Brady of Seattle said, "I saw about twenty-five skiers and they were all making S-turns across the snowfield, and it was like somebody was there with a machine gun. Every second there was a big splash of snow."[9] The spectacle created a media blitz and attracted thousands of spectators. Radio coverage was provided by the Columbia Broadcasting Company and Universal Newsreel filmed the event. Nothing else in the United States, perhaps even the world, could compare.

Wolf was in top form in 1934 at the inaugural Silver Skis Race, and had it not been for the breaking of his ski during a wipe-out, he might have won. Still, he settled for a respectable fifth place. He recalled the event years later in a retrospective piece for the 1963 *Mountaineer Annual.*[10]

WE ALL STARTED TO PUSH OFF, that historic day, onto the convex-sloping roof below Camp Muir, being rapidly pulled, as in a vortex, toward the first hidden gate near Anvil Rock, still a half mile away. Overly-waxed skis with a shellacked base coat prepared for the slower snows of lower elevations began to accelerate us with deceptive smoothness. Everyone was bent on escaping the inevitable traffic jam of the other sixty-five runners, funneling and crowding in from the original spread-out starting line. In these first seconds there was little chance or desire to check our speed until the ranks would thin out on each side. I had gone into Spartan training, doing deep knee-bends during weeks of preparation in order to prevent the cramping effects of a deep crouch position against expected head winds. While this paid off in the later stages, the extra speed cost me both poles, goggles, and a broken ski, which was still hanging precariously together with a steel edge fastening[11]—the result of a somersault at near sixty miles per hour. I was leading at the time, but my spot of reckoning also became the Waterloo for many behind me, in some instances with serious consequences. Most of us had waited too long to check our speed and change course because of the traffic on all sides. When slowing down became imperative, the smooth snow surface suddenly changed to shingled windrows and waves, bringing about a fearsome explosion of cartwheeling humanity. It was not until the race was over that I learned how others behind me had spilled at the same time and place. Somewhat dazed, I picked myself up, deciding not to waste time looking for my poles and goggles, and immediately got under way again. My wax was still working well enough to keep me moving rapidly past Anvil Rock, as long as I kept my weight off the broken ski. I had a lucky break in successfully negotiating the intermediate gradient in midcourse without occasional assistance from poles. I well remember my head clearing and my confidence returning when I heard the P.A. system at McClure's Rock control point announce that I had moved into fourth position. With the weakened ski, I could not afford a high-speed descent of the face of Panorama, and my chances of catching up began to fade. One satisfying experience still was to come my way, nevertheless. Amid encouraging cheers from loyal rooters for whom I meant to uphold The Mountaineers' honor, I somehow found the audacity to trot sneakily but lamely around an unsuspecting cross-country champion in the sickly flat below Panorama.[12] Squatting immediately in the main fast track to Paradise Lodge (later finishes were in Edith Creek Basin), I challenged each subsequent passing attempt from behind to the bitter finish.

Wolf coasts at the finish of the Silver Skis Race on Mount Rainier in 1934. He placed fifth, despite a broken ski and the loss of both poles.

Don Fraser of Seattle Ski Club, who was later to make the Olympic ski team, won the race. No finer competitor could have led the parade.[13]

On the Nordic front, The Mountaineers initiated a grueling eighteen-mile race between its Snoqualmie Lodge and Meany Ski Hut in 1930. This event ran for six years as a club event, and then became open to outside competition until its end after 1941. The Ski Patrol Race, dubbed "the nation's longest and hardest ski race" by *The Seattle Times* in 1936,[14] was patterned after popular military patrol races in Europe. Like the Silver Skis, it also received heavy media support, though the nature of the course precluded heavy spectatorship. Well marked with orange tin markers, the heavily forested route included long climbs and short schusses, with occasional open runs. Following the military model, it was a team race, with each team

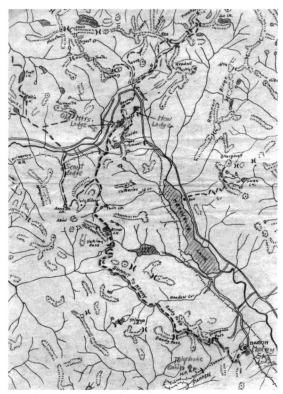

Map of the Mountaineers Ski Patrol Race, 1930–1941.

comprised of three members, all of whom were required to finish within one minute of each other. Each competitor was required to carry a pack weighing at least ten pounds, which included certain provisions for survival: first aid supplies, food, spare equipment, and designated clothing. Though in optimum conditions the course was, on rare occasion, covered in five hours, in adverse conditions it took as long as two days, with a bivouac on the trail. Despite the serious challenges of the course, and intense competition, practical jokers had their fun. Wolf recalls, stopping short of a confession, "the case of two unwitting stalwarts who carried rocks and bricks in their rucksacks all the way across. These desperation methods failed, however, to achieve their purposes, as no one ever suffered in the standings as a result. That one of these victims should turn out to be Paul Shorrock was a more or less foregone conclusion to anybody but him, as his perpetual good nature invited practical jokes out of pure affection. Hans Otto Giese never did find out who-dun-it, but it didn't slow him down in the slightest." In the first year of the Patrol Race, Wolf had not yet reached the required minimum age of twenty, and had to settle for breaking trail for the contestants. But his day would come in the event.

I WELL REMEMBER THE MORE LEISURELY EARLY PACE of these races when one flopped down on the trail to eat a filling lunch until the puffing of the next patrol came too close for comfort. Five club Patrol Races were held before 1936, at which time the race was opened to outside competition. That year, Bill Miller, Chet Higman and I established a club race record[15] of just over four and a half hours. Using narrow cross-country racing skis and dispensing with the three-course coffee break, the race became a hard-fought open chase with little time or inclination to enjoy the sweat-blurred scenery. If it accomplished anything, the Patrol Race certainly made this region more accessible and popular for a considerable period in the thirties, especially after the permanent trail markers were installed. Bob Higman and I learned winter bivouacking the hard way one year when we made the trip under somewhat less than ideal conditions. After building a cooking and warming fire in the wind-protected space under the branches of a fir, we found ourselves slowly melting into a seemingly bottomless sinkhole. As this became untenable and we started to claw our

(Left to right) Wolf Bauer, Bill Miller, and Chet Higman, holders of the unbeaten course record for the Ski Patrol Race, stop for lunch during the race on the day of their victory, 1936.

Wolf rooster-tails uncharacteristic powder in
Commonwealth Basin near Snoqualmie Pass, 1930.

way back up, the branch above us let go, and an almost effective lid was put on a couple of squashed and nearly suffocated Rover Boys. Along with such self-inflicted hardships, there were invariable compensations, such as, in this instance, the rare sight of a cavorting aerial troupe of flying squirrels putting on a show above our heads.

By 1936, Wolf was at the front of The Mountaineers' ski pack. Under the auspices of the club's Recreational Ski Committee, he taught a Ski Touring course, which included a structured curriculum for technique and safety. He led ski tours and crafted tour maps of the Snoqualmie Pass area. Eddie Bauer (no relation to Wolf), whose famous sporting goods store eventually became today's national clothing retail chain, gave Wolf free skis as a kind of sports endorsement deal. That way, when people asked Wolf where he got his skis,

(Left to right) Scott Osborn, Wolf Bauer, Bill Miller, Tim Hill, and Don Blair—The Mountaineers Ski Team in front of Mount Shuksan, 1936.

Wolf — Mtrs.
Slalom Gates in the Thirties
Gate Poles were small

Wolf skis right out of the frame during the slalom event at the 1935 Olympic Trials at Mount Rainier.

he could honestly say "from Eddie Bauer." Andy Anderson's article in the club's 1936 Mountaineer Annual, "Skiing in Retrospect," reads like a Curriculum Vitae of Wolf Bauer's victories, including: "Wolf Bauer was crowned triple crown champion by taking both the men's slalom and downhill in addition to his earlier success in the cross-country"[16] at the annual Meany Ski Hut competition.

At the top of his game and ever mindful of the cultural torch he was bearing, Wolf was loath to leave a single pleasant skiing tradition behind. In tribute to the father of it all, Wolf organized a Fox Chase in 1936 like the cinematic one in the Engadine, and a *Seattle Post-Intelligencer* headline declared:

"STAMPEDE CHASE" DUE
Bauer is Fox; Mountaineers, Pack

'STAMPEDE CHASE' DUE

* * *   * * *   * * *

Bauer Is Fox; Mountaineers, Pack

Wolf Bauer introduces it: The Mountaineers' first "Stampede Chase," designed to set a pack of skiers after one lad with a long stocking cap who tries to keep away.

It's on tomorrow at Stampede, with Bauer the fox, and any energetic skiing members of the Mountaineers the hounds.

Bauer starts at daybreak. The rest of the skiers stay in the ski hut for an hour. They don't peek. At the end of an hour they start after Bauer. Being just about the best skier in the club, Bauer may elude the hounds. His stocking cap must be pulled from his head if one is to win the trophy offered for his capture. He has until 3 p. m. to return.

It is a popular skiing sport in Europe, and a novice skier may have as much fun at it as an expert. All he needs to do is catch the fox.

Notice of the Fox Chase in an undated 1936 edition of the *Seattle Post-Intelligencer*.

Sadly for posterity, when asked whether Wolf the fox was ever caught, the truth must be told; the chase never came off, due to treacherous conditions and poor weather. But Wolf's role in promoting the sport was in no way diminished by this bad luck. He was, whether literally or figuratively, the leader, daring the pack to catch him. Yet, he remained comically fallible on occasion, as his memories from the last of his major competitions in 1936 can illustrate. Wolf was a member of a three-man team competing for The Mountaineers.

WE WERE AT THE CULMINATION of the four-way Pacific Northwest International Ski Championships at Mount Baker. Three events were already in the books. Our Mountaineers team was still in serious contention. Only the jumping remained in the two-day meet. We were decidedly on edge, what with the effort of downhill, slalom and cross-country still aching in our weary bones. It was a matter now of getting up the nerve to jump, for the first time, on a "class B" size hill against veteran Scandinavian jumpers who wanted to get revenge after the earlier Alpine events.

Late into the night I had studied and translated aloud an inspiring German jumping manual that would help us in our hour of need. As we climbed to take our first good look at the impressive hill, our team declined to take practice jumps. Would it not be far better to make every jump count before disqualification or injury? Such were our dark thoughts and prudent decisions.

As the first on the team to jump, I stood waiting for the signal that would send me flying toward those specks of people forming the outrun boundary below. We had all decided to simply schuss over the take-off—to

Wolf's first major successful ski jump at the Pacific Northwest 4-way Ski Championship, 1936. He jumped 104 feet.

heck with distance and form. Like an actor stepping onto the stage with every eye upon him, I hopped onto the inrun. I could not, I would not, disappoint my friends, the team, or the officials. But as I approached the take-off, my eyes caught sight of my heirloom gold watch swinging precariously by its chain from my trouser belt. The mind can evidently weigh many factors in the blink of an eye when confronted with an emergency. At the last instant, I swerved to throw myself sideways to miss the lip, landing pathetically in a heap alongside the take-off. The next few seconds were among the longest in my forty years of skiing. As I furiously scrambled to my feet, foolishly holding my dangling watch toward the judges' stand, I could feel and hear the mixture of pity and laughter stirring from the onlookers. I had obviously chickened out at the last moment.

It was one mad young would-be jumper who, having finally convinced the judges of the real reason for the debacle, made his two official jumps with a vengeance, and had the satisfaction of placing right behind the first four Class-A jumpers in the meet. Thus the inevitable ribbing that followed was easy to take.

Wolf remembers his mortification. But for the record, prior to that event, no one on The Mountaineers team had jumped more than fifty feet. On his final jump, Wolf jumped one hundred four feet. Embarrassment is a fine motivator.

At this point in the chronology, Wolf appears to fall off the map for a while, thanks to graduation, marriage, and a move to the island life of Roche Harbor, Washington. By 2006, most of Wolf's companions in these exploits of yesteryear had long ago passed into legend. But the legends have endured. Art Iodice of The Mountaineers Backcountry Ski Committee, and ski historian Lowell Skoog (himself a ski mountaineering legend-in-the-making), organized an outing on February 25 of that year to retrace the route of the Patrol Race. Though the old Snoqualmie Lodge burned down in 1944, a new one was built further east at Snoqualmie Pass in 1948, and some variations in the route were made to accommodate it. Participants in the event were invited to come to the "new" lodge for a dinner the night before the 6 a.m. start time. By happy coincidence, this was Wolf Bauer's ninety-fourth birthday, and so it was more than fitting that he should have been the keynote speaker, sharing his tales of the original race.

At the bottom of the quarter-mile uphill slog to the lodge, skiers began to arrive on that Friday night, organizing their gear for the walk in. A white Subaru pulled up and out stepped a wiry older man, all business, in a ski cap, wool pants and a gray Nordic sweater that likely pre-dated most of the skiers. "Ready?" he asked as he bounded up the snow steps in the plow-wall. Whispers abounded: "Is that him?" "That can't be Wolf; that guy's not ninety-four..." "Look at that guy climb this hill!" "Man, do I feel old..." and, of course, "Incredible!"

In his element, Wolf stood in front of the great stone fireplace, spine straight as a Douglas fir, and regaled the audience for a full hour with his recollections of the good old days of Northwest skiing. His concluding advice: "The trick is to die young ... as late as possible."

The fourteen participants on the tour the following day departed on schedule at 6:00 a.m. and arrived at Meany Ski Hut at 6:00 p.m. Lowell Skoog announced in admiration, "Wolf, your record is safe for another year!"[17]

Wolf visits the "new" Snoqualmie Lodge in 2006 to regale backcountry skiers with tales of the old Ski Patrol Race days. A group of modern skiers left the following morning to retrace the route of the race. Note the poster on the wall behind him of Wolf's former student, Jim Whittaker, at the summit of Mount Everest. PHOTO BY LOWELL SKOOG.

Have you ever sat with your 'sidekick-in-strife'
Like a lazy god on a sun-warmed peak?
No matter your niche down below that's called life,
Up here you command and you find what you seek!

Have you ever felt of a free-swinging rope,
A crampon that bit, or a piton that held?
Have you looked with despair, and then with new hope,
When a tug brings assurance of a brotherly weld?

Have you ever steered through an icefall by night,
Or bivouacked by storm on a slippery ledge?
Sought scarred old blazes by candlebug light,
Or dug for the lost in an avalanche-wedge?

Have you ever thrilled to the feel of a hold,
Walked on airy arêtes with the sky white and blue,
Or looked back at the summit just turning to gold?
If you have, you will know why the climber is true.

Why true to his learning, his companions, his gear,
With respect for the mountains, to which bends his ear;
But if you have never, climb up and scale high,
And when you return, then let's talk, you and I!

—WOLF BAUER

FOUR

Berg Heil!

I̶T IS AN OVERCAST DAY in September for the 2007 Rainier Mountain Festival, an annual event for climbing aficionados in Washington State. There are cars, people, and exhibition tents all around the property surrounding the Whittaker Bunkhouse in Ashford, Washington, outside Mount Rainier National Park. This is the seat of RMI (Rainier Mountaineering Incorporated), for many years the sole licensed climbing guide service on Mount Rainier. Started by mountaineering legend Lou Whittaker and now run by his son Peter Whittaker, it is the hub for serious climbers in the Cascades. Legions of world-class climbers have gotten their start as guides here, as the 14,410 foot Mount Rainier proves an excellent training ground for even more challenging and extreme peaks around the globe. The festival gives the general public a chance to listen to and schmooze with RMI's illustrious alumni, as well as with Jim Whittaker, Lou's twin brother, the first American to summit Mount Everest.

Wolf has been invited and chauffeured to the festival by the Whittakers. He is first seen standing ramrod straight, like a Marine as always, watching harnessed and helmeted young climbers work their way up a free-standing climbing wall. Maybe he is thinking of his boyhood in Kreuth and the forbidden Leonhardstein, with all its natural dangers. Here, ready belayers focus intently on their intrepid charges. No danger here. Safe yet exhilarating fun—precisely Wolf's lifetime bequest to mountaineering and paddling.

Around his neck he wears the nametag of a festival presenter. Instead of listing a job title, it simply says:

WOLF BAUER
Mountaineering Legend

Wolf is very popular here, and it is no time at all before Lou and Jim Whittaker and their wives, Ingrid and Diane, come up to embrace their old teacher. The affection of this extended family is clear and palpable. They go back more than sixty years; Wolf began to work his magic on these twins when they were still teenagers, back in the 1950s, in the early days of the Mountain Rescue Council. Despite significant fame in the climbing community and beyond, the brothers are gracious and warm people, the way a man can afford to be when he has proven himself to himself.

Atop the kids' climbing tower at the 2007 Rainier Mountain Festival, Wolf lets his co-author know how he feels about being told to get down.
PHOTO BY LYNN HYDE.

When Wolf tells Lou that he and I are working on Wolf's biography, Lou whispers, "Talk to me later—have *I* got some good stories to tell *you!*" Later, Wolf will tell Jim the same thing, to which he will reply, "I have a lot of good stories about Wolf, but I can't tell them to you!" They claim they are mirror twins: one is left-handed, the other right-handed; one was the first American to scale Mount Everest from the South; the other was the first American to summit from the North. On the issue of sharing insider Wolf lore, they have opposite angles as well. Where they coincide is in their reverence for their teacher. "What he really taught all of us was the ethics of climbing," one or both of them tell me. "He taught us *how* to climb, but what he really taught us was *what it means* to climb." Lou clarifies, "He is such a gentleman, and what we learned from him didn't just apply to the mountains; it applied to all of life."

All day at the festival, Wolf is routinely whisked away, launching an on-going search for him throughout the day. After one particularly frustrating search, he is finally located nine feet in the air, sitting on top of a large climbing rock with a tribe of youngsters—King of the Hill—his youthful demeanor causing him to blend right in. They accept him as one of them. Although their parents surround Wolf to spot him when he finally clambers down, he is oblivious to them. He certainly doesn't need *their* help.

Most of the people here are too young to know who Wolf Bauer is, but the Whittakers have invited him to be a part of their panel of Everest climbers, even though he has never done any technical climbing outside the United States. They want the audience to pay homage to the man who started it all in the Northwest. Wolf's full importance is not really understood until hearing the remarks of RMI guide Ed Viesturs, the extraordinary renowned climber who was the first American (and only fifth in the world) to summit all fourteen of the world's 8,000 meter peaks *without* supplemental oxygen. In the introductory remarks of this evolutionary anomaly, Ed traces the foundation of his career back through the Whittakers—who taught *him* how to climb—directly to the fair-haired boy himself, Wolf Bauer. Every climber who had never heard of Wolf before that moment had now been duly informed of the import of this legend.

Hubert Bauer was a geographer, a man who enjoyed adventure, so it was to be expected that his son would follow in his footsteps as an explorer of the planet. Bavarian boys worshipped their mountain guides the way modern boys worship professional athletes, and when Wolf was a boy, mountain guides had been taking people through the Alps for ages. It was hardly a novel pastime. His first "summit" was with Hubert in 1922 to the top of the 5,492 foot Hochfelln near Chiemsee in eastern Bavaria. As he recalls, those climbs were nothing technical, scrambles at best, but the effort still deserved a fine reward: the feast at the summit. The full schedule of supplies on the climb was rye bread, cheese and an alpenstock; they relied on melted snow to quench their thirst. ("In those years, snow was clean!" Wolf informs.) Ten years later, in 1933, his first major Cascade summit was the 9,131 foot Mount Shuksan with German

Wolf's first major peak, Hochfelln, 1922.

Wolf makes his way to the top of Mount Shuksan, his first major climb,
in 1933. His partner, Hans Otto Giese, snapped the photo.
PHOTO BY HANS OTTO GIESE.

compatriot Hans Otto Giese, and likewise they celebrated a true
Bavarian-style summit with rye bread and cheese, though with an
ice axe standing in for the alpenstock.

Hubert Bauer had christened the Cascades when he took Wolf
and his sister Mabel on their first American climb in 1926, to Guye
Peak near Snoqualmie Pass. The passion for climbing transplanted
successfully, its new shoots appearing in Wolf's leadership role in
the Boy Scouts. In 1928, as a young high school student, Wolf was
a cubmaster for a troop of forty Cub Scouts as well as a senior patrol
leader for Boy Scout Troop 145 in the Wallingford neighborhood of
Seattle. He had taken them on an outing to scale the sand bluffs at
Fort Lawton (today's Discovery Park), and encouraged by the experience, he approached the Chief Seattle Council of the Scouts with

Wolf's Cub Scout pack waves from their perch on the sand bluffs of Seattle's Fort Lawton in Discovery Park, 1928.

a proposal to teach older scouts about mountaineering. Wolf's technical knowledge was already lagging behind that of the climbing community he had left in Bavaria three years prior, but with youthful enthusiasm and self-confidence, he was certain he could put together basic instruction to interest the high school outdoorsmen in the Council. (This "Rover Clan" was among the forerunners of the Scouts' Explorer program, and eventually some members would break away from the Scouts and become the Ptarmigan Climbing Club, for whom the Ptarmigan Traverse in the North Cascades is named.) The Council agreed Wolf could try.

In what today is the Wedgwood neighborhood of Seattle lies Wedgwood Rock (also known as "Big Rock"), a glacial erratic dragged and dropped by the Vashon Glacier from Canada during the last glacial period. Once a Native American trail hub in dense old-growth forest, the rock's home is now a quiet, tidy middle-class neighborhood. But in the late 1920s, the area was still undeveloped, just a cow pasture northeast of the University of Washington. When Wolf discovered it, he immediately gleaned its potential as a training ground. At nineteen feet tall, and seventy-five feet around, one could trace as many as twelve climbing routes on the massive boulder. He tried to convince The Mountaineers to buy the land it sat on, suggesting construction of an adjacent climbers' lodge. But Wolf's vision did not infect the ruling elite of the club, and so others were ultimately able to purchase the land, which remains private property to this day. In 1970, the City of Seattle passed an ordinance prohibiting climbing of the rock (worth a one hundred dollar ticket at the time), and today it is nestled snugly in a grove of trees, where no one can get in trouble doing what Wolf's ilk did.

Wolf demonstrates technique to his Rover Clan students at Wedgwood Rock in Seattle, 1933.

But while the going was good, Wolf ran a successful course for the Boy Scouts, training them on the rock, over a mattress moat. He demonstrated rope work and basic techniques for his charges, who were only a few years younger than himself. When he felt they were ready, he and his pack co-leader Bob Higman (Scoutmaster Harry Higman's nephew) received permission to take the boys on their first climb near Snoqualmie Pass, not far from where Interstate 90 cuts through the Cascades today. Not altogether upfront about their exact destination, he must have aroused the suspicions of the Scouting elders, for they followed him secretly to observe the outing.

Wolf and Bob took the dozen or so boys to McClellan Butte, a 5,162-foot peak that provided an energetic hike with some notable exposure and technical requirements at the last one hundred feet of elevation. Wolf decided to take the boys off-trail to approach the chimney of the butte, and they were faced with some convincingly prohibitive thickets of devil's club. But the undaunted youths bush-whacked through the treacherous obstacle, and went on to a successful summit. The success was duly witnessed through binoculars by the council elders, whose stealthy reconnaissance had been thwarted by the same devil's club. They had to concede that Wolf and Bob had led a safe and responsible climb, despite their concerns. As it turned out, the Boy Scout climbing program was just Wolf's warm-up act.

Face to Face with Rainier

In 1933, Wolf's old Skagit timber companion, Hans Grage, along with Wendell Trosper and Jarvis Wallen, made an unsuccessful bid to summit Mount Rainier from the north side, via Ptarmigan Ridge. Though Rainier had been summited on the south and northeast sides multiple times since the first successful expedition of 1885, the northwest side that faced Seattle remained unsullied by human feet. Incredulous about this fact, Wolf looked up at that face each day and felt the mountain daring him to climb it, and when he thought of the indignity of Europeans coming over to usurp the honor, he began to set his own sights on it. "I thought, 'some Swiss is going to come along any day and show you how to do it!'" he says. With the

Wolf tags the top of Mount Stuart in the 1930s.   Wolf gains experience at the Dulfersitz rappel in the 1930s.

experience that Hans had from his own previous attempt, he was a natural choice for a partner. They believed that climbing in pairs was the most efficient way to attain success, though they later decided that was a mistake.

He and Hans made their first attempt on Ptarmigan in June of 1934, gaining an elevation of 11,000 feet, but they were beaten back by a blizzard. Unabashed, they made a second attempt in September, late in the season, when they hoped the avalanche danger would be lower. This, too, proved unsuccessful, but his subsequent article in the 1934 *Mountaineer Annual* provides us with one of Wolf's most eloquent climbing accounts.[18]

"The North Face of Mount Rainier"

THE CHALLENGE OF THE UNTROD MOUNTAINS is an open challenge. If accepted by the climber, a struggle on even footing ensues, provided the mountain does not enlist the services of the weather gods. Only once may an unclimbed peak hurl that great challenge. Yet after the battle, the conquered peak still rears its head unbowed. In admiration, the victorious climber looks back at the giant, who tauntingly seems to fling another challenge: "Approach me, if you dare, from the front."

Every mountaineer who has caught the spirit of the mountains knows when the mountain looks him straight in the eye. The peak lies vaguely cold and distant, passive and unconcerned, when he approaches it from the bulging back or sweeping sides. But if he steps into the shadow of its front, he can feel the massive head look him over, he can feel its breath, hear its rumbling throat, and sense its inherent power.

Mountaineers who have lived and breathed under the shadow of Rainier's front face recognize its final challenge. Yet the challenge still stands today. Hans Grage, who started an attack with a party last year, was rebuffed. The next year I, too, caught the challenging eye of the face that watches the northern lights. Joining forces with Hans Grage, who had some knowledge already of part of the planned route, we made the attempt. The mountain, however, would not face us alone, and threw us back down its sides in a driving blizzard. Two months later, with yet greater determination, we approached the mountain again, hoping for at least an even break in the contest.

A mild September afternoon found us climbing through the trees in the Mist Park and Seattle Park areas. As we stepped out upon the moraines of Russell Glacier and up towards Echo Rock, the mountain looked at us with friendly eyes as the last rays of the sun raced past us up toward its peak. Skirting along the east side of Ptarmigan Ridge, we stopped long enough in the darkness to cook hot soup and enjoy a couple of hours of sleep at an elevation of 9,500 feet.

A thin sickle of a moon and the stars threw enough light to enable us to push on up to the ridge. Working carefully down the west side of the top of Ptarmigan Ridge by flashlight, we crossed the bergschrunds[19] of both sides of the upper eastern end of North Mowich Glacier. Crampons and doubled ropes were pushed into service. Thanks to the moonlight and stars, little difficulty was encountered in finding a schrund-gap that could be crossed.

At last we had come to the first of the three thrilling moments in a climber's day—coming to grips with the mountain. Our face here consisted of three lava ridges spreading fanlike down the slope. The middle ridge separated two steep talus slopes, which were covered with glare ice for more than a thousand feet straight up. For the next three hours, our ice-axe picks beat a steady tattoo up the steep ice. All the movements had to be slow and cautious, requiring constant balance and watching of the partner's maneuvers. At the top of this face, we paused to blink into the rising sun and look down into the still-dark depths of the great Willis Wall amphitheatre. It was here that we sensed for the first time, the enormous latent power of Rainier. To verify our feelings, ice and rock fragments began their hissing and erratic bombardment from above, the sight and ominous sounds of which were to be our evil companions throughout the rest of the climb and descent. It is this factor, and that of poor and rotten climbing rock, that make any climbing routes on this side of Rainier prohibitive to larger parties, which tend to dislodge more debris. Closely pressing ourselves against the crumbly cliffs, we made a horizontal traverse to the east, and planned our next route up an ice-covered chute leading directly to the foot of an overhanging wall. Working under the cover of large projections up the right side of this chute, which was in the direct path of falling rock and ice, we crawled on hands and feet along the foot of this overhanging wall in an arcade-like undercut from the ceiling, from which long icicles hung suspended. Coming out into the sunlight again on the east edge of this wall, we discovered that it was the end of a long rock rampart, the highest exposed ridge on that side of the mountain. Our crampons were at last removed, and we began our rock-work up the east side of this rampart. Within an hour and a half, we stood opposite the uppermost glacier, which slopes gradually to Liberty Cap. We had at last climbed through the face and up to the top snow fields. This point, between twelve and thirteen thousand feet elevation, is directly west of the upper brink of Willis Wall. From here, the route lies up the gentle slope of this glacier, which forms part of the summit dome. We finally decided with great reluctance that there was insufficient time to walk up the snowfields to the summit and climb down out of the face before darkness set in.

Descending for about fifteen hundred feet whence we had come, we continued our descent to the west of the fan-like face, thereby avoiding the long and difficult glare ice we had encountered during the night. This led us down the uppermost ice tongue of the North Mowich Glacier. Crossing this hanging glacier at 10,000 feet, above its ice-fall into the mother glacier, we skirted a half mile to the west above the North Mowich Glacier in an attempt to find a schrund crossing. It was now late afternoon, and we were kept constantly on the dodge by hurtling and singing rocks. Ducking the last shrapnel successfully as we sprang upon the glacier, we found our voices again and gave vent to our feelings. The certainty of having to unravel the maze of crevasses ahead of us up the North Mowich Glacier to Ptarmigan Ridge, in oncoming darkness, was nothing compared to the relief we experienced in being rid of the uncertainty of rock bombardment, against which even the best-equipped climbing team is powerless. After traveling a half mile in four hours up this crevasse-gapped glacier, we again topped Ptarmigan Ridge in darkness, sleeping for an hour on top, and plodding, tired but happy, down the moonlit snow slopes to the green parks below. Once more we sank into the heather for an hour's rest before descending to the Carbon River.

It was a climb that neither one of us will ever forget. It taught us at least one lesson, namely that the best mountaineering is not always good mountaineering. Although our goal, Liberty Cap, was not quite reached, Rainier's north side was conquered for the first time. And that puts to an end the ever-present challenge Rainier has flung at us when our wondering gaze swept its face.

But Wolf was not completely honest in his implication that he had come close enough to summiting to suit himself. He tried again the following season with Jack Hossack, and the pair successfully completed the route. What is important about Wolf's article, besides his romantic, yet sincere, personification of Mount Rainier, is the twenty-two-year-old Wolf's loyalty to his friend Hans Grage. In this and all his subsequent writings and interviews, Wolf always maintained that after the arduous ascent of Ptarmigan Ridge, it was the lateness of the day that kept the pair from summiting. It was not until 1992, long after Hans passed away, in his interview in Malcolm Bates' book *Cascade Voices*, that Wolf revealed the truth publicly for the first time.

During their second 1934 attempt at conquering the north face of Rainier, it was at 12,000 feet that Hans Grage fell ill and could not go on. "Hans was strong as a horse," Wolf said, "but he wasn't really a technical climber." Wolf blamed it on the fact that Hans was a heavy smoker and the altitude got to him. But whatever the cause,

Hans went limp. The original plan had been to return via the same route they had gone up, but there was no way for Wolf to bring Hans down that way. Moving west to the North Mowich Glacier made it possible, despite the inherent dangers even there, for Wolf to assist Hans Grage down the mountain. "Boy, we had a helluva time getting down," he still mutters with a frown, shaking his head, and then moves quickly to another subject. For nearly sixty years, Wolf kept that secret to himself.

—⬝⬝⬝—

In the early 1930s, when a young new generation of climbers felt ostracized and neglected by the ruling Climbing Committee of The Mountaineers, they created their own renegade group of "outlaw climbers." The older climbers were completely self-taught, and guarded their hard-earned knowledge jealously. As a result, the next generation, eager for the fruits of their elders' experience, considered them cliquish. Wolf remembers that they "had learned climbing the hard way, their own way. They had never seen a piton before. They were doing shoulder belays. They were older, and were sort of a clique. They kept to themselves. When I got in, they would never teach me anything. I was just an upstart, a kid. They believed you had to learn it for yourself. Because of that, I felt that somebody should be teaching mountaineering techniques, and not holding them to themselves."[20]

Not content to wait under the table for scraps from their predecessors, the young outlaws organized climbs unsanctioned by the parent club. Wolf aroused their curiosity with the European-style instruction he was giving to his troop of Explorer Scouts, and invited them to a demonstration at Wedgwood Boulder. Duly impressed and hungry for what the Europeans were doing, they asked Wolf, one of their own, to instruct them in a formal climbing course. Wolf was thrilled to take on the challenge of developing the course for this new wave of Mountaineers, but he knew he had a lot to learn before he could teach. He had left Germany before the new technical wave had reached him, so he would have to learn all his technical knowledge from books.

He turned his eyes towards Europe, specifically to a famous German alpinist and popular movie actor whom Wolf admired. Luis Trenker seemed to be the public face of modern European climbing, and so Wolf contacted the celebrity, asking for advice and reading materials on cutting edge alpine techniques. Graciously, Trenker sent books and gave him the leads he needed to learn more, putting him in touch with a publisher who could help. Devouring the books, Wolf recalls, "I really took fire."[21] All the current texts were, naturally, in German and had not yet been translated. Wolf became the bridge, translating the instruction for delivery to Northwest neophytes.

As he told historian Harry Majors in a 1974 interview, "I felt I was really in the saddle as far as knowledge was concerned, not because of myself, but because of the help I'd gotten and the peculiar—or you might say unique—position I held in my relationship to the old country, where these things were so far ahead."[22] He devoured every book he could get his hands on, but he admits he was never more than a week ahead of his students. He practiced every technique over and over until he was sure he had it, often just in the nick of time to teach it. In 1935, on the evening of his first Dulfersitz rappelling demonstration in the downtown Rialto Building that held The Mountaineers clubrooms, he glibly concealed the fact that he himself had rappelled for the very first time just several hours earlier—off the old Cowen Park Bridge, over what was then a very deep Ravenna ravine.[23]

Approximately thirty new students gathered all along the stairwell railings to watch their new teacher demonstrate the first free rappel in the Northwest, using cowboy lariat ropes he had soaked in a tub the night before. Wearing a mask of false composure, inwardly sweating pitons over the shaky iron railing he anchored to in the Rialto stairwell, Wolf wowed his acolytes with his casual descent down the four stories to the marble floor below. "My heart was in my pants,"[24] he allowed. Wolf said he was "scared as hell going down that thing... The marble slab was all laid out for me at the bottom in case anything happened."[25] But the charade was successful, and the course took off. "After that night," Wolf smiles, "the Little Si overhang was a cinch."[26] The elders were skeptical, but some were secretly intrigued. They could not help but see where the future of climbing was going. Before long, club veterans Bill Degenhardt, Jim Martin, and Herbert Strandberg had defected and were with the program.

The first Basic Climbing Course Wolf ran was a seven-week class that included lectures, demonstrations and field trips—all compulsory, followed by a stiff college-style exam created by Wolf. Students were expected to provide standardized written descriptions of the climbing routes they had used, which would become the basis for printed "Climbing Guides," cheap reference booklets made available for everyone's benefit. Lectures focused on elementary mountain travel and safety, while in practicum students worked on knot-tying, friction belaying and rappelling. Their first outing was to Wedgwood Boulder for rock practice. At Fort Lawton came rope technique and axe work in anchoring, glissading, and step-cutting.

Wolf Bauer (left) and Jack Hossack practice rock belays at Lundin Peak in 1935. PHOTO BY OTHELLO PHIL DICKERT.

Wolf Bauer (right) and Jack Hossack practice rock belays at Lundin Peak in 1935.
PHOTO BY OTHELLO PHIL DICKERT.

Next they were off to Lundin Peak (6,057 feet) for rock and body belays, to be followed by the Mount Si (4,167 feet) rappelling practice—150 easier feet than Wolf's effort in the Rialto stairwell. But there was still little, if any, use of hardware at this time, despite the fact that pitons were established in Europe, and were being tested by Sierra Club rock climbers in California. By modern standards, Northwest climbing was still an exercise in friction.

Graduates of the first course included Lloyd Anderson (the founder of REI, who would in turn teach the legendary Fred Beckey in 1939), Jack Hossack, Ome Daiber, George MacGowan, Joe Halwax, Phil Dickert, and Bill Degenhardt—all giant names in the annals of early Washington mountaineering.

By the end of the course in 1935, with plans under way to develop an intermediate course the following year, Wolf and Jack Hossack resolved to settle accounts with Rainier on Ptarmigan Ridge. Choosing to make the attempt in September again, and obtaining special permission from the Rainier rangers, the pair planned their assault, enlisting the base camp assistance of Harriet Woodward, the sporting woman who would later become Wolf's wife. In the era before cell phones, Harriet's job was to watch for

Wolf demonstrates the Dulfersitz rappel in the field for the first time on the Haystack on Mount Si, outside North Bend, Washington, while Bill Degenhardt watches, 1935.

their signal flares on the mountain, like an alpine Paul Revere. One flare meant they were doing fine and planned to proceed—her cue to drive around the mountain to Paradise to await their descent, preferably with dinner ready. Three flares meant they were in trouble and that she should send help.

This time both climbers were fully prepared for the task, Wolf being fortified with the kind of resolve that comes only after multiple failures. In the 1935 *Mountaineer Annual,* he recounts the expedition.[27]

"The Final Conquest"

TO BE ABLE TO WRITE THE LAST CHAPTER OF THE SAGA about a series of three attacks I made upon the front of the white giant is truly a privilege, so it is written not without some pride and thankful appreciation. Pride in the clean safety technique that successfully opposed the often unfair counter-attack of the mountain, and grateful acknowledgment of the weather gods, and of Jack Hossack, the loyal teammate who stood by his man when phys-ical and moral support were needed most. I wish to express additional acknowledgment to Harry Myers and Major Tomlinson of Mount Rainier National Park for their efforts and goodwill in sanctioning the climb during the late season; and, last but not least, the patient and trustworthy ground crew in the person of Harriet Woodward, who stood by on Ptarmigan Ridge during the cold night and early morning hours with binoculars and flares, prepared to receive and transmit signals during the difficult and, at first, uncertain phases of our work on the lower glare ice chutes and verglass-covered lava outcrops of the main face. The climb could not, therefore, and did not fail, although forty-eight hours were needed to complete the tra-verse of the mountain from Carbon River to Paradise Valley.

Many pages could be devoted to a climb of this type in describing in cold detail the various techniques employed in working out the many problems and immediate difficulties such a varied route, with its ice pitches, rockfall chutes, lava cliffs, crevassed cornices, icefalls, schrunds, and ice chimneys, has to offer. But I will present the trip from a general interest standpoint.

Outfitted to face Rainier for at least four days, we were equipped with spare food concentrates such as cheese, figs, butter, and dates; a Primus cooker and soup concentrate; a small flask of alcohol; sleeping bag covers; headlights and flares; red cloth schrund markers; detailed waterproof aerial photographs for the whole route; and the usual tools and safety equip-ment. Half of a 120-foot rope was carried by the last man in his Bergen rucksack, the remainder serving to rope up the team, with stirrup loops for the axe anchoring maneuvers.

It was the weekend following Labor Day. Meteorological conditions pre-vailed that were similar to those we encountered the year before. A high, steady barometer, small and scattered southward-sailing cirrostratus clouds, and a low first-quarter moon left the mountain to rely on his own resources to defend his unconquered side. Never had I felt so certain of success before a difficult climb. We agreed that if the climb of the face was done at all, it would be done with credit to the mountaineering art, even if it took three days to climb through the face to Liberty Cap. This meant reaching the face of the top rampart before the sun had thrown the rock and ice bombardment into high gear. A four-hour sleep on the arête of Ptarmigan Ridge above the upper cirque of the North Mowich Glacier found us rested and eagerly anticipating the night's and morning's assault.

Descending down the crumbly west side of Ptarmigan Ridge by flash-light, and crossing the upper North Mowich Glacier and its ice bergschrund, we decided to make a stab at the tremendous icefall of the snout of the hanging glacier that descends from Liberty Cap onto the divide between the Carbon and the North Mowich Glaciers. The chute fringing the west side of the icefall proved, however, too exposed to rock and ice fall for the prolonged operations necessary in that location. A con-tour traverse to the west back onto the face had to be made. Here a flare signal was given to our lone ground crew member saying that conditions were okay, and the team would carry on over the top. This signal carried with it the further significance that there would be a hot meal waiting for us at Camp Muir should we get there that evening. The crew came through, but we didn't.

The next two thousand feet consumed eight hours, most of which were spent cutting steps into the steep glare ice slope of the face and its chutes. Because anchoring was almost wholly confined to body and ice axe belays, large footholds and frequent knee and handholds had to be chiseled. This work proved to be slow and tiring, since the cutting was done under an intermittent, but often furious, bombardment of hissing rock and ice frag-ments, necessitating constant cover and quite restricted working positions. At noon, the point along the uppermost rock rampart, which terminated the previous climb, was reached. The next five hundred feet consumed almost four hours. The key to the problem of reaching the top of this ram-part proved finally to be a narrow inclined ice chimney and a detour over a verglass-coated névé roof. Deep ice belays had to be cut here as neither pick nor shaft gave anchoring security on the exposed surface. From this point on, it was only a matter of chopping through a small fringe of seracs before we could step on the wind-crusted névé that overlaid the rampart top. The face was again conquered—this time completely.

Twenty-four hours had elapsed since the Carbon River was left behind, of which thirteen had been spent on the face from the Ptarmigan Ridge bivouac. At this elevation of 12,500 feet, the slope angle to the top changes to half of that encountered throughout the face proper. A sense of freedom and happy satisfaction stole over us as we looked at the world below us through the rose-colored glasses that the afternoon sun had slipped over our eyes. No more step cutting. No more bombardment. No more rotten rock and glare ice pitches. Our crampons bit securely into the crusted snow boards as we slowly pushed our way around a few more crevasses and cornices, up over the Sunset Amphitheater, and on to Liberty Cap, which we reached at about nine o'clock Sunday night. A temporary bivouac of seven hours' duration was quickly established on a small spot of lava gravel near the Cap. Crawling into our sleeping bag covers and cooking hot pea soup on the Primus, we prepared to weather the icy blast. A warm little eruption from the old boy that night, we agreed, would have been a welcome disturbance. However, having been fairly beaten, there was nothing he could do about it now except make us as uncomfortable as possible. And here we give Rainier his due credit.

Blinking airplane beacons and a brilliantly lighted-up St. Helens from the reflection of a nearby forest fire presented a rare sight. The next morning a unique spectacle greeted our amazed eyes. The whole cone-like shadow of Rainier hovered projected in the air to the south. It seemed as though the black shadow represented the malicious soul of the old boy, the presence of which we had been kept aware of throughout the previous day. And now that this ominous soul and spirit had departed, there was nothing left but the glorious white head in the crisp morning air, and the rising sun greeting us in celebration of our victory. Though it was probably the most wretched, it was truly the most inspiring and scenic bivouac I had ever set up.

Wolf leads the way up Ptarmigan Ridge during the first ascent of Mount Rainier from the north side in 1935. His partner Jack Hossack snapped the photo.   PHOTO BY JACK HOSSACK.

After two hours, we reached the north rim of the crater. Steering leisurely through the crevasses to Gibraltar Rock and proceeding through the chutes to Camp Muir, we reached Paradise Valley at 3:30 p.m. Monday afternoon. The peak was in our rucksack, and the Mountain had, for the first time, been climbed and traversed from Ptarmigan Ridge.

With a cheery yodel we descended under a lazy afternoon sun down into the green valley, which, after the cold deadness of the upper ice world, seemed truly a Paradise Valley to our hungry eyes.

On September 30, just three weeks after Wolf's September 9 summit, Ome Daiber, Will Borrow and Arnie Campbell made the first ascent of the north face of Rainier via Liberty Ridge, only to find a climb register that declared in Wolf's unmistakable hand:

No Omee, You're not the last!
Wolf Bauer } **Mountaineers**
Jack Hossack **Berg Heil!**

To which Ome good-naturedly added:

By golly We are the last—I hope–
   Ome Daiber   MTNER
   Will H. Borrow Jr.
   E. Arnold Campbell

Truth be told, despite his enduring and genuine commitment to humility, when the playing field was fair, Wolf wasn't completely above giving his own little version of a victory dance. His consoling remark that posterity would show Ome ahead of legions of future climbers may not have comforted Ome much. Ome, however, would have the satisfaction of setting the standard classic climb on the north face. Though it would be twenty years before either route was climbed again (Ptarmigan wasn't climbed again, until July 1959 by Bill and Gene Prater), the Liberty Ridge climb became the preferred and classic climb for many years. When Wolf told people he wouldn't recommend Ptarmigan, they listened to him, and until

The Mount Rainier summit register showing both the Bauer-Hossack first ascent via Ptarmigan Ridge and the Ome Daiber-Will Borrow-Arnie Campbell first ascent via Liberty Ridge three weeks later.

modern equipment helped alleviate the route's difficulties in more recent years, it was not often climbed.

Still, Wolf recounted with pride that he now "could look Mount Rainier in the face and not feel ashamed."[28] Later in life, when he purchased a home on Vashon Island in Puget Sound, he kept Ptarmigan Ridge in his sights from his living room. A watercolor of the mountain's northeast face painted by friend and fellow climber

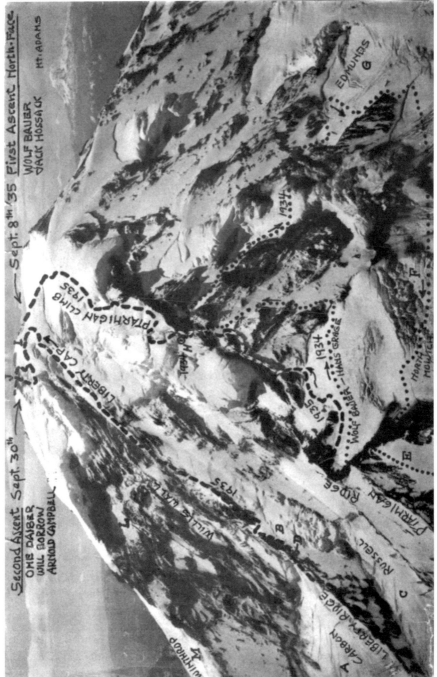

Early U.S. Navy aerial photo of the north face of Mount Rainier, showing both the Ptarmigan Ridge and Liberty Ridge routes.

Dee Molenaar has long hung over his mantle. The mountain will forever be a member of his family.

The effect of these climbs and the overwhelming success of Wolf's first climbing course set the hills ablaze with Climbing Fever. Wolf may have stressed that the competition for first ascents was not important, and his students may have even affirmed it within his earshot, but deep down, everyone was manic to bag a first ascent of their own. After all, no mountain could have more than one, and they weren't making any more mountains in the foreseeable future.

Wolf, on the other hand, satisfied with his victory on Rainier, threw himself into developing the Intermediate Climbing Course. What drove him was what he later called "an almost frantic effort to catch up with the Alps."[29] As a Bavarian native son, it was a matter of honor for Wolf that his Cascade climbing culture should keep pace with European techniques and technology. And his climbing course included an overview of geology, flora and fauna, a telling indicator of his personal appreciation for and relationship with the mountains he would climb. For Wolf, that old Bavarian alpine ethic trumped the competitive need to compile a resume of personal achievements. It was always a bit disappointing to Wolf that that romantic ethic did not naturally transplant to American soil.

The second-level climbing course covered winter travel and weather, including snow and ice, avalanche readiness, winter camping, search-and-rescue techniques, and leadership situations. At Fort Lawton, where sand stood in for snow, they practiced "snow" climbing, self-arrest, and crevasse rescue, using ice axes and rope. Sand was hard on both ropes and clothing, but it was the next best thing to real snow. Field trips to McClellan's Butte and Commonwealth Basin took the difficulty factor a notch higher, and provided experience in overnight snow camping.

Enlisting the graduates of the first year to help teach the second Basic Climbing Course in 1936 was a stroke of inspiration, as in any field one does not really know the subject matter until one has had to teach it. This help enabled Wolf to teach both the Basic and Intermediate Courses, while also helping to launch condensed basic climbing classes in the Olympia and Everett branches of The Mountaineers. He added more technical components as he "imported" the technology, most importantly the use of pitons. He eschewed the hard Tricouni nail boots in favor of soft French climbing shoes, called "Kletterschuhe" in Germany. In addition to corresponding with European climbers, he traded his ice techniques to the Sierra Club in California in exchange for their rock techniques. Many of the techniques Wolf was teaching at this point were virtually unknown in the United States. His only worry now was making sure that he did not flunk out of the University of Washington.

The use of ice axes on Ptarmigan Ridge helped confirm the end of the alpenstock era, even if Wolf and Jack Hossack found themselves continuously hammering back the prongs that were bent by the rock-embedded ice. Wolf imported his first vertical and horizontal rock pitons from Munich, and had a Ballard blacksmith forge him some ice pitons to order, despite his life-long ambivalence about using them. (Even 70 years after the climb, one thinks twice before bringing up the "P" word around Wolf Bauer.)

As opposed to the later climbing style of long pitches with pitons, in those days the style was short pitches with finger holds. To a purist, the extra time and patience required for finger traverses and rock belays was worth the trouble, for ethical reasons. "My philosophy was not to knock iron into the breast of the mountain," he explained. "I felt that was an unfair advantage. I could never countenance a direct aid. It was absolutely against anything that I would want to do ever in my life. In fact, it was tough enough to put a piton in, you know, and even pull on it here and there. But to step on it—that was completely out of the picture. I've never been accused of that. But pitons were a necessary evil as far as I was concerned."[30] Nonetheless, Wolf was the first climber in the Pacific Northwest to import pitons, and to use them, albeit sparingly, on Mount Goode.

Mount Goode is a 9,220-foot fortress of a mountain at the head of Washington's Lake Chelan in North Cascades National Park—the highest peak in the park. In 1936, it was one of the most coveted first ascents in the Cascades. Many of The Mountaineers elders had attempted it, and shared the lessons of their failure, but none had succeeded. These included a veritable "Who's Who" of Cascade climbers, such as Hermann Ulrichs, Everett Darr, Norval Grigg, Art

Winder and Forest Farr—all thwarted at the peak's famous chimney with its huge chockstone—an irresistibly formidable obstacle. And so the secret dream of a stunning first ascent engendered a graduation climb for four of the graduates of Wolf's Intermediate Climbing Course: Jack Hossack, George MacGowan, Phil Dickert and Joe Halwax, with Wolf leading the way. This was not just their culminating recital, but the triumph of the new over the old—their badge of ascendance over the old guard that had been so stingy with their knowledge. It was an alpha climb for the climbing crown in The Mountaineers. The future power balance of the club would ultimately be determined by it.

Graduates of The Mountaineers Intermediate Climbing Course, Jack Hossack (left) and George MacGowan were part of the party that made the first successful summit of Mount Goode in 1936. PHOTO BY OTHELLO PHIL DICKERT.

(Left to right) George MacGowan, Joe Halwax, Wolf Bauer, and Jack Hossack crossing Lake Chelan en route to Mount Goode.
PHOTO BY OTHELLO PHIL DICKERT.

For this ascent, Wolf conceded the narrative report duties to George MacGowan, and his article "Goode Conquest" in the 1936 *Mountaineer Annual* is an interesting account of the technical process. However, Wolf did offer a snapshot narrative of the climb for Malcolm Bates in 1992.[31]

I HAD NEVER BEEN UP THERE [to Mount Goode] before, but you got to hearing about all those guys trying to climb it. It got bigger and bigger in your mind. Here was this chimney with a huge chockstone—the ideal thing. Climbers were always stopped there. The funny thing was that when we went up to climb it, there was a [party of two Mazama climbers] who also wanted to be the first on Goode. It was one of those rare coincidences. We were on the same boat going up Lake Chelan and [at Stehekin] there was

(Left to right) Jack Hossack, George MacGowan, and Wolf contemplate the attempt at Goode.
PHOTO BY OTHELLO PHIL DICKERT.

only one car to take you to the end of the road. Well, I had made arrangements for the car ahead of time. So we got to the dock and here were these guys with climbing gear. They, too, were going to the North Cascades, and that was fine. But slowly it came out that they wanted to be the first to climb Mount Goode. We didn't tell them what we were doing. It turned out we were trying different routes, and we got the car and a head start.

The summit of Mount Goode is characterized by its daunting chimney, a basalt intrusion where weaker rock has eroded faster than the underlying basalt tower. This particular tidbit was no doubt learned as they climbed, as part of what MacGowan later called (with only a polite hint at irony) "the endless fount of geological knowledge that Wolf dispensed" during the climb. Being a recent University of Washington graduate, with a minor in geology, Wolf could hardly be expected to resist.

MacGowan described the climb[32]:

> It was our plan to use the same route that had been tried several times before, as we had considerable information regarding it, and knew that it led to within a few hundred feet of the summit. Accordingly, we crossed over snow fields to the right of the main

peak into a couloir, which cut back as nearly as we could tell directly toward the summit. The couloir was cluttered with considerable debris, and at about 8,900 feet narrowed into a chimney formed by a basalt intrusion, which had eroded more quickly than the rest of the rock, a typical formation on Goode, as other similar ribands were apparent on the face of the cliff, marking the walls at various curves and angles. The rear wall of the chimney sloped back at an angle of fifty to seventy-five degrees, and was covered with ice and snow. The side walls were also verglassed, making friction climbing impossible. Wolf worked his way up, driving pitons wherever possible, having considerable trouble in making them hold in the ice-filled cracks. The fact that the party moving up had poor footing and could make no move to avoid falling rock made the utmost care necessary, but in due course the entire party arrived at the top of the chimney, which was about 150 feet high, and ended in an overhang.

The right wall was vertical for one hundred feet, and the left six or seven hundred, slanting back to a ledge thirty feet higher. With some difficulty Wolf stemmed up between the walls, here about five feet apart, crossed and scrambled to the ledge above, where he drove a piton, to belay the remainder to his side. Here we thought our difficulties were over, as the ledge led to the left in a most promising manner, but on exploring we found it ran onto the face of the cliff and we were forced to return to our original position on the ledge.

Thirty feet higher a break in the ridge looked like a probable solution to our difficulty, and while dubiously realizing that the first man would have very little protection, Wolf spied a crack in the granite ten feet above. The second flip of the rope caught, and ascending with prussic knots, he found himself on a narrow sloping slab with no close holds. With considerable effort he was able to drive a piton far enough to his right to protect himself until he worked over to where a finger traverse was possible. A few anxious moments, and he was on the ridge and announcing that the way was clear to the summit. Accordingly we quickly moved up, Wolf and Jack on the first rope, and myself, Phil and Joe on the second.

Wolf's sense of humor got the best of him at this juncture, and quickly building a small cairn, he informed me as I came over the top that the Mazama boys had made the ascent before us. This

Jack Hossack takes over camera duties to let Phil Dickert into the victory shot on the summit of Mount Goode. (Left to right) Phil Dickert, Joe Halwax, George MacGowan, and Wolf Bauer.

added no touch of gaiety to the occasion, but I had sufficient curiosity left to desire to see their record, and the truth was admitted. It seems characteristic of human conduct that when one has been taken in, he does not recover his self-esteem until someone else has been caught in the trap, so I passed the "news" on to Phil and Joe, and we all stood around the cairn consoling each other until the deception became apparent, and the clouds of gloom rolled away.

Looking back on it now, Wolf says with a mischievous smile, "You should have seen the look on their faces." He was probably lucky they did not pitch him off the summit.

A view of Mount Goode from the southwest, showing the route of the first ascent by Bauer, Hossack, Dickert, Halwax and MacGowan.

It was a symbolic act of fate that on that very same day, Mountaineers elders Norval Grigg, Don Blair and Forest Farr were making the first ascent of the southwest summit of 8,900 foot Dome Peak nearby: the future starting point of the iconic Ptarmigan Traverse. It would be their last major climb, and inevitably eclipsed by the victory on Mount Goode. The Goode climb, Wolf declared, "proved that the [outlaws'] climbing course was up to snuff and [we] could conquer where others had failed."[33] (Norval would take it with grace and dignity: "You've got to give Wolf Bauer a lot of credit..." he would later say.[34]) Wolf had, for better or for worse, (remorsefully or not), pounded the first pitons to establish a new route in the Cascades.

Mountaineering historian Harry Majors would say of the day, "On that tranquil July day during the summer of 1936, the Stone Age of Northwest climbing quietly came to a close on Dome Peak; while to the north, on the fierce precipice of Mount Goode, with the ringing of metal being driven into rock, the Iron Age had begun."[35]

By the time of the next climbing season, Wolf was newly married and beginning a new career in the San Juan Islands, with children not far in the future. His mantle of climbing professorship would be passed onto others, most notably to Lloyd Anderson, who documented and formalized the instruction, delegating certain areas of instruction to course graduates with particular expertise. To this day, this transcription and cataloguing of curriculum remains the basis for the course.

There were other technically advanced climbers around the country, many in clubs such as the Sierra Club and Appalachian Mountain Club. Many of them had already begun using ropes and pitons in the early 1930s, perhaps even offering elementary instruction, but it was Wolf's creation of the structured Mountaineers' Climbing Course that was a pioneering development in the United States. Climbers in the Northwest were not forced to learn skills on their own by risky trial-and-error in the mountains. Now they could enter the field with a strong foundation in skills and techniques, with lots of practical experience in controlled settings. By 1940, The Mountaineers Climbing Course was the largest mountaineering education program in the country—perhaps the largest outside of Europe. In that year, Lloyd Anderson would compile the curriculum in *The Climbers' Notebook*, which in turn would become the basis for The Mountaineers' classic textbook *Freedom of the Hills*, without question the most important textbook on mountaineering ever published in the United States.

⎯⎯ ∙ ⎯⎯

BACK AT THE RAINIER MOUNTAIN FESTIVAL IN 2007, Wolf was now being pursued by father climbers with their young sons, hoping perhaps for a kind of papal blessing—a spark, a flash, a dot-dot-dash of whatever it is that one generation has to inspire another. And Wolf has already inspired several generations before these youths. His ascent of Ptarmigan still gets a smile and an enthusiastic head shake from Dave Hahn, nine-time summiter of Mount Everest, not just because Ptarmigan can be a rotten and unpleasant climb, but because the most sophisticated equipment Wolf and Jack had was an ice axe, and the most sophisticated safety devices they had were hazard flares and homemade ice pitons, not so much as a hard hat. For this alone, he garners respect; even the pros avoid going unprotected into a chute of perpetual rockfall.

The fact that Wolf made three runs at a route he would advise everyone else to avoid is a bit problematic. That persistence in the face of a bad risk might make one wonder if his focus on safety might have been something that came to him later in life. But, in fact, it was always first and foremost in his mind, as he asserts in "The Final Conquest":

THE TRUE MOUNTAINEERING ART IS, after all, a safe and sane art and sport or recreation. It is no more "death defying" or "dangerously hazardous" than any other publicly accepted occupation or sport, such as swimming, skiing, flying or automobile driving. If climbing and true mountaineering is to become an accepted art and sport in our Northwest, as it has become recognized on the Continent, then the public must be made aware of that fact. It cannot be done by misleading and unsound pictures and statements extolling the wrong sort of bravery or nerve. A risky climb, a dare-devil thrill picture, or a serious accident due to lack of preparation can be of more harm directly and indirectly to our climbing fraternity and climbing future than seems to be realized by many climbers along the West Coast. Our Northwest will surely become one of the great skiing and climbing centers of the world, and it is up to us to set a standard and foundation for the spirit and ideals of mountaineering, both winter and summer, that will give our Northwest country and its climbing public the right type of recognition and publicity, and give us climbers the realization of our goal, namely, a mountaineering-conscious public that will be helpful in developing our many climbing districts, and a Northwest climbing fraternity that knows better than to regard the mountain world as a place to defy death, and its peaks as an apparatus for gymnastics and new speed and endurance records.[36]

He was also aware that unlike the great "notoriety" climbs, such as those in the Himalaya, Mount Rainier was ultimately in the backyard of millions of people. Route assessment would become extremely important to the National Park Service and the public. Wolf's study of Air Force photographs of and the history of weather patterns on the mountain, along with the route familiarity born of his two failed attempts and his final success on the northeast side of Mount Rainier, set a baseline for mountain knowledge that was invaluable to all who followed.

But of course, he wasn't going to let Ptarmigan beat him personally, either.

The primary focus of Wolf's mountaineering career was to develop the cultural foundation that would allow any and all to access the mountains for the kind of spiritual and aesthetic pleasure that he derived there. Indeed, the curriculum vitae of Wolf's climbing career is not a long bulleted list of peaks from around the world, extolling his courage and strength. Wolf climbed in a time when the Cascade and Olympic mountains were virtually untapped. It was primarily the closest and least difficult peaks that had been conquered. There were plenty of first ascents to go around for everyone.

Wolf's greatest first ascents were, rather, metaphorical: the "Everest" that Wolf climbed was to sow the seeds—spark the genesis—of a safe and fraternal climbing culture for all the generations that would come afterwards. By focusing on formal instruction and safety, he poured the foundation upon which legions of other climbers would foster one of the best arenas for climbing in North America. As Jim Kjeldsen said of early instructors in *The Mountaineers: A History*, "Numerous course leaders were willing to sacrifice their own ambition for the good of the course. [Lloyd] Anderson and [Wolf] Bauer both admit they could have achieved many more first ascents but were primarily interested in teaching the skills to others."[37] Mountaineer and historian Lowell Skoog echoes the sentiment: "His standard-setting climbs on ice and rock would, by themselves, earn Wolf a lasting place in Northwest climbing history. Yet his efforts to teach others had a far greater impact."[38]

As would become true in every other arena of Wolf Bauer's public life, his energies went not into his own personal self-aggrandizement, but into providing something for the public good.

PART III

Professional and Married Life

FIVE

A Family All His Own

I T WOULD TAKE MORE THAN AN ORDINARY GIRL to keep up with Wolf Bauer. Harriet Woodward was not ordinary. When Scoutmaster Harry Higman suggested she could out-hike any boy, he knew how to hook Wolf's curiosity, but it was more than clever marketing. Harriet's upbringing had prepared her for a boy like Wolf, with her world travels and a conspicuous absence of girls in her generation of the family. Her mother was a member of the Daughters of the American Revolution, and though they were old stock, the Gray family was restless. They had blazed their way to Oregon City, Oregon—the terminus of the fabled Oregon Trail, at the confluence of the Willamette and Clackamas Rivers and at the foot of Mount Hood. When the Fairbanks Gold Rush broke out in Alaska in 1902, the whole family bolted north, parents and grand-parents alike.

Harriet's father, G. Carlton Woodward, came from Philadelphia Quaker stock. They had beat William Penn to Pennsylvania, hailing from Plymouth, Massachusetts, in their flight from the tyranny of the Puritans. It was Harriet's father and his brother who heeded the siren call of the Fairbanks Gold Rush. As it panned out for most, the misty apparition of sudden wealth eluded their grasp. But they found something else. Most importantly, Carlton found Harriet's mother, Reva—an eighteen-year-old beauty eleven years his

Reva and Carlton Woodward, Harriet's parents.
PHOTO COURTESY OF HARRIET BAUER.

younger. And he established his worth. Possessor of a mimeograph machine, he helped put out the first "newspaper" in Fairbanks, the *Fairbanks Miner*, in 1903. In the classified ads of the first issue, he advertised his services succinctly as "Woodward the Stenographer— First Avenue—Fairbanks." Emerging as a respected member of the Fairbanks community, when the U.S. Consul to Canada went on vacation, Carlton was asked to fill in for him.

So positive was this experience that he was invited to train for the consulship himself, and the newly married Woodwards set off for consul training in Philadelphia. Here, Harriet's brother Warren was born, and soon after the family boomeranged back west with Carlton's first post: Vancouver, British Columbia. Though never a Canadian citizen, Harriet was born in Vancouver five years after her brother, and lived there until she was six. Horrified by the taunt that she was actually an American, Harriet refused to believe it. With the gentle pedantry that characterizes older brothers, hers took it upon himself to lock her in the closet until, after much power-wrangling, she admitted she wasn't Canadian.

Carlton served as Consul to Canada during World War I with such notoriety that he received a letter from abdicated Kaiser Wilhelm after the war thanking him for ensuring that German prisoners were treated kindly during the war. Vividly, Harriet recalls being in New York City on Armistice Day at the war's end in November 1918 and sitting atop her father's shoulders while the parade advanced down Broadway, a blizzard of confetti snowing upon their heads.

After British Columbia, the family moved to Mexico for a term, back to Canada to Campbelltown, and ultimately to New Brunswick. Mother and children were stationed south of the border in Brookline, Massachusetts. Harriet attended school in Boston, where she recalls with both embarrassment and pride that, the first time her class undertook to sing "My Country 'Tis of Thee," she naturally began belting out the lyrics to "God Save the Queen" instead, both songs being sung to the same music. Ultimately posted back in British Columbia's Prince Rupert consulate, the family headed west once again; this time the family stayed stateside without their father in Seattle. Like her future husband, Harriet moved to her new home in Seattle in time for eighth grade. It was in junior high that she remembers meeting Wolf for the first time, on a bird walk with the Harry Higman clan.

But until college, she was busy enough charting her own territory. In an era when few girls were involved in athletics, Harriet was the catcher for the Roosevelt High School softball team and an avid member of the school's basketball team. Her son Larry would remember watching his mom play basketball in the late 1940s, when she was in her late thirties. She had learned how to ice skate in New Brunswick, and loved roller skating. She took up fencing as a student at the University of Washington and was an avid cyclist in the early days of her parenting career. In later years, she would become a competitive curler and the National Singles Lawn Bowling Champion in 1974 and 1979. Harriet liked to win.

Harriet Woodward, in the uniform of Girl Scout Troop 1 in Seattle. PHOTO COURTESY OF HARRIET BAUER.

The irrepressible Ms. Woodward was also a Girl Scout in Seattle's historic Troop 1, and loved camping. She camped with her church youth group at the Christian Science Church in the University District of Seattle, a youth group that included Chet Higman and Ome Daiber, two young men who were, or would become, friends of her future husband, Wolf. As a counselor at the Girl Scouts' Camp Robbinswold on Hood Canal, she had the honor of taking First Lady Mrs. Herbert Hoover on a tour of the camp. When her boys were small in St. Louis, where the family moved in 1942, she was a Troop leader, and Larry joked that the boys were Girl Scouts long before they were Boy Scouts, coming along to troop meetings for the games and playing ball on the empty school courts.

If ever there were a girl qualified to take on life with Wolf Bauer, it was Harriet Woodward.

Harriet and Wolf grew close at the University of Washington, when Harriet, a sculptor and painter, frequented "Lower Slobovia" to use the kiln of the Ceramic Engineering Department. Now in her nineties, Harriet recalls with pleasure Wolf's invitation to Snoqualmie Lodge to hear him play the accordion. She was there when the Victrola played on the frozen Lodge Lake while the moonlight shone down on the alpine skaters. She was there when Wolf demonstrated rappelling in the Rialto building downtown. She was there when he dumped off the ski jump to save his watch, and she was there to console him after his unsuccessful try-out at the 1935 Olympic Ski Trials. She was there, along with her mother, a neighbor, and their 1936 Packard, waiting at Paradise while Wolf was picking his way up Mount Rainier's Ptarmigan Ridge. Perhaps the height to which she was willing to go to prove her own mettle can be detected in Wolf's recollection of a climb she made with him on Columbia Peak in the Monte Cristo area. He is still proud to relate that Harriet was the first woman to sign its register. "She enjoyed

Harriet Woodward, the first woman to climb Columbia Peak.
PHOTO COURTESY OF HARRIET BAUER.

the climb," Wolf recalled, "but she didn't want to sit on the ledge for the photo." Harriet Woodward was a very good sport.

She received her degree in fine arts, and while Wolf was taking his fifth year at the "U," Harriet tucked in a year of business school. When both were done and Wolf had secured his first job, the only thing left to do was get married.

Applied Psychology

THE SUMMER OF 1935 saw the first hints that the Great Depression was on its last legs. Being involved in the establishment of a Boys Camp on San Juan Island, I had occasion to visit the owner of Roche Harbor Lime and Cement Company, across Westcott Bay. This lime plant was in the process of gearing up for a planned operation. I was advised to come back the next year for a possible engineering position. This came to pass, and my career had its unlikely start. It was here, at this unique operation in one of the most beautiful seascapes of the state, that Lady Luck again showed me her hand.

Getting acquainted with this multi-faceted operation and personnel took up the fall months. I was temporarily housed in the historic Hotel de Haro until a cottage could be readied for me on the sloping hillside behind the hotel. On my occasional walks exploring the surrounding countryside, I came upon an adjacent small lime-burning operation of the Orcas Lime Company that just had exhausted its quarry ore. The land had been bought by a Scottish lady sheep-rancher and farmer. In order to make her payments, she had to sell some of her waterfront lands, including a small pocket-beach cove near the Roche Harbor boundary on Mosquito Pass. It didn't take me long to recognize a great opportunity, especially since a small cabin also occupied the three acres of land. It would be only a ten-minute walk from the plant. What a Shangri-La, especially in view of the fact that my future wife was also an outdoors-oriented individual. But how to convince Paul McMillin, my boss, to make an exception to the company policy that mandated in-house employee residence? Because of my growing responsibilities, it was especially important that I be readily available, in case of emergency.

Well, I waited some weeks until I found him in a good humor one day, and asked him whether my position was permanent enough to get married on. He assured me that he had full confidence in me, and that yes, by all means, I should settle here with a wife. I then asked him for some "fatherly" advice as to whether I had been offered a reasonable price of one thousand dollars for three acres of waterfront land, including a small cottage. Being unaware, at this point, of what I was driving at, he assured me that it would, indeed, be a good bargain.

Thanking him for his "expert" advice, I then enthused about all the shared outdoor interests that this place would offer us, and our possible offspring. Furthermore, I assured him that I could not only hear the emergency horn at the plant from the property, but that I would be able to reach it by shortcut trail or by car within ten minutes. Paul McMillan was hard put to say no at that point, and, to my relief, he reluctantly agreed to give it a try. I vowed to prove to him that he had made the right decision.

Labor of Love

IT WAS NOW TIME FOR ME TO START WORKING DOUBLE-SHIFT DAYS. I gave Harriet the good news, and we agreed we would get married just before Christmas, giving me but two months to make the cabin livable. Luckily, our plant maintenance and repair man, Henry Schultz, was not only a jack-of-all-trades that knew about welding, blacksmithing, diesel, electric, and plumbing, but also a man of German extraction. In my job of modernizing all phases of plant and quarry operation, he became my right hand man, and we developed a good cooperative relationship. Thus, he was more than happy to help me get my living quarters in shape after work hours. This included my well and hand-pump water system with storage tank and tower, a water line to the house, a shower room addition and house plumbing, a fireplace with a steel hood, bedroom addition with a skylight and built-in bed, and a privy shack with a twin-hole seat bench. The only missing amenity was electricity.

In those months before Christmas, we put in at least six hours every evening, so that upon my return from the holidays on the mainland, I could carry my new wife confidently over the threshold into a livable domicile.

Still, there were questions. How would she take to a pioneer-type life that included taking turns at:

- Hand-pumping well water twenty feet up to the fifty-gallon storage tank, rain or shine.

- Cutting or gathering bark or wood daily for the kitchen stove to cook and to heat the cabin and water for washing, showers and laundry.
- Lighting kerosene lanterns and pressure-pumped glow-mantel lamps that need constant trimming care, every evening.
- Doing the weekly washing using a washtub and scrubbing board, and indoor and outdoor clotheslines.
- Racing through rain, freezing temperatures, and darkness to the outdoor privy.
- Living without a telephone, and with only one neighbor, at the nearby sheep ranch.

Well, this would be the cost of an "idyllic" life, but it was our choice.

Wolf and Harriet Bauer, newlyweds, 1937.

Harriet at Roche Harbor on San Juan Island, where she found their wedding present of two goat kids. PHOTO COURTESY OF HARRIET BAUER.

On December 23, 1936, I arrived in Seattle to be married in a civil ceremony, with a close friend in attendance. If that sounds like a hurry-up occasion, it was—for two very different reasons. When Harriet's father learned that his daughter no longer wanted to abide by Christian Science dogma, I became persona non grata—unwelcome in his house. Thus, our marriage, for the time being, had to be secret. As for me, I, too, wanted to keep it a secret from my parents, but only so that I could surprise them by hanging our marriage certificate on their tree the next night on Christmas Eve. A joyous shriek from mother announced its discovery, and there was a subsequent celebration. It was not until a year later, when our first son was born, that Harriet's father relented, and become a proud grandpa. Father Time, I've learned, is a universal healer.

Lizzy now proudly carried us back to the island, and to the little cabin, with its fresh coat of whitewash. To our great surprise, we found two little white kid goats tethered to the front porch. They turned out to be a wedding gift from the plant foreman, which we eventually raised to a milking output of more than two quarts per day. Although milking them became a necessary chore, their loveable antics easily made up for it, even despite some mischief. They followed us everywhere—or at least they tried to!

A view of the Bauers' Eden at Roche Harbor, San Juan Island.

Our Island Life

IN RETROSPECT, having had seventy years to compare them with, these first three years of married life on San Juan Island become ever more treasured memories. Within a year or so, our fist son, Rocky, was born, with both pomp and anxiety. When Harriet announced that her water had broken, we rushed out of bed to Lizzy for the flight to Friday Harbor. Arrangements had already been made for a bed and nurse. I also had seen to it that Lizzy was ready to roll. But when we rounded the first major curve on the road, the headlights suddenly went out. I hit the brakes like mad in the blind darkness, and the lights came on again as we straightened out—followed by a loud "boom" from the muffler, where accumulated unburned gasoline re-ignited. This unnerving sequence repeated itself several more times, but this was no time to stop and check out the engine. Years later, I recounted to Rocky how

Rocky Bauer, with his parents and one of the goats, 1939.

his arrival in Friday Harbor had been noisily announced by Lizzy's last belch. A loose wire between the distributor and plugs had shorted because of the centrifugal force generated on the tight curves, thus giving Lizzy a voice with which to advertise the occasion. Not until the next morning did Rocky's lusty greeting show whose decibels had won the celebration.

Sasha No. 2

BY THE TIME THE SECOND YEAR ROLLED AROUND, and Rocky had turned from quadruped to biped, his world and ours became ever more exciting. We had acquired Sasha No. 2, the spitting image of my Bavarian boyhood companion. She had learned to keep an eye on Rocky whenever he showed an early wanderlust. Sasha kept herself between the toddler and the eight-foot bank above the beach, and she barked loudly when Rocky was trying to pat the neighbor's bull in the field. Sasha instinctively became his guardian. Harriet had Rocky dressed in a bright red jumpsuit so that he would be easy to find, but this bull luckily didn't "see red" at his appearance.

I recall an unusual incident that took place in our little bay. This dog loved swimming, to the point of floating without making any frantic motions to stay afloat. That summer, we occasionally saw a seal checking out our little cove at Mosquito Pass. One day, to my amazement, I saw two grey heads and snouts curiously circling each other in the eddy—one had ears, and the other, whiskers. What a rare camera-shot that could have been! I'm still wondering whether that was their first encounter.

Ma

OUR SCOTTISH NEIGHBOR, who didn't mind us calling her "Ma" (which, when we called her, may have made us sound a little like her sheep), frequently needed a little help, for which she reciprocated in kind with butter,

Mrs. Nellis Houde, "Ma," with one of her sheepdogs.

eggs and milk. One time, she hurried over, asking for help in dislodging an apple stuck in her cow's long throat. The bulge showed its position in the wheezing animal. While I held a piece of lumber against one side, Ma smacked the other with a heavy rock, evidently an old-country trick that worked like a charm.

In return, she came over in a hurry the day that I found one of our goats lying on the ground with a balloon-sized swollen stomach, popping eyes, and labored breathing. She had somehow gotten into a sack of oats, and after gorging herself, evidently added injury to insult by drinking her fill of water, generating the bloating gas. When I described her condition to Ma, she immediately grabbed one of her darning needles, and we hurried to the patient who, by now, seemed on her last legs. Expertly fingering for a spot between the goat's ribs, she confidently punched in the needle, and with a swoosh, the heaving balloon deflated, with little loss of blood. Ma's Scottish Highland shepherd friends would have been proud, and Harriet and I looked on in grateful amazement. "Now we're even again, Wolf," was her only comment. The following cold winter, she showed us another amazing trick of animal husbandry.

Ma had a wool buyer in British Columbia who, in order to get a jump on the market, would give her a better price for an early shipment of her wool. Early breeding meant early sheering, as sheering was always done after the lambs had matured and were less reliant on their mother as a source of warmth. This meant that her lambs were thrown in February, with snow on the ground that year. Lambing is a harried twenty-four hour period when, in some instances, Ma had to be on the spot to save an abandoned newborn by keeping it warm and alive. In such circumstances, it was sometimes possible to skin a dead lamb, drape and tie the skin over a rejected lamb, and offer it to the foster mother in disguise. Searching for such lambs with a night-lantern, I gained new respect for a shepherd's life.

The Swing

MEMORIES OF OUR ROCHE HARBOR LIFE invariably return to the almost daily thrill of swooping down and out over the bay's water on a trapeze-type swing. Early on, I noted the ideal happenstance of a tall fir at the top edge of our shore bank, leaning precariously over the high-tide water. What a "skyhook"[39] opportunity! Taking off from a raised platform on the tree, one would drop vertically twenty feet down toward the beach, and then sail out over the water. Only at high tide would you get your feet and fanny wet. That provided great hilarity when we would urge an unsuspecting new-comer to try the ride at such a time.

When we wanted a quiet, undisturbed meal, we would strap Rocky into the swing in a special seat with a supply of rocks and sticks to entertain him-self and Sasha above the water's edge.

The Boat

BEFORE THE ADVENT OF MODERN KAYAKS, rowboats and canoes were the all-purpose manual propulsion crafts. Living on the water's edge without a boat was a necessary evil until some hard-earned money could be spared for such a luxury. Friday Harbor Shipyard, though very busy, was willing to build me a cedar rowing dinghy with keel-box if I provided an adequate design. Drawing on my eighth grade era sailing experience on Lake Washington, I knew just what I wanted—and they built it for us. I then added a mast, centerboard, rudder and sails—we were finally in business,

Rocky in the front "yard" with the Bauers' sailboat at Mosquito Pass.

ready to explore, fish, and sail the surrounding waters. Our shipyard foreman at the plant had, in the meantime, dragged some logs into our cove.
These I converted into a floating dock that could rise and fall with the tides,
held in place by two roped anchors. In major storms, the boat could be carried up the rocks out of harm's way. Many happy rowing, fishing, sailing,
and exploring hours occupied our free time. Often on our return, we were
greeted by an enthusiastic welcoming committee of dog and goats, all trying to jump into the boat in a rush to greet us.

Ferry Farce

IT WAS IN THE 1930S, on San Juan Island. I had to attend an important
Seattle meeting, and Harriet and I were pushing our 1929 Ford to make the
ferry on time. We had just heard the double-blast for its departure, as we
entered Friday Harbor four blocks from the landing. We raced to the end of
the dock with frantic toots of our horn, both for people in our way and for
the captain's ear (the ferry had already reached the outer pilings of the
berth, some hundred feet from the ramp). Unbelievably, the captain must
have seen and heard us, since the ferry reversed engine and started to come
back. Then the dock attendant stepped on my running board and asked,
"Where're you going, Bud?" I said "Anacortes." He scowled and said,
"That's the Sidney Ferry!"

Putting Lizzy into reverse in chagrined humiliation, to the snide remarks
and gestures from dockside witnesses, we snuck back up the hill to the
Anacortes ferry line. I'm sure that was the last time that ferry captain
reversed his engine as a goodwill gesture. I owe the island an apology.

Labor Unrest[40]

1938 MARKED THE "YEAR OF THE STRIKE" at Roche Harbor. The push for
unionization came from many directions. Most of our customers were
already organized industries, where union workers questioned the use of
"scab" lime products from Roche Harbor.

Visiting union organizers from the Cement, Lime & Gypsum Workers
Union pointed to shortcomings in safety, pay and health insurance. When
Paul McMillin was thus confronted, he said to us on the staff: "Shut 'er
down—we'll show them." A strike ensued.

Wolf (standing second from left) with his fellow management "scabs" during the strike at the Roche Harbor Lime Company in 1938.

I was on very friendly terms with all the employees, working closely with them every day, and I was very sympathetic to their cause. Many of them became good friends through First Aid courses I taught, and they came to me with personal problems that did not merit an audience with McMillin. So when I was forced to become a "scab," the men didn't hold it against me. They knew I couldn't risk losing my job.

And so the salaried personnel—bookkeeper, salesmen, all the foremen of the quarries, plant, shop and engineer—we all rolled up our sleeves and kept earning our pay that summer in the quarry. With the lime kilns down, we just broke rock and shipped our output. I well remember when we backed the first loaded truck up the ramp to dump into the scow while Paul McMillin stood alongside with a loaded shotgun to show the surprised strikers that he meant business. Nothing happened, and for about three months we toiled at hard labor until the strike was settled. It was the first time that the McMillin authority had been challenged, and as members of the new Union, the workers had found their voice. No longer had the island isolated us from the industrial policies of the mainland.

Moving On

DURING MY STUDENT YEARS, I had occasion to test the raw materials and products of the Washington Brick & Lime Company of Spokane. The new president of this manufacturing business, Neal Fossen, was, like my boss Paul McMillin, a son of the former owner. Unlike Paul, Neal graduated from the University of Washington's Business School about three years ahead of me, and was also similarly involved in the Boy Scout organization. He bought lime from my employer for resale and use in his operation, so it was natural that we should meet and become acquainted.

It was in the late summer of 1939 that Neal wrote to me inquiring whether I might consider working for him, especially as he was toying with the idea of getting into the lime manufacturing business. How could I not accept? After all, my career was just starting. It was also an easy decision for Harriet. "Just think," she said, "we can have light and heat just by pushing a button! Also, we'll soon have another arrival." The future looked rosy, but the next five years would test us both.

Harriet with younger son Larry at the beach, 1942.
PHOTO COURTESY OF HARRIET BAUER.

Design Opportunity

WE MOVED INTO A MODERN RENTAL APARTMENT IN SPOKANE, and returned to city life. Neal Fossen, my new boss, made me feel like a friend and team member right from the start. During the rest of that year, I became thoroughly familiar with his clay products operations, which was in my field of Ceramic Engineering. In the spring of 1940, our second son, Larry, was born and by that time, Neal and I had decided that the business climate for getting into lime products manufacturing looked encouraging.

There was a somewhat dilapidated single-kiln plant sitting in the Okanogan Highlands near the old mining town of Republic. After he and I looked into its history and its modernizing and business potential, Neal became enthused and said, "Wolf, let's get busy." Little did I guess what highs and lows lay ahead, but the die was cast. For the next six months, I spent my weeks at Republic, redesigning and rebuilding the operation, and driving back to Spokane on weekends to be with my enlarged family.

I was free to design and put to the test several technical innovations at the plant. For example, I redesigned the fireboxes to produce some unburned gas that would ignite later with recuperated hot air from the kiln cooker, raising the combustion temperature and kiln output. To increase efficiency further, I capitalized on the steady winds sweeping through the narrow valley in which the plant was located. Rather than paying to create a draft with a motorized exhaust fan, a swiveling "venturi-elbow" on top of the exhaust stack boosted production down the line on windy days.

While I must confess that being able to create such innovations was a technical highlight in my life, at the time that did not really compensate for the business and family pressures that weighed heavily on me during this period from 1939 to 1941. For Harriet that winter, our new life was no picnic. After the initial set-up of the plant, she and the boys had left Spokane and joined me in Republic. Living in a two-room motel cabin in a former mining town without friends or recreation, but with lots of diapers and chores, as well as a tired and often frustrated husband returning late at night, was not the idyllic married life we lived in the San Juan Islands.

Nevertheless, the plant was running and making acceptable products that stood up to the competition, and I had developed a dependable crew and superintendent to take over. Most important of all, Neal Fossen was satisfied with my work in making the operation profitable. In fact, I was most surprised when he told me that he now wanted to expand his lime-products market into Oregon, a plan that hinged on purchasing a small unprofitable operation in that state and putting it on its feet. Goodbye, Washington; Hello, Oregon!

Oregon Plant

THE SMALL LIME PLANT near the town of Williams, Oregon was located at the northeastern terminus of a series of limestone lenses that extended across the Oregon-California border, part of which became famous as Oregon Caves National Monument. Unlike the grey mottled limestone at Roche Harbor and Republic that burned into white lime, this limestone was white to begin with, and thus had additional potential uses in the broad industry of "mineral fillers."

Unlike the defunct lime plant that we started with at Republic, the Oregon plant was still operating, albeit with limited markets and capital and questionable profits. Neal saw increased market potential, and I saw possibilities for improved earnings with some technical modernizations and improved operating practices. Our speculations proved accurate, even as war clouds began to darken the political horizons.

During my nine months of engineering work at Williams, Neal provided us with a company car. He also took care of the continuing rent on our Spokane apartment. When compared to our life and quarters in Republic the year before, Williams was a major improvement. Our cabin was part of a pleasant working farm that was near the lime plant, as well as the village of Williams. Our growing boys were ever easier to take care of and to keep entertained, what with farm animals and free-time trips to the nearby countryside and ocean coast. My own work, too, was less stressful, even though I sometimes had to "pull rank" on an older plant superintendent when it came to technical decisions.

Saltwater Cure

THE SUMMER OF 1941 WAS A HOT ONE, and in the process of doing field surveys at the new plant in Williams, stripped to the waist, I came down with a serious case of poison oak infection. Covered with blisters, I drove all the way down to a Portland clinic, where they applied liberal quantities of potassium permanganate over my skin. I was informed I would be cured in a week with daily applications and dressings.

As I was driving back on the long coastal highway, imagining how the cold water would feel, I said to myself, "To heck with it. I'm going in, bandages and all!" I stopped at the first isolated beach spot, and sans clothing, I plunged in, remaining immersed until my skin turned blue, and my teeth began to chatter. As I staggered back out, with almost all the bandages having washed off, I drove home without a single itch, and got the first comfortable night's sleep I had since the infection set in. The next morning, I had only rings where the blisters had been, and by the next day, I seemed cured. I phoned the Portland doctor, letting him in on my "secret" cure, and suggesting he test the idea with a bathtub full of iced, salty water. I don't know whether he did it, but I like to think that I contributed a cure for poison oak to the field of medicine. How self-satisfied can you get?

Staying Alive

LIFE IS LIKE THE WEATHER—UNPREDICTABLE. Harriet and I had bought groceries in Williams, and were driving back home one day, when suddenly an oncoming car swerved directly into our lane, smashing into us head-on, at an angle. When I came to, I squeezed out from behind my bent steering wheel to reach Harriet, who was bleeding on her forehead from getting cut by broken window glass. After tending to her bleeding (a cut that needed subsequent stitching) and thankful that the boys were not in the car, I ran over to the other car, where a seriously bleeding and unconscious woman lay slumped across her steering wheel. Finding the nearest pressure point, I stopped the heavy blood flow, and luckily kept her alive until an ambulance crew that had been called by a passerby arrived to take over.

Both cars were towed off, and Harriet and I were checked out at the local clinic. I was released, but Harriet was hospitalized for a week with her injuries. Thankfully, she made a full recovery. At the later trial, we learned that the lady in the other car was subject to fainting spells, and should not have been driving alone. Our company car was fully insured, and we both felt extremely lucky, especially that the boys had not been involved. Now it's just a faint memory, but it serves as an occasional reminder of modern life's ever-present hazards.

Listening to Wolf and Harriet reminisce, it is both amusing and *be*musing to reflect on the absence of complaints about hard Depression-era circumstances, whether it was breaking quarry rocks with a diploma, raising babies without plumbing, or living a virtual widowhood stranded in a desolate motel cabin. A modern middle-class couple would likely have been insulted and embittered, offering a litany of scathing observations about the unjust indignities they endured. The daughter of a diplomat and son of a naval officer and university academic, these two could easily have felt that their circumstances were beneath them.

But seventy years ago, our modern American sense of entitlement had not yet matured. Americans still understood the value of their blessings and the utter naturalness of hardship and challenge. And Harriet and Wolf had more than just the stoic personal discipline of the era. Even for their time, both seem possessed of a calm confidence in their own ability to handle whatever trial or contest life might place before them. If they recall being frightened or insecure, they are not able or willing to give expression to it for this narrative. Fearless, humble, and focused, they were ready to face the national and international trial ahead: World War II.

At the Mountain Rescue Council Convention at Snoqualmie Pass in 1949, mountain rescuers from Oregon practice using a "Bergtrage," or mountain litter, adjusted to carry a sitting victim.

Jack Hossack poses in front of Mount Rainier with the "Stokeski," a variation of the Stokes basket litter, which he designed and built with Wolf Bauer. Wally Burr built the ski attachment, which was later redesigned to have tips at both ends, like a snowboard.

Wolf takes a sample of water stratification in the brackish waters of Snohomish River sloughs near Everett, Washington. He designed the Tyee I kayak, built by Linc Hales in 1961, and painted both vessel and paddle with native motifs. One of the earliest fiberglass kayaks built in the United States, it is now in the care of Seattle's Museum of History and Industry, along with the paddle.

Wolf assembles a foldboat in the 1950s.

The foldboating fleet congratulates Susan Meredith on catching their dinner on the coast of British Columbia, 1950s.

Young male California sea lions charge Wolf and his friend Tom Steinburn in their fragile foldboats on the west coast of Vancouver Island. Luckily, they were bluffing.

In a first contact by foldboat, the fleet visits a native summer fishing camp at Active Pass, on the southeast side of Vancouver Island.

The Washington Foldboat Club conspires to save Dunn Canyon on the Cowlitz River by showcasing its recreational value in the media, in this case *The Seattle Times*, 1958.
PHOTO COURTESY OF SPRING TRAIL TRUST.

The characteristic rapids and pools of the
Green River Gorge.

Daisies accent the drama of rock and river
at the Green River Gorge.

Harriet Bauer relaxes at a gravel beach campsite after a day of paddling on the Green River Gorge.

Towering sandstone formations dwarf a kayaker navigating the Green River Gorge.

The spit at Tolmie State Park prior to restoration by Wolf Bauer.

The same site after restoration.

The south beach at West Point in Discovery Park prior to restoration by Wolf Bauer.

NEW WEST PT. BEACH BERM (After Storms)
Aug. 83

The same site after restoration.

SIX

The War Years

WOLF'S BOYHOOD FRIEND, Richard May of Kreuth, followed in the footsteps of his forefathers and became a doctor. Like Wolf, he was of draft age at the onset of World War II, and so found himself a physician conscripted into Hitler's army. His talents were put to work during the horrific Siege of Leningrad, and Richard credits his survival to an accident. Just prior to the retreat of the German Army, he fell from a horse and broke his back. Evacuated ahead of the army, he had the good fortune to escape the fate of his healthy fellow officers at the hands of the Soviet Army.

Another of Wolf's friends, Alois Kreckl of Wasserburg, similarly found himself a tank commander in North Africa under Erwin Rommel during the war. He recalled the day he and Wolf Bauer had dropped a great snowball into the stack of a locomotive, but unlike Wolf's deja vu during a ski trip, Alois remembered it as he watched a direct hit on a locomotive in the desert, raining bodies rather than snowflakes in the sky. Later, he found himself, like Richard May, at the disintegrating Eastern Front, encamped near Leningrad in what is now Poland. When the order came down from Hitler that anyone trying to retreat should be shot in front of the troops, Alois and his men had a good laugh. "They knew the war was over," Wolf relates. "They weren't going to listen to that crazy guy." As a group, they discussed how, when and where to surrender. Alois and one other

decided it was worth the long journey to Northern Italy to surrender to the Americans; risking capture by the Soviet Army held no
appeal. He told his men they were free to go and left them to fend
for themselves as best they could. Then, leaving the equipment
behind, he and his lone companion began stalking the Yanks, with
white flags at the ready. Traversing the Alps at night, the two made
it to Italy and executed a successful surrender to the Americans.
Within a few weeks, the war was over.

Of the twenty-three boys in Wolf's and Alois' Wasserburg class,
only three came home alive.

"The odds are not very good that I would have survived," Wolf
reflects.

⟶⟨⟩⟵

LIFE IN THE UNITED STATES FOR A GERMAN-AMERICAN had its own
challenges. During World War I, Woodrow Wilson had invoked the
Alien Enemies Act of 1798, which, during the War of 1812, had
given President Adams additional power, during a declared war, to
control the lives and property of its "enemy alien" population. (This
act is still on the books, and still grants the president this power.) In
Wilson's war, it allowed for the curtailing of multiple civil liberties
for foreign residents in the name of, for lack of a better phrase,
homeland security. Un-naturalized foreign-born residents who were
citizens, subjects or denizens of the hostile country were "liable to
be apprehended, restrained, secured and removed, as alien enemies." Anti-German sentiment during World War I was so high that
Lutheran churches dropped German-language prayer and "ham-
burgers" were renamed "liberty steaks." Germans and German-
Americans, regardless of citizenship, were routinely harassed and
humiliated, were fired randomly without cause by suspicious
employers, and were often the victims of mob violence. It was a
national embarrassment, especially considering that then, as is still
true, more Americans claimed German ancestry than any other eth-
nicity, including English.

There was little time between the wars for the collective retrieval
of civility and propriety before the old prejudices came rushing

back. With World War II on the horizon, attitudes were further exacerbated by the media and a tidal wave of blatantly xenophobic movies, such as *Confessions of a Nazi Spy* (1939), with Edward G. Robinson, Charlie Chaplin's The *Great Dictator* (1940) and *Ghosts on the Loose* (1943), where Nazi spies come up against the patriotic wiles of the Bowery Boys.[41]

With the outbreak of the Second World War in 1939, and Wilson's precedent in place, Congress passed the Alien Registration Act of 1940, which required all aliens to be registered, photographed and fingerprinted with the U.S. Post Office, and for all over fourteen years of age to file a comprehensive "resume" and a record of their political beliefs. When President Franklin Roosevelt created the Emergency Detention Program in 1939, and commissioned J. Edgar Hoover's FBI with its implementation, the die was cast for one of the least-known witch-hunts in American history. Most Americans are aware that 120,000 Japanese residents, many of whom were citizens, were sent to internment camps in the western United States after the attack on Pearl Harbor. What is less known is the fate of many Europeans in America at the time of the war.

What began as the compilation of an Enemies List was to evolve into a system of Enemy Alien Detention Camps, wherein 11,000 unnaturalized residents of German descent, and 3,300 residents of Italian descent found themselves sitting out the war behind barbed wire and watchtowers manned by armed guards. Many were sent there simply at the scurrilous charges of paranoid neighbors and were often ignorant of any charges against them, with due process of law summarily suspended. Citizens could not be interned, but often they voluntarily accompanied their un-naturalized parents and spouses into the camps. Homes and fortunes were often left to scavengers, teenagers were seized and handcuffed in their schools, and young children were often sent to orphanages. Families were broken, and careers and lives were ruined. And returning to their now-hostile communities after the war was rarely a happy return to a former life.

For naturalized German-Americans, there were other potential nightmares. In Wolf's Seattle circle, Hans Otto Giese had arrived in the United States in 1923, attended the University of Washington and become an American citizen. As an attorney, he offered his services to the German Consul in Seattle, an affiliation that ended up causing problems for him. When the war broke out, the FBI tried to revoke his citizenship, alleging he was a Nazi sympathizer. He was successful in defending himself and his citizenship in court, but he and his American wife were forcibly relocated to Colorado nonetheless, his law practice and home abandoned. It was simply deemed too dangerous to have German natives living on either the Atlantic or Pacific seaboard.[42]

Fortunately for Wolf, his family was not subjected to this level of humiliation, but the context of widespread American sentiment is important to note. Despite his native fluency in English, his residual accent still betrayed his lineage at every utterance. His mother was born a U.S. citizen, and his father became one. Wolf thus became a citizen when he turned eighteen. The percentage of German aliens who were interned was mercifully small. There were more than three hundred thousand who were left alone. And until after the war, very few people, including the Bauers, knew anything about the internments.

Harriet does recall that in the early days of the war, some anti-German sentiment was expressed to the Bauer family, but it did not last long. The most noteworthy episode came with "the knock on the door" in St. Louis, where Wolf and his wife and family moved in 1942. It is still with bewilderment that Wolf recalls his questioning by two government agents. He was presented with and asked to explain a picture of himself at age twelve in Germany. In it, he is wearing a swimsuit with a "hackenkreutz" insignia sewn on the waistband—a "hooked cross," or swastika. "How did they find me? That photo was taken in the twenties!" he still blurts in amazement. "Where did they get it?" He shakes his head. "Back then, Hitler had been considered a good guy. Things were very bad in Germany after the first war. He was a man of the people. Everyone was pro-Hitler then; he gave them hope. We didn't know what was to come." His parents were terribly unsettled by the incident when he related it, and likewise were mystified about how the United States government had come to be in possession of this personal family photo. The resulting feeling of distrust and humiliation compounded Hubert Bauer's growing disenchantment with his adopted country, and likely contributed to his decision to return alone to Germany after the war, leaving his wife and grown children in the United States.

At twenty-nine years old, Wolf was certainly of enlistment age, and his loyalty was one hundred percent true blue American. But he was not particularly keen on the prospect of trying to kill the likes of Richard May or Alois Kreckl. His career had taken him to the Midwest, where he was contributing to the war effort in the defense industry, and with two young children at home, he was loath to leave his family. He was on a six-month call with the Selective Service, but likely through the machinations of his new boss, he was never called up. Still, Wolf always felt that he had somehow let his adopted country down by not taking up arms personally in her defense.

Convincing Wolf to speak about life as a German-American during World War II is like trying to wrestle the secrets of the cosmos from a single blade of grass. He slides deftly away from the subject at every turn. His non-response is a response in its own right. As an eternal optimist and an all-American boy, Wolf has decided to let this dark and conflicted era fade into the quiet past, choosing instead to chronicle the day-to-day experiences with his family and co-workers. "We were all people, after all," he explains. "What does politics have to do with human feelings?"

War Clouds

THE REAWAKENED U.S. ECONOMY had obviously gotten much of its energy from an upbeat President Roosevelt, who apparently hoped to keep the United States out of any political re-alignments in Europe. Europe, however, was less optimistic, and had begun to react to the ever-more-obvious despotism and ambitions of a Hitler Germany, a communist-military Russia, and a heavily armed Japan.

The St. Louis Connection

THE NON-METALLIC MINERALS INDUSTRIES were served by two competing trade journals, "Pit & Quarry" and "Rock Products," the latter featuring patented lime kiln designs and operations by a Mr. Victor Azbe of St. Louis.

I had occasion to read some of his writings, and was convinced he was a top man in the field. I had written to him about my wood-gas fired lime kiln in Republic, but without any reply on his part. Thus, I was greatly surprised, three years later, to receive from him an inquiry as to whether I would consider working for him. It certainly seemed a timely opportunity. To my relief, Neal Fossen congratulated me on landing an engineering position with worldwide involvements, and was satisfied that they could now carry on without me. So off we went by train, the four of us, to start an unpredictable life during the war years.

Unlike Neal Fossen, Mr. Azbe (emphasis on the "mister" throughout our association) had lost the technical engineering assistant on whom he evidently had heavily depended in his design and consulting work. It was not until a year or so later that I surmised the reasons for this man's departure, as I, too, eventually became disenchanted with the position that I at first eagerly embraced.

The lime industry was beginning to feel the strain of trying to meet growing war-induced demands for metallurgical and chemical lime products. About a dozen lime plants in the United States and Canada were clients of Azbe & Associates, all demanding instant higher production. Thus, I was immediately thrown into a frantic schedule of plant visits, during which time Azbe not only acquainted me with the plant operations, but also, at the same time, demanded consequent engineering and design work at the office. Hectic months on the road by train were interspersed with short family visits. For the fact that I kept my sanity I can thank the draft board. While Azbe had convinced them that I was critically important to the war effort, I nevertheless remained on their call-up list, because of my age and my two-year ROTC training at the university. I can probably also thank my two little sons for initial deferment consideration within those war years. I had, nevertheless, already made up my mind that if I was drafted, I would try to be signed up for the Japanese engagements, in view of my remaining family and friends in Germany. After the Pearl Harbor attack, I at least became more directly involved, by working on camouflaging a Hawaiian lime and carbon dioxide plant in Honolulu in case of a follow-up Japanese bombing raid. This work, in turn, led to my post-war assignment to design and build a modern lime plant at nearby Waianae, but under my own name as consultant.

I spent three professionally frantic war years increasing production of critically needed lime and carbon dioxide gas products in the East, Northwest and Canada. For me, this difficult period provided an ongoing education, also gaining me friends and respect that would be invaluable in the post-war years.

I always felt very strongly that as long as I was being paid for my services by a boss, that I owed him complete loyalty and trust. This was not an easy resolve to adhere to when Mr. Azbe's clients and their engineers complained to me of shortcomings and costly problems experienced with the installed Azbe-designed kilns and techniques. I would be caught in the middle, trying to make it work, but getting a cold shoulder from my boss when I suggested solutions that were not in line with his patent claims. I was beginning to suspect the likely reason for my predecessor's decision to leave Azbe. No matter. I was determined to remain to the war's end, looking at the positive aspects of the job: feeding my family, aiding the war effort, and gaining valuable experiences for the future.

Family Life in St. Louis

IT SHOULD BE SAID, IN RETROSPECT, that Mr. Azbe also had his good sides. He lent us his double-seater collapsible kayak (called a "foldboat") that we could transport by either streetcar or bus to a lake or to the Missouri and Mississippi Rivers. And his wife, who was a figure skating judge with the St. Louis Club, gave us a club membership that got us started in mastering the first- and second-year "school figures" at the ice arena.

Mr. Azbe's office was located in University City, a suburb of St. Louis. We had found an apartment within a relatively short walking distance of the office, and next to a wooded park and playground for the boys. Even without car transportation, the family was well located. Summer heat and humidity, of course, had to be tolerated without air conditioning—often by sleeping naked without bed-covers during heat waves. By the same token, winters could get icy cold, particularly in my work in unheated plant environments. Of one winter, my right hand still reminds me now and then.

It was during one of those icy winter days, when I was collecting lime samples at a processing machine in Pennsylvania, that the gauntlet of my right-hand glove got caught by a rotating blade. As it started to pull my arm, and then me, into the machine, I had to save my life by jerking my arm out in a desperate backward leap that landed me on my back on the concrete floor below. When I pulled the torn work glove off my hand, I saw my ring finger and my little finger hanging from my hand only by the skin. I was in shock, so I felt no pain. I was rushed to the hospital, where a specialist did all he could to set the bones and reattach the tendons, nerves and skin, to the best of his ability. For several months, my hand and arm were in cast and sling, and I was required to learn to dress, eat, write and draw (at half-speed) with my left hand. A partially straightened ring finger, with limited circulation and flexibility, still reminds me of the incident on cold days.

River Interlude

ONE SUMMER WEEKEND, Harriet and I deposited our two boys with a neighbor, grabbed the two big bags in which Azbe's folding kayak was stuffed, and set off on our first river adventure on the mighty Missouri. A trolley would take us about ten miles upstream, from where we could then float

Harriet prepares to embark on the Bauers' first foldboat adventure on the Missouri River in St. Louis, 1941.

down past our University City, and another five or so miles to St. Louis, near the junction with the Mississippi.

After using a coal barge for a handy launching dock, all went according to plan until we stopped paddling and had a late lunch on a grassy flat meadow. Harriet had wandered off a bit, when I heard her cry for help, saying that she was sinking into the mud. I had heard about river quicksand, but never experienced it until I noticed the suction on my bare feet as I hurried to her aid. By the time I reached her, she had made the situation worse by standing alternately on one foot while trying to pull the other out. There was no time to lose. I had her sit, then lie down to spread out the weight, and eventually I was able to pull out one leg at a time. It was a close call, and never forgotten experience. Later, when I asked Azbe why he didn't warn us about it, he said, "I didn't tell you to eat lunch in quicksand!"

A bit shaken, we continued downstream in the approaching dusk that the quicksand episode forced us to contend with. Now we were entering a river-reach where we could no longer hug the stream bank, but had to paddle out past long, current-control pilings stretching toward the main channel. In the approaching darkness, it often was only the gurgling sound of the current against the channel marker pilings that kept us out of trouble. Soon the lights of the industrial waterfront became the "light at the end of the tunnel" for us, and searching for a proper landing spot was more of a relief than a worry.

Easter Bunny

IT WAS THE EARLY DAWN OF AN EASTER MORNING that found me surreptitiously hiding Easter eggs in the adjacent park. The boys, for whom this bleary-eyed effort was undertaken, were still asleep. For Larry, the youngest, this hunt would be great fun. I wasn't too sure whether Rocky, two years older and in Kindergarten, still believed in an Easter Bunny. I went on the assumption that he did. Excitedly, I roused them out of bed, reminding them that it was Easter, and we better hurry out to the park to check whether the St. Louis Easter Bunny had been about.

Steering them toward a large tree stump where I had hidden the first eggs, I saw Rocky take hold of Larry's hand, seriously explaining where, by that stump, he might first look. He then looked at us and grinned an all-knowing grin. Uh-oh! The neighborhood kids had evidently gotten to

The Bauer boys, Larry (left) and Rocky, on scooters in St. Louis, 1944.
PHOTO COURTESY OF HARRIET BAUER.

Rocky ahead of me and told him the truth about the Bunny. Then, unbelievably, a rabbit jumped from the stump as Larry rounded it, and disappeared into the park thickets. Wow! Larry, of course, was not impressed.
Why should he be? But Rocky, the beginning "unbeliever," now had to
spend the next day convincing his friends that the Easter Bunny was the real
McCoy. The powers that be had obviously pulled a fast one. For Harriet and
me, it was a reminder of our own childhoods. It certainly topped my "older
brother" effort on the farm in Bavaria, where I had rigged a basket on the
back of one of my rabbits to fool little sister Gita.

Wolf succeeded in remaining with Azbe until the end of the war as a matter of principle, but when it finally ended, both he and Harriet knew that the Midwest was not the place for them to raise their children. The great amount of time Wolf spent on the road, away from home and family, took a tremendous toll on all the Bauers. During his brief visits home, he was tired, and reluctant to fulfill the paternal role of disciplinarian. Harriet once again was living as a de facto single parent, earning money on the side by running a telephone wake-up service, and seeking a recreational outlet in leading a Girl Scout Troop. Mr. Azbe had proven to be a difficult boss, and the prospect of working as his partner held little appeal for a man who knew his own talents and expertise could only lead to conflict with the headstrong head of the company. He had, in short, outgrown the job. In the service of Mr. Azbe, Wolf had gained the connections and established the expertise that signaled the end of his unspoken apprenticeship. Ready to liberate himself from the constrictions of a boss, and to return his family to its native soil, Wolf resolved to hang out his own shingle as a consultant back at home in Seattle. The family would never look back.

PART IV

Return to the Northwest

SEVEN

Coming Home and Diving In

W ORKING FOR MR. AZBE, the number one lime engineer in the world, had been great experience, and it put Wolf on the map professionally. Victor Azbe offered to make Wolf an equal partner in his business. But partnership in any form can slow a dynamic person down. For example, part of Wolf's job was to travel to plants around the country to make sure a patented Azbe system worked. The problem was, it often didn't. Wolf had to learn how to make a malfunctioning system work, without implying to his boss that his design might be faulty. It taught him two important lessons: 1) how to navigate human business relationships diplomatically and 2) that to be most efficient and productive, he had better work solo—not just without a boss, but without underlings as well. Nevertheless, he understood loyalty and timing, and despite the attempts of clients to persuade him to moonlight for their companies, Wolf closed his tenure in St. Louis with honor. He never burned bridges.

Harriet recalls that the family could not get back to Seattle fast enough, pulling up stakes in 1945 as soon as the war was over. The Bauers moved into a house in the "U-District," on 11th Avenue Northeast and 52nd Street, directly across the street from Harriet's parents (at Wolf's suggestion). Not far away, on University Way in Ravenna, Elsbeth Bauer would take an apartment after Hubert returned alone to Germany for good. Sadly, "Mutti," as her children always called her, would not live long after the war, succumbing to cancer before long.

Wolf commenced to hang out his own shingle as a consultant and slowly developed a clientele that spanned the globe. He soon obtained his Professional Engineering license and Rocky and Larry enrolled in public school. Harriet worked for the area Post Office and in her own basement. There Wolf built her a bookbinding workshop, where she made book repairs and bound music for the University of Washington, specializing in gold leaf. At the YMCA she taught Bookbinding and Ceramics (putting her art degree to work), and at home she worked as Wolf's manager in arranging climbing slide shows for groups. She raised the boys and organized ski trips for the PTA. And for fun in the summer, there was always the great outdoors. Woe to the Bauer boys if they didn't like the mountains.

Post-War Independence

THE "WAR TO END ALL WARS" WAS OVER. Victor Azbe wanted me to stay and become an equal partner. No way—I could do better on my own. With mixed feelings I took stock of my future, and also my conscience. By luck of emigration, I had escaped early conscription into Hitler's army, and, despite U.S. Reserve Officers' Training time, also was passed over for the American military call-ups. And while my war-effort-related absences from my family and industrial injury will never quiet my conscience of not having served on active duty, I would at least try to become involved, as much as possible, in the rehabilitation of post-war industry, both here and in Europe. I would also get my family re-established in Seattle.

Harriet's parents were, of course, happy to see us back, especially since we were lucky to find a house in the University district kitty-corner from theirs. This had a number of advantages, in that the grandparents and I could take turns with the boys while Harriet supplemented my irregular income with library stints away from home.

A modest but most helpful financial boost during this period of independence came from my decision to write for a monthly publication. There has always been a reluctance by certain professionals to advertise their talents, although that is probably less so now than in the past. Writing about your own successes could be construed as a form of bragging. By writing in a teaching mode, I could at least do so with a clear purpose. When I approached the editors of "Pit & Quarry" trade journal, I was surprisingly invited to become a contributing editor, writing a monthly series of technical articles useful to the non-metallics mineral industries. In retrospect, and without question, the subsequent one hundred illustrated articles that were published over the following fifteen years proved to be the catalyst that launched me into a worldwide engineering career.

After a few more years in my own business, my consulting work was beginning to pay off. On the basis of my ten years of engineering projects, and supporting recommendations from clients, I received my Professional Engineer title and a license to practice under my own name. My ceramic engineering professors, who had kept track of me, invited me to teach a senior class in what I had learned, what the new technical field of non-metallic mineral engineering required, and what it had to offer. In turn, the University of Washington allowed me to make use of their lab facilities for my own research. This arrangement was also a two-way street, in that students could earn tuition and living-expense money and gain hands-on experience working for me on research problems. Such practical involvement was especially valuable to foreign exchange students, as their letters to me, years later, indicated.

Oahu Interlude

IT WAS NOT LONG AFTER THE WAR'S END that I was commissioned to design and put into operation a new coral-lime burning and manufacturing operation at Waianae on Oahu. The job required that I leave my family behind for several months in 1947 and 1948, an absence which I would make up to Harriet on a pleasure trip to Hawaii several years later. The lime produced at the plant was to be used for neutralizing acids in the Island's cane sugar and pineapple industries, as well as for other agricultural purposes and uses in the building industry.

I had worked closely with a friendly crew of native Hawaiians, and after supervising the testing of all equipment, pronounced us ready to start up the new operation. Lime burning, or calcination, is a twenty-four-hour-a-day, seven-day-a-week operation. It is carried out in a rotating furnace or kiln, at a temperature of 2,200 degrees Fahrenheit. Everything started out smoothly, but by afternoon, the wind had begun to pick up, and by ten o'clock that evening, it had turned into a seventy-five mile-per-hour rainstorm, and all hell broke loose. First the power went out, then all the machinery and motors in low spots got flooded, and the hot kiln had to be rigged with a wrapped cable and tractor motor so that it could be periodically rotated to prevent warping.

The next morning, most of the crew wouldn't talk to me. When I asked the foreman why, he patiently explained that before all major undertakings in the islands, the gods must, traditionally, be appeased with some Luau-type celebration. "Now he tells me," I thought. It didn't take me long to get a couple cases of beer for the workers' lunch that day, as we rolled up our sleeves and repaired the mess. Who was I to challenge the gods? Sure enough, everything went like clockwork on our second time around. Some gods are easy to please.

The present popularity of religious beliefs that include a promised afterlife is understandable in view of the finality witnessed in all life on earth. Despite the wars and killings that happen in the name of gods, even to this day, many religions have obviously had positive effects on the psyches and lives of the sick and oppressed. As for me, I consider myself lucky to be free of any afterlife expectations or worries. At my age, every day is a gift to be embraced, and much of my joy comes from cherished long-term friends.

Dutch Interludes

IN 1948, I WENT ON A THREE-MONTH ENGINEERING TOUR in post-war Europe. My first project was a Dutch clay-processing operation. A new industry was forming, based around the fact that certain clays and shales could be heated at high temperatures to form a pumice-like aggregate for use in light-weight and insulating concrete when mixed with cement. Having designed an operation in Canada and the United States already, I was qualified and ready for Europe. Two Dutch clay-product manufacturers read one of my technical articles on the subject, and asked me to design a factory to make such a product in Holland. In my testing facility at the University of Washington, I proved that their clay was suitable, and my plant design was approved by the Dutch government. In view of the scarcity of U.S. dollars in Holland, much equipment and machinery had to be found secondhand in the United States, because war-torn Europe could not yet supply such items. Foreseeing this, in 1947 we toured the western

States, finding and buying as much low-priced used equipment as possible, which I then redesigned or had repaired before shipment to Holland.

Occasionally, the luxury-starved Dutchmen gave in to a pent-up urge to splurge, be that on hotels, meals or gifts. One incident that I've never forgotten occurred when we were checking out of a swanky hotel in Salt Lake City. During the morning checkout rush in the huge lobby, it was evidently normal practice for the dozen or so uniformed busboys to stand in a long line, waiting to be assigned to one of the arriving or departing guests. As we were leaving, I noticed one of my Dutchmen busily handing out silver dollars to each surprised attendant in line. Could this have been a European custom, or was part of their buying spree generated by the fact that no Dutchman could use U.S. money in Holland at that time? I didn't dare ask.

A year later, I was at the new plant in Aalst, near The Hague, eager to start up the new operation. I had been warned not to speak German in front of the crew, for obvious war-memory reasons. None understood English, but their foreman spoke German, and my teachings and explanations had to go through him out of the crew's earshot. Frustrating, but we made the best of it.

Speaking in Switzerland

DURING MY TIME IN HOLLAND, I also had some time to visit Swiss and Italian clients. The Swiss cement firm Holderbank had read about my processing patent and invited me to make a presentation to their technical staff. Having had little opportunity, since my 1925 arrival in the United States, to improve my German vocabulary, especially the technical kind, I now had to rely heavily on hasty blackboard schematic diagrams for this lecture. I was sweating and stuttering along toward the end of my talk when one of the engineers in the audience called to me and said, "Mr. Bauer, why don't you speak English? We all understand it." I thought, "Now you tell me!"

Italian Translation

WITH RENEWED CONFIDENCE, I resumed my journey, heading to Milan. I was to confer with a Portland cement consultant who also had read some of my technical articles, and felt I could be of assistance. In view of the fact that we had both corresponded by mail in English, I entered his office with a confident "Good morning," which to my surprise he answered in Italian. "Tit for tat," I thought. But when I started to speak in English, he shook his head, and I realized that his letters must have been through a translator. Trying German also produced an exasperated expression. So here we were, ready to go to work on a three-day safari to several clients' cement plants, without a means of communication. Hurriedly engaging a translator, we sat him between us in the chauffeured limousine, and off we went.

Slowly but steadily, we gained confidence. Many technical compound words have a basis in Latin, and that's also true of Italian, and my two required school years of Latin in Germany made his speech more intelligible over time. Additionally, as anyone can tell you who has witnessed Italians seriously engaged in lively conversation, body language is a basic component. Thus, as unbelievable as it may sound, the last evening of our three-day visit found us sitting for three hours in a swanky wine-and-dine restaurant, engaged in continuous animated technical "conversation," sans interpreter, but with pad and pencil support.

I was reminded of this new skill a few years later when the University of Washington School of Engineering asked me to design and teach an upper level course based, essentially, on the idea of making a pencil do the talking via schematics.

Dutch Life Vignette

I FONDLY RECALL THE EVERYDAY VILLAGE LIFE around me in Holland. One incident in particular revolved around the use and life of wooden shoes. The dike surrounding the village and clay plant was as high as most roofs, its crest forming a narrow roadway. One day I heard bell ringing coming from the top of the dike, announcing the arrival of the local shoemaker, ready to sell or repair wooden shoes. His two-wheeled dog-drawn cart was loaded with new shoes and all kinds of patterns, designs, repair materials, and tools. Villagers with children were arriving from below, forming a line as he expertly and patiently tended to his trade. As youngsters took off and handed him their shoes, he would rapidly chisel out some more toe room for a growing boy, smooth a pinching spot for an adult, or repair a crack in the wood with copper rivets or plates to give it added life. No wonder the new shoes often were so thick when first bought. Wooden shoes are still standard footwear in many farm communities and barns.

Peruvian Interlude

I WAS IN LIMA, IN THE ANDES MOUNTAINS, discussing the design of a new type of cement plant with a client, when he suggested that I take the Saturday off, and experience a typical market day at a mountain village, high in the backcountry. His two teenage sons would take me up in their Volkswagen Bug, and show me the sights. "Great!" I thought.

The boys and I soon got used to each other's language difficulties as we explored our interests during the steep canyon drive. When we reached the pass, which lies at an elevation higher than the peak of Mount Rainier, they stopped the car and suggested that I would get an excellent view of glaciers and the valley if I walked up the visible short trail. They would wait here in the car.

So off I went, at a good pace, but almost immediately felt my breathing become labored in the thin air. Glancing back at the car, I saw that the boys were now standing next to their car with binoculars fixed on me. Then I got it. I evidently wasn't the first one to fall for their little game, But I wasn't about to play it by their rules. Shortening my stride but keeping my fast-paced rhythm, I continued to the top. I then fast-walked back to the car to the obvious consternation and disappointment of my guides. One of them asked whether I was a distance runner. Obviously, we each had kept our own secrets.

We continued on down to the busy Saturday market in the village, with its local produce, pottery, weavings—and no tourists. I was impressed by these short-stature mountain people: women carrying babies strapped to their backs and wearing shading hats, and deep-chested men bartering goods and livestock.

Back down in modern Lima, I was also surprised by the "normal" closure of most large businesses for the two- to three-hour midday siesta period, which created a second daily roundtrip traffic jam. Most stores and offices featured heavily steel-shuttered doors and windows to thwart the night shift of thousands of professional thieves. That situation has hopefully improved there in this new century.

Mystery Flight

ASIDE FROM WORD-OF-MOUTH, most of my consulting work was generated from my monthly technical articles in the "Pit & Quarry" trade journal. One day, I got a call from representatives of a company in Pocatello, Idaho, asking if I would be willing to meet them at the airport in Idaho for an inspection trip to their manufacturing operation. When I asked about their product, I got an evasive reply, but they assured me that my expertise was needed. With some misgivings, I agreed to meet them. Yet the thought remained: Was this some illegitimate enterprise I was being drawn into? Landing at the airport, I was met and hustled to their waiting Piper Cub, and off we took.

We were heading east into the great desert, and I knew of no town in that direction, and wondered, "Hey, is this an abduction?" Then suddenly, the man sitting in front of me handed back a large double-layer paper bag with the printed inscription: "Kitty-Cat Litter Mix." So, the dark secret was out. They had been worried that I wouldn't be interested in the work. We landed at their isolated diatomaceous earth deposit in the middle of nowhere, and I subsequently helped them increase the profitability of their processing operations. However, I never felt motivated to advertise expertise in the absorption of feline deposits.

Clearly it was an exciting time for Wolf, as his career took off. A thriving practice and professional notoriety in a trade magazine provided great satisfaction, and his expertise even led him to obtain a patent for a process for liquefying sand with air. But Wolf was an outdoor man, and from 1945 to 1965, he never let up with his outdoor pursuits. The mountains still beckoned as they always had, and now he turned his sights to new challenges there. He returned to The Mountaineers to chair the new Mountaineering Development Group, an ambitious congress of sub-committees charged with development of a broad spectrum of mountain life arenas. Member Cam Beckworth was in charge of better organization and implementation of climbing courses. Fred Beckey put his energies into developing advanced climbing training. John Klos tackled leadership training. Keith Rankin, Ed Kennedy, and Jim Crooks all took turns at developing safety policies. Art Winder was in charge of climbing area development and Toni Sobieralski undertook the expansion of activities related to the natural and cultural history of the mountains. The compilation of outing and climbing guides and outreach to organizations with tandem interests were also a primary focus of the group. This "who's who" of Mountaineer forefathers always held in view that they were laying a foundation for future generations in what Wolf called "the Mountaineering Arts," as much a philosophy as a set of skills.

But the greatest hook for Wolf's mountaineering energies came during his 1948 trip to Europe, when he had occasion to visit his old schoolmate, Alois Kreckl, and to catch up on the latest recreation and mountain trends in the German Alps.

Germany was still in a shambles in 1948. Many areas were still bombed out, including Wolf's old haunts in Wasserburg. Together, Alois and Wolf visited their old friend Billie—Wilhelmena Mayer—whose family ran a restaurant and "gastehaus." Wolf was mortified to learn that the American occupying forces were not particularly sensitive, either to the value of historical artifacts or to his former neighbors, even though they were civilians. The army had been confiscating furniture, even ancient antiques, to be used as firewood, and his friend's family had lost most of theirs. Wolf intervened on Billie's behalf, driving forty miles to Munich and demanding an audience with the commander there as an American citizen. As a journalist, he explained, he was inclined to write an article for Reader's Digest magazine, exposing the incivility of the American army to innocent civilians in occupied territory. He expected more of Americans. Two weeks later, all of Billie's family furniture was returned to them, still undamaged. The timely bluff worked.

And the side trip paid off as well. Exploring Munich, Wolf found a bombed out bookstore that was still in business, and by the time he was done perusing, he had his arms full of yet another cultural harvest. As in the days when he imported German climbing manuals to create course curriculum, Wolf was again engaged in relaying Alpine wisdom to the mountain lovers of the Northwest, a bequest that ultimately spread across the nation and beyond. It was called Bergwacht—Mountain Watch.

Mountain Rescue

THE 1935 FIRST ASCENTS OF MOUNT RAINIER'S NORTH FACE and the 1936 conquest of Mount Goode represented my last efforts with experimenting and teaching mountain climbing techniques, and proving to myself that safe and sane mountaineering can be taught in a proper sequence of training and experience. It was not until after the war and another decade had passed that the general public was to learn that lesson. It soon became apparent that search-and-rescue was a necessary by-product of a recreation in which you cannot always separate the danger from its beauties and challenges.

It was during one of my engineering trips to Europe in 1948 that I had the opportunity to acquire some technical books on mountain rescue techniques and equipment in a bombed-out Munich bookstore. The German "Bergwacht" manual by Dr. Fritz Rometsch, and a guide to mountain rescue techniques by Wastl Mariner of Austria were treasured finds that would be invaluable in getting us started. (Mariner's text was then translated by Dr. Otto Trott and Kurt Beam and published by The Mountaineers Books under the title *Mountain Rescue Techniques*.) I also located a short Bergwacht training film that got us fired up. In recent years, friend and fellow climber Ome Daiber had been keeping an informal list of volunteer alpinists who could be called when someone was in trouble in the mountains. It was now high time to relieve Ome of some of his self-appointed duties and, by all means, encourage his wife Matie's "Call Girls" (who summoned help during mountain emergencies via a phone chain) to keep their phone bills paid.

With a million postwar Puget Sounders watching the sun rise over the Cascades, and set over the Olympics, all an hour's drive away, we had to become ready. The evolving skiing sport played a major role getting the public into the mountains in both winter and summer with the attendant obvious weather hazards and conditions. While the established National Ski Patrol could take care of injured people with immediate First Aid, including toboggan-type transport, they were not equipped to handle wilderness search-and-rescue. Thus, an organization had to be formed and trained for year-round mountain emergencies.

It also became obvious that we would need cooperation from public agencies that should be involved, such as the National Forest and National Park Services, local and State Police and Sheriff units, as well as any available air search-and-rescue personnel and equipment. While we wanted to continue as a strictly public service system with expenses coming out of our own pockets, it was nevertheless important to keep agencies and the public aware of needed equipment and operation expenses.

To that end, The Mountaineers took a lead role in establishing the original Mountain Rescue & Safety Council, later shortened to Mountain Rescue Council, and now officially called Seattle Mountain Rescue. The organization was initially staffed predominantly with our club members. Dr. Otto Trott of the Mount Baker Ski Patrol, in particular, became a guiding element in the organization. It was natural for Ome Daiber to head many of the search-and-rescue missions, for Otto Trott to tend to medical matters in the field, and myself to act as the catalyst in designing and improving equipment and teaching field techniques. I ran annual conventions and training sessions, and during the early years, gained governmental input, acceptance and public support. In return, we all profited from the creation of lifetime friendships, and the satisfaction of having promoted safe travel habits in our Pacific Northwest mountain world.

Northwest author and legend Harvey Manning is credited with saying that "to have a mountain rescue, you have to have Wolf for philosophy, Ome for spirit and Otto for plasma—and the Whittaker twins to get the body out of the crevasse or down the cliff."[43] Ome Daiber, a widely known and respected climber, had been in the first party to summit the north side of Mount Rainier via Liberty Ridge (with Will "Jim" Borrow and Arnie Campbell), just two weeks after Wolf and Jack Hossack had done so via Ptarmigan Ridge. Eventually a carpenter, he started out as a climbing gear vendor and inventor, designing the Penguin sleeping bag and Sno-Seal waterproofing solution, among other things. Ome's Penguin bag had openings for feet and hands, so that one could work around the campsite "without getting out of bed." It was apparently the bag of choice of Admiral Richard Byrd, as testified in the Arctic explorer's personal letter of praise to Daiber.

Ome had been involved in search and rescue since 1936, shortly after the dual Rainier summits, when a twenty-two-year-old Seattle

(Left to right) Kurt Beam, Otto Trott, Wolf Bauer, and Ome Daiber
display components of the Stokeski rescue litter.

man named Delmar Fadden had attempted to climb Mount Rainier
via the Emmons Glacier by himself. When he failed to return, Ome
was called in to help search for the young man, both for his climbing skills and because he kept a "pocket-list" of other mountaineers
with the skills and inclination to do search-and-rescue at odd hours
in inhospitable places. Once he was called to duty, Ome's wife Matie
and the wives of other climbers became the "Call Girls," rousing all
available rescuers for business.

Sadly, Fadden had perished on his descent, the camera in his
pocket proving he had attained the summit. But the search for
Fadden had attracted national attention, and the result was the
broad public understanding that some formal process needed to be
implemented to deal with the increased numbers of people in the
mountains. The operations of Ome's army expanded, and in 1939
The Mountaineers officially formed The Mountaineers Rescue Patrol

from the ranks of its Climbing Committee, specifically for rescues requiring technical mountaineering skills. (It would later be reorganized as the Mountain Rescue Council when it became a region-wide entity.) Yet until Wolf returned from Munich in 1948 with his framework model from the German-Austrian Bergwacht, it remained a largely informal affair. (The Bergwacht was established in 1920 in a Hofbräuhaus in Munich.) The master of efficiency began to do his job. Though Ome, Otto and Arnie Campbell ran it for years, it was Wolf who changed the MRC from a call-list to an active rescue organization with training and public education.

The name Ome Daiber sounds European, and it is, but not as European as one might think. Born German-American in the United States, Ome was named George Daiber, but used the childhood nickname he earned when he asked the lunchroom lady to "Owe me a nickel" so he could eat lunch. This story seems to clearly illustrate Ome's particular amiable charm, and, as such, he remained the front man for the Mountain Rescue Council, acting as spokesman and dealing with the press. His charisma was his greatest tool for furthering the cause, but he was known for his uncompromising ethical standards as well. In a tribute to Ome published in *The Seattle Times* after his passing in 1989, Ben Groff wrote that Ome "reserved his wildest fist-pounding invective for volunteers who will go out to rescue a climber, but not a hunter... 'You can't discriminate between people in need of help. Even that horse's ass Hitler—the murderer—I'd rescue him, too, if I had to.'"[44]

When Wolf returned from Europe, loaded with enthusiasm, books, and film, he called a group together to take mountain rescue to the next level. The third member of the Mountain Rescue Trinity recruited at this time was Dr. Otto Trott. Like Wolf, Otto was born in Germany, studying medicine in Freiberg and Munich, Germany and in Innsbruck, Austria. He was a skilled climber and skier, having served his apprenticeship in the Alps—particularly the Dolomites—and by the mid-1930s was a doctor in the German Army. But being part Jewish, he foresaw dark times coming, and immigrated to the United States in 1937 to set up his practice. Serving his residency in Syracuse, New York, he headed west in 1939. In Seattle, he became best known in the outdoor community as "the mountain doctor," a founder and major persona of the Mount Baker Ski Patrol for some thirty years. The "Ottobahn" run at the ski area is named for him. Mountaineering historian Harry Majors pays homage to his climbing as well, noting that his revolutionary ascent of the Hanging Glacier on Mount Shuksan in 1939 made him "largely responsible for introducing European ice climbing techniques into the Northwest."[45]

Ira Spring tells a story about Otto in his autobiographical *An Ice Axe, A Camera and a Jar of Peanut Butter*. He writes, "As an ex-German soldier, [Otto] was monitored by our intelligence authorities and once, to his disgust, was called in to explain a postcard of Mount Shuksan he had mailed to his family in Germany showing a new climbing route he had pioneered, a big X marking the bivouac site. Failing to penetrate the minds of nonclimbing, nonintelligent officers, he blew up and told them the line on the photo was a tank route to the top of Mount Shuksan and the X was a gun emplacement to rid the world of intelligence officers."[46]

We can enjoy Dr. Trott's bold sarcasm, but unfortunately he spent the war in an internment camp in Tennessee. However, unlike many embittered Germans, Otto appeared to take his fate in stride, spending his tenure there as a camp doctor, and developing an anti-venom serum for black widow spider bites. Upon his release from the camp in 1946, he pursued and earned his U.S. citizenship. His hope in all his volunteer activities was to make a contribution to the welfare of his adopted country. As one of the three founders of what would ultimately become the national Mountain Rescue Association, responsible for the successful rescues of thousands of people over the years, Otto Trott most certainly achieved his goal.

Where Wolf was a tremendous organizer, and Ome was a great spokesman, Otto was the cool and competent physician, advancing understanding of the effects of exposure in alpine conditions. Wolf himself, though he was the chairman of the MRC for the first six years, was not the most comfortable of the three on a rescue mission. Many of the efforts were, as they no doubt will always be, on behalf of young people who wandered too far out of their element. Reflecting on rescues that became body recoveries, he becomes very somber. "Those are the stories you don't want to hear about. When you're looking for a high school kid, and you come along and you see a hand … or a leg sticking out of the snow … and it's already blue…" He shakes his head. "You don't ever want to see that. I could never sleep the night after we found someone. Otto Trott, he was the doctor. As soon as we would come upon one, he would make some kind of a joke. Not about the person, but about something completely different—to keep it light, so we could do our job. But I could never be a doctor. I could never take all those people to bed with me. You have to be a certain type of person. I could never do it." As a result, his admiration and respect for Otto was considerable.

The Trott Chronicles

THERE ARE MANY WAYS TO DISTINGUISH TRUTH, or fact, from assumption, as illustrated by an anecdote about a Supreme Court judge who tried never to make assumptions. He was riding on a train, when his companion pointed to the window and remarked, "Look at all those sheared sheep out there," to which the judge dryly remarked, "Well, sheared at least on this side." Just like a scientist sorting for the truth, the judge had been trained to make deductions based solely on hard evidence. My old friend Otto Trott was very much like that, always seeking the view from the "other side" before making a judgment.

I'm reminded of a riddle Otto posed at an appropriate moment—namely, What is the difference between an atheist, a believer and an agnostic? The atheist, he said, jumps into bed without further ado; the believer kneels and thanks God for all the good things that happened, or might yet happen; and the agnostic kneels down, imploring, "Dear God, if there is one, save my soul, if I have one." I guess that's really hedging your bets. While Otto Trott was not on "speaking terms" with the gods, no more self-less and humanitarian individual influenced us in our Pacific Northwest mountain world of climbing, skiing, and search-and-rescue. Time and again, it was his dry humor during some of our most tragic and difficult situations that pulled us through with our psyches intact.

As his name seemed to indicate, you never knew whether Otto was coming or going. Others have already written about his participation in our year-round mountain emergencies. A few other personal stories might further define this remarkable man and close family friend.

Tit for Tat

WITH OTTO, THERE WERE FEW DULL MOMENTS, and eventually, one learned to expect the unexpected from him. Whenever he gave first-time visitors a ride to his Mount Baker cabin, he liked to treat them to his unique brand of humor. The pre-freeway route led through Arlington and past the famous Giant Cedar Stump that, in those years, one could actually drive through with inches to spare (the stump is now located at a freeway rest stop[47]). Approaching the location in the evening hours, he would suddenly swerve off the paved road, heading for the stump. At the last second, he would turn off his headlights as the car squeezed through the opening, pretending he was confused as his passengers braced for the crash. Then he would open the car doors and say in a calm voice, "Go ahead and relieve yourselves."

Dr. Otto Trott's famous ambulance in the mountains.

After my initiation via this ritual, I couldn't let the incident go without a mental resolve that I would get even with him some day. That opportunity came during a rescue mission on Mount St. Helens, when I was driving our rescue truck off the mountain, down the winding gravel road. By pre-arrangement, Otto and one of the fellows would ride the first half of the trip in the windowless back compartment, with the remaining three of us in the front seat.

As earlier planned, I had my companions up front pretending to loudly criticize my driving every time we came to a tight curve, at which time I would initiate sudden stops and jerky steering, while they hollered conflicting instructions, loudly marveling each time how lucky we were that we didn't go over the edge. By that time we heard Otto yelling "Stop the truck and let me drive!" I stopped the truck and calmly said, "OK, Otto, it's your turn to relieve yourself." Give him credit. He countered with, "Too late. I'll send you my cleaning bill." Such was life with Otto.

Dog-gone Incident

ONE MORNING OTTO GOT A CALL from our "Call Girls" to check an injured prospector stuck up on the upper west side of Mount Si, and he asked me to help him to get up there before the rescue team could be organized. When he picked me up in his car, I saw he had his pooch, "Pepper," along. Knowing we would be up in one of those rock avalanche chutes on the side of the mountain, I thought there might be problems with having the dog along. Otto, the optimist, said not to worry.

Without a trail, we scrambled up to the old prospector, who was lying in a loose slide trough. There was little room for all four of us. Otto tended to the man's superficial bleeding and sprains. His medical rucksack and Pepper were between us, and when Otto asked me to reach into his bag for some medicine, Pepper suddenly had my arm in his teeth and wouldn't let go. Otto almost had another patient, because the dog and I tumbled backwards down the chute. After Otto checked out my bitten arm, I informed him that on any future search-and-rescue missions that Pepper came on, he would be designated as "emergency food"—first to go! Anyway, all four of us eventually got off the mountain, with help from the back-up patrol.

On Second Thought

I HAD BEEN UP AT MOUNT BAKER helping Otto with some work on his cabin. After work, in the late afternoon, we made a few last-minute ski runs that, in the woods, took us below his cabin. Otto wanted to take a shortcut down to intercept the highway switchback. But as we got deeper into the darkening timber, I told Otto that, on second thought, we had better backtrack, as we might miss the highway. He insisted that we would be OK, until, as an argument clincher, I pointed out the ignominy of a search party looking for the founders of the Mountain Rescue Council! That did it, and we followed our tracks back to his cabin with resolve to practice what we preach.

Having lived in both Europe and the "New World," there is no question in my mind as to which people are endowed with the best sense of humor. Usually it's the Americans who are better at kidding. Yet, Otto's propensity for making down-to-earth remarks in stressful situations, as well as his ability to take a ribbing, were remarkable, considering his Hitler war and American internment experiences. Often his initial answer to a direct question would give you momentary pause—"Is he serious?" you would wonder. I'm sure his five daughters learned early on the value of repartee. Why can't more physicians bring such a gift along with their black bag?

These three men—Wolf, Ome and Otto (yet another Teutonic Gang-Up)—took mountain rescue to a whole new level. With their collective drive at the head, they were able to recruit many new climbers to the cause. Arnie Campbell, Kurt Beam, Max Eckenburg, Dorrell Looff, and ham radio wizard Irving Herrigstead were active and committed members, insuring the success of the fledgling operation. All of these men made outstanding contributions to the cause.

The newly convened Mountain Rescue & Safety Council (later, "Safety" was dropped from the group's title, though not from its mission) was sponsored by The Mountaineers, the Washington Alpine Club and the Northwest region of the National Ski Patrol. Wolf's first task was to organize a conference that would attract all the major climbing clubs in Washington, Oregon and British Columbia, and any other invested organizations, to collaborate and participate in developing a more universal system. This included solving the problem of coordinating a whole army of agencies. Wolf

Seattle Mountain Rescue Council helicopter training in 1949 at Snoqualmie Pass with the U.S. Coast Guard. Standing from left: Chuck Welsh, Dee Molenaar, Coast Guard pilot, "K" Molenaar, Max Eckenberg, Ome Daiber, Coast Guard crewman, John Thompson, and Lou Whittaker. Kneeling from left: Wolf Bauer, unidentified rescuer, Jim Whittaker and the unnamed Coast Guard pilot.
PHOTO COURTESY OF THE SPRING TRAIL TRUST.

was the driving force in this aspect of the operation, as well, bringing in the National Park and Forest Service rangers, police and sheriff's departments, the Coast Guard, and the military. Enlisting the Coast Guard's helicopter services for rescues was pivotal. Mountain rescue is hardly a coastal operation. Yet they were enlisted for four different field practice sessions, the first one at the second annual conference at Snoqualmie Pass, and subsequent sessions at Mount Rainier and Mount Hood.

Wolf recalls the nightmare of communication problems caused by the fact that each of these agencies communicated on different radio frequencies. One particular rescue of a young man in tennis shoes on Mount Pilchuck called for a saw that the rescue crew did not have, but that the Ranger Station did have. Though they could see the Ranger Station down the slope, requesting the saw required

During crevasse rescue training on the Nisqually Glacier at Mount Rainier, Dee Molenaar receives help from Ome Daiber (left) and Wolf Bauer (right) in raising an unfortunate "victim," 1950s.   PHOTO COURTESY OF THE SPRING TRAIL TRUST.

placing a short-wave radio call all the way to Seattle, which in turn triggered a phone call back to the Ranger Station.

Wolf made sure that rescue volunteer training received increased energy and focus, just as he had trained climbers in the Climbing Course. Also on the MRC agenda was public education, and to this end, a film called "Mountains Don't Care" was produced, along

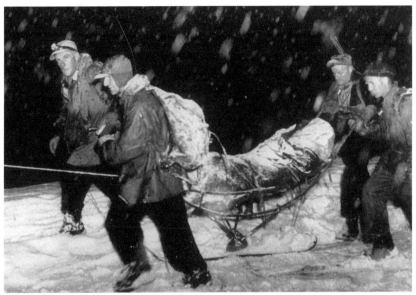

(Left to right) Kurt Beam, Otto Trott, Al Krup, and Wolf Bauer rescue Bill Degenhardt, who suffered a broken hip after an avalanche on Snoqualmie Mountain in 1952. The double-ended Stokeski is visible.

with pamphlets and journal articles, for distribution and viewing at dozens of public venues. This combination of accident prevention and skills preparation was the trademark of Wolf Bauer, a constant theme in all his public outdoor ventures.

When accidents occurred, the MRC responded with vastly improved efficiency, coordination between agencies, and advanced rescue techniques and equipment. The "Bergwacht" film that Wolf had brought home showed equipment far better adapted to alpine terrain than the boat-like Stokes stretchers in use by ski patrols. But with the help of Jack Hossack and Wally Burr (later to gain notoriety as the leading designer of water skis in the Northwest), Wolf improved even upon the German litters, or Bergtrage, designing what they would call the Stokeski. Starting with a basic Stokes stretcher, Wolf adapted it for diverse terrain by resting it on interchangeable single keel-like supports—a wheel for ground and rock and a ski for snow. This extremely maneuverable transport was lightweight and collapsible, easily carried by two men in pieces strapped to their packs.

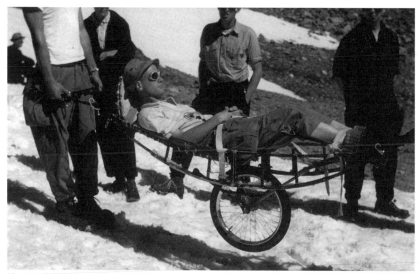

The Hood River Crag Rats demonstrate the functionality of the European Bergtrage at a 1950 Mount Rainier rescue training.

Because of the collaboration of the MRC with groups such as Oregon's Hood River Crag Rats, satellite mountain rescue groups sprang up all over the west, and eventually across the country. The natural result, in 1959, was the creation of a nation-wide umbrella organization called the Mountain Rescue Association. All the member groups of the MRA retain the familiar original logo of the MRC, a blue mountain peak with a white inset first aid cross—the logo originally designed by Wolf Bauer[48]—his tangible mark on our "safe and sane" mountaineering culture.

The 1953 incarnation of the Mountain Rescue Council logo, as published on the cover of the pamphlet "Can You Handle an Emergency?" by The Mountaineers.

In 1977, Jacqueline Kennedy Onassis, U.S. Senator Robert Taft Jr. ,and presidential aide Sam Beard initiated the Thomas Jefferson Award as the premier honor for outstanding volunteers in the United States, and it continues to be conferred annually by the American

Institute for Public Service. In 1985, all three of these inspiring men—Ome Daiber, Dr. Otto Trott and Wolf Bauer—received the coveted Jefferson Award for their contributions to the mountaineering community and the public. A quiet honor in a noisy world, it is a fitting recognition for an achievement that has saved and will save untold legions of outdoorsmen.

Jungle Island Seafari

North of the Salish and east of the Nootkas,
A fringe-land of islands awaited our paddle,
Ancestral seascape of Kwakiutl people,
It drew us up north from Salish Seattle.

As we entered the gate twixt Cracfroft and Hanson,
We left the arterial of Johnstone Strait,
To the north lay the maze of mysterious islands
Called "the Jungle" by natives, quite abandoned of late.

Midst squalls and rainbows, a moon in a hurry,
Midst golden kelp in a sunset glow,
We could feel the ghosts of the ancients scurry,
On the white-shelled middens of long ago.

The splash of an otter, the croak of a raven,
The furtive glance of a mink on the beach,
These were the totems that peopled our haven,
This did we come for, so oft out of reach.

The snore of a whale, 'hind a moon misty curtain,
Frankie's laughing echo from a necklaced loon,
The tattoo of raindrops, the tide so uncertain,
This dream did we dream, and wakened too soon.

—WOLF BAUER

EIGHT

Launching the Boat

O NE WOULD THINK THAT THE ESTABLISHMENT of a new independent business and a nationwide alpine rescue organization would keep a person fairly busy. And it did. It kept Harriet, the working mom, busy as well, what with her new job as an MRC "Call Girl." But something else had greeted Wolf upon his return from St. Louis in 1946 that would consume his energies with an even greater passion.

The Kayak Connection

IT WAS IN THE POST-WAR YEARS OF THE LATE FORTIES, after we had resettled in Seattle, that I became suddenly aware of the manifold Pacific Northwest waterways—made to order for a paddle sport. Flash back now to my Bavarian boyhood days when, crossing the Inn River on the way from school, we boys made our first contacts with the new "foldboating" sport by trying to hit our paddling targets below with, you guessed it, our spitfire. Many years later, in the early days of Northwest paddling, I was leading a trip down the Skagit River from Newhalem. The whole surprised town turned out to watch the spectacle from their cable suspension bridge, as we passed underneath. With some trepidation, I warned my gang that it might be smart to keep our heads covered.

Just as in mountaineering and ski touring, river touring would also be a sport in which you could not separate the danger from the fun and beauty.

I soon felt it was up to me, as an engineer, to study river hydraulics, in terms of both safe navigation and rescue techniques. This I did above and below water, using a wetsuit, mask, and snorkel. It also led to my happy discovery of the multi-faceted eddy system, in which kayakers could surf, spin, and plane in what I called "play-spots." This led not only to conducting our first river slalom competition, but also to the exploitation of tidal currents and kayak sailing on the Sound.

For our first river slalom course on Humpback Creek east of the mountains, we stretched clotheslines and climbing ropes across some whitewater spots so that we could hang gate flags. We reached a similar level of "technological advance" in sail rigging. Although German foldboat builder Klepper made complete sailing rigs for his double-seaters (jib, main, and mizzen), we just wedged a bamboo stick against the forward gunwale for a mast, using surplus red "emergency sails" that were available in the postwar Navy stores at bargain prices.

The developments we made to further this new recreational sport are the legacy of an enthusiastic group of outdoors-minded friends, many of them from The Mountaineers, the early skiing crowd, and Scouting. By 1948, the time had come to organize into a club. Since it was the first of its kind in the area, we claimed the name Washington Foldboat Club, in reference and deference to the German language "Faltboot," or folding boat, where the sport and boats had become popular twenty-five years earlier.

I must confess that I was again put in the role of "copy-cat"—having earlier been exposed to climbing, skiing, mountain rescue and foldboating in Europe during my boyhood years in the Alps. Adapting these activities and equipment to our Pacific Northwest conditions, with the help of my outdoor friends, became, nevertheless, a source of pride, especially in terms of safe and sane practices and growth. To that end, it was fortunate that the Seattle YMCA allowed us to make use of their downtown facilities for a seven-week River Touring course geared toward the general public. We named the course "river touring," as a counter to the offshoot "whitewater" sport that would come to scare off many people and families. This springtime class became very popular, growing each year from twenty to more than a hundred students, half of whom became club members. The course furthered safe practices, as well as public recognition and acceptance. "Seattle Times" photos and articles also acquainted the public with the sport, as we invited reporters to come along on our outings. By the early 1960s, we were designing and building our boats out of rigid fiber-glass, and had changed our name to the Washington Kayak Club. This group was the catalyst that would open lakes and coastal waters to the general public of the Pacific Northwest. The seed took hold.

Wolf's thumbnail history of his experience in the kayaking movement is a bit understated, and begs some augmentation. "The seed" started with old friend and mentor Harry Higman—the man who had been most responsible for introducing Wolf to the Northwest mountains, as well as to his wife Harriet. On reconnecting with him after the war, Wolf discovered that Mr. Higman had found a new means of exploring the vast natural wonderland of western Washington. During World War II, while his protégé Wolf was in St. Louis, Mr. Higman had taken up the German sport of fold-boating: paddling in folding kayaks (the only kind available in the 1940s). By some political wrangling, he was one of the very few civilians who were allowed to paddle around Puget Sound, somehow circumventing the national security restrictions banning such pleasure craft. Once he was exposed to the sport, which had begun in Germany at the turn of the century, Mr. Higman undertook to follow the historic 1792 route of Captain George Vancouver in the pioneering explorations of the *HMS Discovery* on Puget Sound, as described in the ship's original log. Perhaps he foresaw the explosion of development that would soon obliterate the wild shorelines that greeted the celebrated explorers, and he hoped to come as close to seeing what they had seen as any man ever would again.

When Wolf returned to Seattle in 1945, it took very little persuasion on Mr. Higman's part to get Wolf into the water. He was already well acquainted with the sport of foldboating from his childhood in Germany (and from his ill-fated trip with Harriet on the Missouri River). Foldboating had begun to gain popularity in Wolf's native land around 1905, at the same time that the skiing movement was taking off, when a German tailor named Hans Klepper bought a German student's patent for a collapsible kayak design. Klepper began to manufacture his folding boats for the public's recreational use in Rosenheim, a Bavarian town in between Wolf's two boyhood

homes of Kreuth and Wasserburg—smack in the middle of Bauer
territory—seven years before Wolf was born. The concept of the
folding boat, one that could be broken down to fit into two portable
pieces of luggage, evolved in a time and place where few had auto-
mobiles, and rivers were reached by train, streetcar or bicycle. Being
able to haul a boat in compact form was essential to participating in
the fun.

Despite the setbacks to the movement caused by both World
Wars, foldboating was introduced to the world of international
competition in the 1936 Olympics in, of course, Germany, and even
World War II could not unring the bell. The first events were the
10,000 meter solo and tandem races, the former won by Austrian
Gregor Hradetzky in 50:01.2, and the latter won by Swedes Sven
Johansson and Eric Bladstrom in 45:48.9. (The whitewater slalom
would not make its debut in the Olympic Games until 1972, and
would not become a standard event until 1992.)

As far behind Germany as the United States was in skiing and
mountaineering, it was even farther behind in foldboating. German
émigré entrepreneur Jakob Kissner brought his company, Folbot, to
New York and began providing boats to a few American novices in
the 1930s. The sport, however, would not gain a foothold in the
United States until after the war. (The company, like Klepper
Folding Kayaks in Germany, is still in business today, though Folbot
is now located in Charleston, South Carolina.)

Of course, kayaks were hardly native German vessels. Evidence
shows that native Inuits and Aleuts were using kayaks as hunting
vessels as early as 1000 AD. Russians exploring the Aleutian Islands
and Alaska in the eighteenth century documented waters teeming
with "baidarka," the Russian word for small Aleut hunting boats
(which is also the meaning of the word kayak). These split-prowed
vessels were made of driftwood or whalebone frames with sea lion
skin covers, waterproofed with whale blubber, buoyed by inflated
seal bladders and all lashed together with whale baleen or sinew.
The lightweight, flexible craft were capable of moving at great
speeds in treacherous waters in pursuit of their quarry: seals, sea
lions, walruses, whales, and sea otters. Hunters waited with har-
poons, spears, and hand-launched darts by airholes in the ice and at

caribou river crossings, as well as in open waters. Designs were modified depending on the requirements of the region and the use of the boat. Shorter, broader boats were built for carrying game and supplies; longer narrower boats were designed strictly for speed to run down prey. As Wolf said of the natives who used the latter, pencil-thin vessels, "They had to part their hair in the middle to stay upright."

Fortunately, when Paddling Fever seized Wolf in the 1940s, he didn't envision violating the future Marine Mammal Act. For both scientists and recreationists of non-native ancestry, there were many unknowns lurking in Northwest waterways. For example, orcas, also known as "blackfish" and "killer whales," were poorly understood. Their relationship with humans was not well established or documented among non-natives, and the misnomer of "killer" created a highly wary public. Upon sight of their dorsal fins on the horizon, the boaters would hide in kelp beds until the pod was out of range. It was simply unknown to the budding kayaking community how orcas, or even sea lions, would react to the presence of defenseless humans in fragile floating skins in their territory.

But this was yet to be tested, as the early days of foldboating took place primarily on rivers. River tourists at that time had more to fear from bears than from orcas, and the irretrievable exhilaration of those trips lay in the uncharted, unexplored nature of those still-wild waterways. Whereas alpinists had explored and charted the slopes of the Cascade and Olympic mountain ranges, it was the kayakers who explored and charted their rivers. Ever the geologist and engineer, and son of a tidal cartographer, Wolf was the first to create a river navigation map for Western and Central Washington. This map, based on his own personal research on the rivers from 1950 to 1965, notes put-in points and river classifications, and is a valuable document still used today by river conservation advocates.[49]

Once Wolf decided to dive in to the new pastime, he sent to Germany for books about foldboating, just as he had done with climbing. But he was interested in more than just learning strokes; he wanted to understand the water the same way he had understood the mountains. Wolf's initial studies of western Washington rivers gave rise to an exhaustive paddling lexicon that described aspects of river hydrology, considering, for example, current speed, gradient and channel configuration. In addition to nearly fifty terms describing conditions and hazards in running water, he also created terminology for paddling technique, adding another twenty terms to the glossary. Borrowing from skiing in some cases, he coined such terms as "eddy christies" and "whirl eddies," and in mastering these terms, the novice paddler gained a tremendous understanding of both the developing sport and the nature of its playing field.

With both novices and experienced paddlers in mind, Wolf created a classification system for rivers, based on both paddler ability and river conditions. The ratings were from one to five, with five being unrunnable and one being appropriate for a beginner. Later in the 1950s, he became aware of a European system of classification, which coincidentally also worked on a scale of five. He compared it to his own system and incorporated some of its concepts, though it remained essentially Wolf's system. Ultimately, this hybrid would be the basis for the official International Scale of River Difficulty that is used today by American Whitewater. Adopted by paddling clubs in the east, it remains the standard river rating system recognized in the United States. Paddling historian Susan Taft credits Wolf's combination of science and sport with distinguishing Northwest foldboating from the rest of the movement. She says "his breakdown of river characteristics was much more thorough than anything that the European system had at the time—or even has now."[50]

As a representative of the Washington Foldboat Club, Wolf was one of the founding members of American Whitewater[51] (founded as the American Whitewater Affiliation) in 1954, along with the representatives of paddling clubs from all over the country. He wrote several articles in the organization's journal on paddling technique, and was a part of the Guide Committee, formed in 1955 to standardize the methods for rating river difficulty for a broader geographic range. (Today, American Whitewater represents the interests of river conservationists and recreationists, and has more than one hundred local paddling club affiliates across the country.)

Predictably, Wolf wasn't content to study the rivers and go kayaking alone; there would be a movement necessary. Techniques must be refined, gear improved, safety practices developed, and people educated. Because of his past and ongoing relationship with The Mountaineers, he approached them first with the idea of establishing a new committee and course for foldboating under the club's umbrella. But the club wasn't sold on the new-fangled pastime, and passed on the opportunity. Kayaking would not become a part of The Mountaineers for nearly forty more years. A Sea Kayaking Committee was finally formed in 1986; Whitewater was added in 1994. Wolf would have to find another venue for his vision.

Thus was born the Washington Foldboat Club. Since most members of the foldboating community were already members of The Mountaineers, the structure of the Washington Foldboat Club was modeled after the structure of that club. The group was chartered in 1948, with the following purposes:

- To promote public good will and understanding of the paddle sport and foster its safe development in the Pacific Northwest

- To encourage exploration and recreational use of rivers and other waters by offering training and instruction, by developing and providing expert leadership, and by scheduling trips throughout the year

- To encourage, aid and give direction to conservation of water resources and adjacent lands for recreational purposes.

Without facilities of their own, and realizing the benefits of controlled pool practices, Wolf approached the YMCA's Adult Hobby School, where Harriet was teaching Bookbinding and Ceramics, and found an organizational home for his first foldboating classes. Harriet shared instruction duties, and according to Wolf, was a wonderful teacher for those with fear or anxiety to overcome.

The first river outings of this core group outside their home state of Washington were on the Fraser, Thompson, Parsnip, Peace, and Kootenai Rivers in British Columbia, and the North Saskatchewan and Bow Rivers in Alberta. Early sea kayaking destinations were along the north coast of British Columbia and both the east and west coasts of Vancouver Island. On these trips, safe technique was learned by trial and error. Wolf recounts their baptism in the sport in more depth in his article "Pioneering a New Sport: Early Club History,"[52] written for the Washington Kayak Club, parts of which are reprinted and paraphrased here:

IN THE EARLY FORTIES, we started more or less from scratch in terms of developing paddle techniques, river navigation, rescue methods, channel stretch classification and terminology, as well as party management. But by the time of the first classes of public instruction at the downtown YMCA in 1950, self-education and experimentation had brought us to a reasonably safe level of paddling rivers up to Class III.

It is somewhat embarrassing now to admit to the repeated tip-overs we experienced until we hit upon the idea of leaning downstream and paddle-bracing across strong eddy currents. Nevertheless, once basic hydraulics were identified, and a working terminology was created to describe them, river touring could be taught. We also pioneered the concept of "playing the river," with the identification of "playspots" where jets, eddies, and rollers provided surfing and planing fun. The skiers in our group were now beginning to feel at home. Snow that provided downhill surfing and stem christies in winter was recycled in summer, offering upstream surfing and "eddy christies" at playspots.

Soon it became apparent how little we knew about river hydraulics and how to navigate them. We also learned that, unlike river canoes, double-seater kayaks were not sufficiently maneuverable in our rocky streams. Even then, most available single-seater foldboats were not forgiving in cross-currents, except, perhaps, for the Klepper T6. They had too little rocker, so their bottoms were too flat to spin and maneuver the way we needed them to.

Susan Meredith, one of the earliest members of the club, remembers that those limitations of maneuverability made the foldboats difficult to land, and that most of the boats were tandems, because it helped to have two paddlers to avoid obstacles.[53] Foldboats were vulnerable to collisions, and tire patch kits and carpentry tools were a must. (And if the boats were a bit fragile by modern standards, the clothing was downright comical: old clothes, sneakers with the toes cut out, and rain ponchos—better at least than the Speedos that were the uniform of choice in Germany. Helmets were unknown, and life jackets (World War II aviator surplus) were only worn by those who could not swim.

Wolf assessed the Kissner foldboats available at the time, but was dissatisfied with their materials and their one-hour assembly time. Klepper boats from Germany, on the other hand, were prohibitively expensive. Wolf met Hans Klepper's son and namesake in New York, who asked him to be the North American representative for the company, but he wasn't interested. He had a better opportunity to set his own compass by collaborating with Martin Geisler of Chicago, another German-American and entrepreneur who was developing the Whalecraft to compete with Kissner. Geisler had come to Wolf with a foldboat design, and after some consideration, Wolf decided he could "fix it." Being a Midwesterner living in lake country, Geisler didn't fully grasp the needs of river boaters, but Wolf, an engineer and a budding hydrologist, could provide the remedy. Thus began a successful partnership, as Geisler offered to build anything Wolf designed. Each year, Geisler produced a model that Wolf would test-drive for the season, and then modify based on his experiences. Best of all, the sticker price was half that of a Klepper boat.

The first Whalecrafts were foldboats made of three-ply neoprene rubber stretched over wooden ribs, topped with a waterproof canvas deck. Wolf described them: "With a broader beam than the imports, for extra buoyancy for the heavier paddlers, the Whalecrafts could be ordered in any deck color. While European decks were invariably blue, we now became a colorful flotilla, according to our individual tastes. A weak point in most folding kayaks continued to be the manner in which the spray cover was fastened to the wooden coaming of the cockpit. Dependable instant release and watertightness were really never achieved until we could design it into later fiberglass boats."

Wolf was at the forefront of designing those fiberglass boats. Many features of the Whalecraft made their way into Wolf's earliest fiberglass design, the Tyee. The Tyee, built in 1961 by Linc Hales, was one of the first fiberglass boats made in North America. Designed with a hatch in the rear deck and a bulkhead, it measured fourteen feet long and two feet wide. It had a large cockpit and a long bilge keel, and could cut through wind and wave as well as or better than many a modern kayak. He recalls Linc's contributions:

LINC HALES DESERVED A LOT OF CREDIT for helping to get us into fiberglass kayaks in the early sixties. We teamed up on the first three designs. On the Tyee I, we each tried for some special features—it was not easy to create a single design and size for both short and tall people varying more than a hundred pounds in weight. We designed the smaller cockpit Tyee II to be similar to the Klepper T6 that Harriet and I started with. One of my contributions was a snap-on skeg fin that acted as a tracking stabilizer when the kayak was used on saltwater, because we couldn't afford two specialized boats. I also designed a pure sea kayak, for which Linc made a mold.

Wolf displays a flatwater kayak of his design from the late 1960s during an interview with Malcolm Bates in 1991.
PHOTO BY CLIFF LEIGHT.

Beyond the nuts and bolts of technique, safety, equipment, and instruction, Wolf was the marketing man for the Washington Foldboat Club *and* its later incarnation, the Washington Kayak Club. Here is the pitch he made in the 1950 *Mountaineer Annual*,[54] coaxing climbers to supplement "first ascents" with "first descents":

"1950 Foldboating Season"

THERE IS LITTLE DOUBT in the minds of those all-around Mountaineers who have trained for, sought, and tasted the thrills (and chills?) of swift mountain stream slalom runs, or the adventure and memory of new river exploration vacations in far-away places—memories of entering unexplored canyons, mastering chutes, rapids, and tight turns, and of campfires along the ageless downhill highways—that foldboating is not only here to stay, but that it has all the earmarks of becoming the climber's and skier's little brother, with growing pains.

A goodly number of Mountaineers associated with the Washington Foldboat Club have helped develop this versatile sport, and it is only logical that a recreation that satisfies the climbers and skiers equally will become a part of their mountain activities. The foldboater learns the art in foldboating courses that teach him about his gear, the antics of the current and its navigation, coping with emergencies (including the use of rope and carabiners, to make the climber feel at home), and the techniques of trip management and scouting. In the field, he graduates from gentle streams to "first descents" on exploration journeys. There are forty foldboat-navigable streams in Washington alone, and many are awaiting us in Oregon, Idaho, and Canada. From the river, the mountains look taller, the country greener, the trail is always downhill and dustless, and the journey is made without retracing one's step, without a burdensome pack, and with an ever-changing panorama and current speed. From the mountains upon which he climbs, the glaciers upon which he travels, the snow upon which he skis and finally to the meltwater upon which he can coast so effortlessly down the valleys, the climber, skier, and foldboater have in common the spirit of the adventure, the test with the elements, and the source of these joys—our mountain ranges. Why not widen your appreciation with a change of pace now and then, and learn to feel the freedom of a light kayak carrying you down our magnificent mountain streams?

Wolf demonstrates an eddy christie on the middle fork of the Snoqualmie River, 1956.

PHOTO BY JOSEF SCAYLEA, *THE SEATTLE TIMES.*

Wolf contemplates the whitewater ahead while foldboating on the Sauk River in 1964.

PHOTO BY PAUL V. THOMAS.

To spread the gospel of paddling beyond the club, Wolf enlisted the photojournalistic talents of Bob and Ira Spring and Josef Scaylea, convincing them to join the adventures and disseminate full color rotogravures and photographs in *The Seattle Times* and various magazines. He authored articles in the *Seattle Post-Intelligencer*, *The Seattle Times*, and *Northwest Boating* and encouraged others to do so as well. In a 1963 article in *The Seattle Times*, he continued to entice outdoorsmen to the water, boasting "we ... can cruise at a comfortable three-knot speed with full camping gear, and with less effort than level walking without a pack." He arranged to have the foldboaters lead Seattle's famous "Opening Day" (of Boating Season) parade through the Montlake Cut from Lake Union into Lake Washington in 1959. And he staged a demonstration club race for the public on Lake Washington, which included not only the paddling, but the disassembling, packing, and carrying of the foldboat across the finish line on land.

With so much to promote (in addition to the Washington Kayak Club, he was still developing the Mountain Rescue Council at this time as well), it is worth noting that Wolf still saw kayaking as something of a "transcendental" experience. He seems at times to channel Thoreau, as he narrates his outings for the reader—a growing tendency that will soon set the course for the rest of his career. In the June 1958 issue of *Northwest Boating World*, the marketing man was at work again. In "Waterways Unlimited," he describes introducing a hypothetical visitor, particularly a "nature lover," to the beauty and magic of river touring.[55]

AS A NATURE LOVER, he might inquire about the wildlife encountered on these close-in weekend tours, and I would recount to him our meetings with the most beautifully colored bird in America, the wood duck; the ever-present merganser, with her bevy of ducklings, skimming ahead of our boats; the fish hawks and bald eagles; black bears and deer; angry, tail-slapping beavers; furtive, sleek otters; and friendly raccoons. I would tell of the spawning salmon bumping our foldboat hulls and paddle blades in their effort to squeeze by us through the same chutes and riffles. No doubt he would hear in amazement of our late autumn paddles down the marshy deltas of our streams, sneaking up on the rare white snow geese, or watching frolicking seals slide down a mud bank chute and disappear under our kayaks.

"As a nature lover," I would point out, "unexpected thrills will be yours, with occasional close-up glimpses of whole flotillas of blackfish whales [orcas], spouting and cavorting with mighty leaps in the larger channels and straits. These mammals [can grow to more than thirty] feet in length, and you may count several dozen dorsal fins steaming by you a few hundred yards away as you sit demurely in your kayak. More appealing are the playful porpoises and curious seals that will swim around and by your kayak most every day, and if you are exceptionally lucky, you may even surprise a sea lion on a rocky reef.

After fifteen years, Wolf and Harriet retired from teaching, but they were hardly retiring from kayaking. They had begun to shift their venue from rivers to sound. With the advent of the fiberglass kayak, they set their sights increasingly downstream to salt water. Perhaps it was the mellowing effect of middle age, but in Wolf's case, we still cannot be sure he had hit middle age at fifty. He had never envisioned kayaking as a high-risk, thrill-seeking sport. Certainly, that was not what he had witnessed on the Inn River in the Alps. He always saw it as "river touring"—a way of backpacking on water, a way to enjoy and bond with nature—something *anyone* could enjoy. "Today, if it's not whitewater, it's not kayaking," he now laments. "How can they *see* anything like that?" Though that may seem ironic coming from a mountain climber and a survivor of the Silver Skis race, it is consistent with Wolf's decision not to pursue the kind of high-risk peak-bagging that so many of his students did. "It shows a lack of respect for the mountain," he reflects with disdain. "It's not a gymnasium."

Leaving the young whitewater sport to its initiates, Wolf took to the Sound with relish. He had known the rivers well enough to chart them, and now sought adventure in new places. Here, there would be no problem with thrill-seekers. The quiet and undisturbed coastlines, especially along the waterways of British Columbia, had never been visited by Europeans in single-seat boats before, and Aleut-style kayaks from far-off Alaska were equally exotic. So the

Washington Kayak Club paddlers were likely the first to visit such places as the Queen Charlotte Islands, and the Broken Islands near Vancouver Island, in kayaks. To the Native Americans still carrying on their lives in their traditional homelands, as well as to the wildlife, these small, silent fiberglass flotillas in rainbow colors must have been an astounding curiosity.

Only ten months after that article in *Northwest Boating World*, he continued in the April 1959 issue with an article called "Paddle-Cruising Our Island Waterways."[56] In it, he documents a club trip to the Canadian Gulf Islands, with a description of the best moment on an excursion—launching "twenty-one windmilling boats with their flashing paddles."

BEHIND US WERE THE HECTIC HOURS of readying ourselves and our party; of catching ferries; of offloading the folded boats and gear onto the dollies at Anacortes, where we parked the cars; of assembling the kayaks to the kibitzing amazement of natives, tourists, and customs inspectors at Sidney; and of waiting for that last anxious moment of launching with tongue-in-cheek to see whether the boat would still float after that last trip to the supermarket.

The Washington Foldboat Club caravans to Barkley Sound, Vancouver Island, British Columbia, 1955.

But ahead lay peace and contentment, and the utter freedom and satisfaction of self-locomotion and crafty use of free rides furnished by mother nature's wind and tidal push. One who has only cruised or moved through water by rowboat or motorboat can little appreciate the feeling of seaworthiness, cozy comfort, and silent ease of travel at a three-knot pace that a single-seater foldboat kayak offers. To let yourself down upon a soft sea of folded sleeping bag against an air-cushion backrest, to button up the instant-release spraycover over your cockpit and around your waist, to grab your feather-light double paddle and feel your responsive craft glide swiftly forward to rise and cleave the oncoming breakers, or to pass waves abeam under the narrow hull without the slightest roll or fuss—such exhilaration and rocking-chair comfort is a combination hard to describe.

And so we paddled and sailed, and chattered and drifted, and poked around along our general course northward to Ladysmith—living for each moment and mood of sky and water, of idyllic campsites and shady noon siestas, of surfing the breakers and lolling in warm-water swimming pools, of making friends with baby seagulls on the Bell Chain Islands or with an Indian family in Active Pass, of coasting along under the tremendous sandstone cliffs and caves of Saturna and Galiano Islands or stroking the edge of Georgia Strait to the rhythm and swing of Viennese waltzes issuing from our portable radio under the deck.

Obviously, with a young-at-heart group of boys and girls of the outdoor type ranging in age from fifteen to sixty we were bound to have our interesting and hilarious moments. The closed fire-season put a damper on our cooking and campfire plans and recurring demands on our little gas, Primus, and canned-heat stoves for one-dish-at-a-time cooking; nevertheless, it was most satisfying to camp on a different island each night. Every beach and driftwood point was another challenge to the esthetic and architectural leaning of each beachcomber building his nest and shelter among logs and ledges. On some of our narrow sandstone shelves, it became a nightly game to place the sleeping bag and air mattress just out of reach of highest tide, and a screech in the night would indicate a slight miscalculation or stubborn last-ditch hold-out against getting out of the warm bag to admit defeat for all to see the next morning.

On Secretary Island, in the middle of the night, a few of us heard a school of blackfish [orcas] snort and cavort by us a few hundred feet off shore from our camp. The vibration was so deep and monstrous that it was unbelievable that all but three of the group soundly slept through the uproar. These three who did hear, however, staged a simulated play-back sound effect the following night just out of sight of the campers. Our decoy gal "in the know" started to paddle out from shore to naively investigate the herd of whales passing by, while scores of stalwarts followed in haste and horror to retrieve her from the darkness and path of destruction. It was a chagrined group who heard the suction whistles and flailing tail splashes turn to human laughter as our "whales" could contain themselves no longer out there in the dark.

More sociable and curious, and swimming around us for a closer look, were the many seals and porpoises we traveled with in chummy companionship during our cruise. While only a few of us trolled for fish and captured crabs, nearly everyone had a chance to pry some delicious oysters off the sandstone shelves in front of our warm-water camp spots. And when, from sheer exhaustion, some of our gabby gals' chatter would subside, we would often drift unobtrusively close among the many species of rare water birds abounding in this region.

Much interest always attended our appearances at small settlements such as those on Saturna, Mayne, and Thetis Islands, where we replenished our water and took on a few green vegetables, etc. Often it turned out to be the "etc." that put the country store back into the black. With the owner's cheerful "Come back soon" still ringing across the water, some boats were hard put to show sufficient freeboard for a convincing reply. Considering the bulk and variety of edibles that were put away under both the decks of the foldboats and the belts of their skippers, I was almost tempted to title this saga "Eating your way through the Gulf Islands."

Whether the pastures are actually greener on the other side of the [United States-Canadian] boundary line will always be debatable, for we cannot sell short our lovely San Juans. [In British Columbia,] the warmer waters, up to sixty-eight degrees Fahrenheit, and the many dazzling white shell beaches, were a welcome bonus. Also, there seems to remain a bit more of the aura of the original Salish people and early white homesteaders. When, in an Indian family's cove on Mayne Island, we exchange mutual interest and admiration for each other's respective cedar and rubber paddle boats; when we are playfully challenged to a burst of speed by a couple of native youngsters in a dugout near Kuper Island; and when we find signs reading "No Trapping Allowed" instead of a brash "Keep Off," we feel strangely content and understanding among these ageless waterways so close to home.

After fifteen years of experimenting, teaching, designing, and marketing, Wolf and Harriet succeeded in germinating the seed and cultivating the young fledgling sport of American kayaking. But if you ask him to talk about the sport, you will not receive a curriculum vitae of his involvement with the organizational history of the movement. He might pause to reflect with pride that no one on any of his trips was ever killed or seriously injured. But what he will really enjoy talking about is his wonderful experiences on the water. Here are some of his favorites.

Wildlife Encounters

WHETHER DOMESTIC OR WILD, four- or six-footed, flying or swimming, animal neighbors are a part of our lives. In the sharing of our little planet, they add comedy or fear, understanding or surprise. Taken for granted are our comforting interactions with domestic animals. With them, our communication is conducted with repeated gestures, touch, and sounds that suffice for both friendly and adversary relationships. In some measure, this also applies to the animals in zoos and wildlife parks. Meetings with animals in their natural environments, however, remain my most vivid and prized memories.

Fresh Off the Shelf

WE WERE ON ONE OF OUR EARLY RIVER SCOUTING TRIPS, having just run the lower canyon stretch of the Snake River. While we were in the vicinity, the tributary Grande Ronde River between Minam and Troy in Oregon, which was just receding from its flood stage, also beckoned to be explored. As we passed a vertical cliff deflecting the current, I spied a shivering lone porcupine, stranded and clinging to a narrow rock ledge just above the water. I saw that his spiny quills were smoothly matted down, and decided that I could probably dislodge him onto my deck with my paddle blade. But as I turned back upstream and got my bow under him, he met me halfway by jumping down onto my deck. So far, so good—as long as he didn't try to crawl into the cockpit with me. He clung on for dear life until my bow crunched onto the gravel bar across the channel, and we parted in mutual relief. It made a hilarious discussion at campfire that night. But what the heck, isn't that what mountain rescue is all about? When someone is "up a creek.". . .

Uninhibited Curiosity

WE WERE ON ONE OF OUR EARLY EXPLORATION PADDLES off the west coast of Vancouver Island. It was getting late in a drizzly afternoon, as we searched for a good camping beach among the many small islands. With hooded jackets and covered cockpits, we were still warm and dry, but tired. Finding a comfortable campsite for a dozen paddlers hinged on access to fresh water. When our bows crunched up against a sandy beach on Wower Island, we were reluctant to jump out of our warm and dry cockpits to make camp. I asked the gang to stay in their boats until I had a chance to check out the water situation.

Crawling through some wet brush past the beach meadow, I found some mossy depressions that would refill when dug into. As I was on my knees digging, a flock of curious local chickadees were chattering above me, watching and getting ever closer, with a few lighting on my shoulders and head to get a closer look. I slowed down my arm motions, relishing the fairy-tale moment. They obviously had never seen a human being—I was just another four-legged animal digging in the ground. Wow! Wower Island had the right name. It still counts as one of my most cherished moments in life.

Hitchcock Revisited

I HAD AN UNFRIENDLY ENCOUNTER with a Ruffed Grouse when I "ruffed" her as she was protecting the young in her nest. It was during my Alaska cannery work in the summer of 1933. I had taken a short hike into the back-woods of Chichagof Island. Working my way up a steep draw, I inadvertently stumbled upon a nest full of grouse hatchlings. Before I could take a closer look, however, I came under what I can only describe as a ferocious aerial attack. I was bare-headed and had to use my hands and arms to ward off the dive-bombing, which left a bleeding hand as proof of my encounter. When I returned chastised and chagrined to the cannery, the crew got their comic relief at my expense. They said I was lucky it wasn't a brown bear.

Is He Bluffing?

JUST AS IN OUR OWN SPECIES, bluffing seems to be a deliberate act to which some animals resort for the purpose of gaining an advantageous position through pretension or intimidation. The trouble occurs when a bluff is not recognized as such. That was the case on a kayak trip along the Vancouver Island west coast.

We were encamped on an island beach. About a quarter mile seaward from us came the steady bellowing and grunting of California sea lions, which were perched on a small rocky island. With binoculars, we could make out the imposing upright figure of the dominant male in the center of his harem. With the capture and domestication of Namu, the "killer" whale, we kayakers had learned the benign attitude of that mammalian species towards us humans, and we no longer would paddle for a kelp bed when sighting a pod. We wondered whether the term "sea lion" might also be a misleading name, and if they would be more in the category of seals. The next morning, I decided to pay them a visit in their own habitat, and at their water level. One of our more adventure-minded paddlers, Tom Steinburn, would accompany me for the close-up, while others in our group would stay further back in case of trouble.

As Tom and I cautiously paddled into a small cove, the dominant bull ignored us. But then a handful of young males suddenly plunged in and headed for us. Territorial defense is nothing new in the animal world. I got out my camera, and when I saw them in the viewer coming full throttle with their mouths open and teeth showing, pushing a bow wave, I hurriedly put the camera under the deck. Tom and I pulled our kayaks together and braced ourselves for whatever might happen. At the last moment they dove under us. Now what? For several minutes, there was utter calm. Then suddenly, as we peered into the water, one of them was floating belly-up to within a couple of feet below the surface, looking us over, then sinking away. What at first seemed to be an attack was evidently a combination of scare-tactic and inherent curiosity. Our northern coastal waters were "becoming" ever more benign. We obviously are not the only species interested in another!

Human Bluff Gone Bad

SEA LIONS ARE NOT THE ONLY ANIMALS that try to bluff other creatures. During my early college years, when I was trying to find myself, and the philosophies of Wordsworth and Thoreau became religion, I often wandered alone in my beloved mountains. (After I became involved with Mountain Rescue, I disabused myself of that foolish habit.) One weekend found me north of Snoqualmie Pass on what is now called the Pacific Crest Trail. I was heading north toward Chikamin Peak when, as I rounded a curve in the trail, I came upon a large black bear eating blueberries. He would wrap his arm around several bushes, pulling them to his chest, and, with a deft side-sweep, pull them through his mouth, and then spit out the leaves. We saw each other at about the same time. He stopped eating and rose up, moving his head from side to side as he sniffed the air. (I learned later that their eyesight is not as good as ours.)

I had always heard that our black bears are not like grizzlies, and aside from females with cubs, they tend to stay out of your way. Deluded by this "rule," I did a really stupid thing that I immediately regretted. I tried to scare him with a loud "WHOOF!" while waving my arms. He wouldn't have any of that, and glared intently at me. I could have bitten my tongue. Very slowly, I walked backwards until I disappeared from his view, around the bend. I had lost my nerve and my hiking goal, but in retrospect, I had gained a better insight into how we need to share this world.

Human Encounters

MEETING WILDLIFE isn't the only way kayaking expanded my world. The people I have met are no less fascinating, and some deserve credit for the gifts they gave Harriet and me.

Going Native

ON ONE OF OUR EARLY INLAND WATER EXPLORATION TRIPS in southern British Columbia in the fifties, I had designed a round-trip where we would drive to Tsawassen, park our cars, and take our foldboat kayaks on board the Mainland-to-Vancouver-Island ferry. This would give us a good look at what we might expect on our return paddle along the same route. As our group of paddlers came on board in a long snaky line, each carrying the stern of the boat ahead and the bow of the one behind, one of the amazed deck-hands shouted, "Don't you trust us? We do have lifeboats on board!"

The route that took less than two hours by ferry required the full following day to paddle back. The exciting return trip led through Active Pass, a narrow passage on the shipping route. We had stopped for lunch on the upper slope of a pocket-beach, with our kayaks parked on the water's edge below us. As we were eating, a couple of fast Canadian Navy ships came roaring past, and were soon out of sight around the bend. Then their big wakes hit our beach, lifting all twelve kayaks in the surf, and then pulling them out into waist-deep water with the return swash. Frantically, we all plunged into the water to retrieve our boats. A lesson learned!

A little farther through the pass, we came upon a small row of weathered Indian shacks. We stopped to inquire whether we could buy a salmon, but as I walked toward the cabins, what natives we saw disappeared into their huts. We were evidently not welcome. But then a portly older man, evidently a tribal elder, came out and, learning of our purpose for the stop, informed me that their fishing boat had not yet returned. I showed him our boats, some with Indian designs, and soon we were surrounded by emerging women and children admiring our fleet. We had literally met them at their level, rather than shouting down from a high yacht. My last view, as we left, was of the elder waving at us as we rounded a promontory and slipped out of sight.

In later trips, sometimes native boys challenged us to race them in their dugouts. Our kayaks, in those early years, were still a novelty. I recall, one time, paddling by a portly woman trolling in a narrow dugout. As we exchanged greetings, neither of us could resist asking the other about stability concerns.

Ceremonies

BILL HOLM, A WELL-KNOWN AUTHOR, professor emeritus of Art History at the University of Washington, and curator emeritus of Northwest Coast Indian Art at the university's Burke Museum, was also a member of our kayak club, along with his wife, Marty.[57] They had designed and built their kayaks, and joined us for paddling trips. One day, Bill invited my wife, Harriet, and me to witness a true native Potlatch, a ceremonial gathering, on Vancouver Island. Although such events are seldom advertised in the local media, Bill had somehow been made aware of this event, and wanted to witness what few non-natives have seen.

We arrived for the Potlatch at dusk, each of us offering a small entry gift of a can of coffee as we were ushered into the mysterious longhouse. We then witnessed a scene that had been played out for centuries at this and other locations on Vancouver Island. Nearly a hundred native people sat on raised and tiered wooden planks surrounding three fire pits with smoke curling up and venting through openings in the roof.

We took our seats up on the highest tier, not only to be as inconspicuous as possible, but also to gain a good view of all the happenings. This was not an orchestrated program, as we understood it, but rather, events appeared to occur on the spur of the moment. The first event we observed was the passing around of several new babies, each strapped rigidly on a board to be handled like a big loaf of bread as each was admired and commented on in turn. Other youngsters in feathery garb were showing off their finery to the rhythm of drumbeats as they circled the fires. Every once in a while, a few adults joined in, especially one gray-haired woman who eventually seemed to reach a trance state, whirling in a dance that seemingly had no end.

As the evening advanced, we heard some announcements being made near one of the fires. Evidently each local head had his greetings and announcements. Then some names were being called out to the audience through the smoky haze. Bill explained to us that this was the beginning of homage gift-giving that was a ceremonial part of the potlatch, when important members were being honored with gifts or praise. He also pointed out that gift-giving plays a big part in tribal status; the more someone gives away, the higher his status becomes. Such practices often affect the economic health of the competing givers and their families.

Mungo Martin was one of the major chiefs in the hierarchy of the Kwakiutl (who are now known as the Kwakwaka'wakw), and was a well-known woodcarver and painter throughout the Northwest. He was also a close friend of Bill's. As Martin continued to call out the names of important people to come down and receive recognition, he kept repeating a name in Kwakwala, the group's native language, with no response. Suddenly, Marty poked Bill in the ribs and excitedly said, "Hey, that's <u>your</u> native name!" Unbeknownst to Bill, Mungo had evidently spied him in the audience. To the astonishment of everybody, an embarrassed white man made his way down to the fire circle to be publicly praised for his efforts in promoting scholarship of Northwest tribal histories and art. He was honored with a ceremonial token. Harriet and I had witnessed a momentous occasion, in more than one sense—a forerunner of the much-deserved recognition that Bill Holm earned in subsequent years.

A Remarkable Friend

BIRDS OF A FEATHER FLOCK TOGETHER, sometimes despite being a few feathers short. When, after the war, I introduced the first public course in kayaking at the Seattle YMCA, a young woman asked me if she could use her Alaskan Baidarka kayak. I told her she would have to tell *me* what she thinks after she graduated. Since the emphasis at the time was on river touring, she soon realized what design features were important, and chose to switch to a more appropriate touring boat. Today, more than a half century later, when fishing from her modern kayak in the San Juans, she might wonder if she got rid of her native boat too soon.

Having joined our group of intrepid and innovative outdoor enthusiasts in skiing, biking, kayaking, camping, sailing and exploring the Northwest, Susan Hull (later Susan Meredith), began to lead an ever more adventurous life. And she did so against remarkable odds—polio had robbed her of the full use of one of her legs, causing a slight walking limp, and some obvious physical limitations. But her ever-cheerful enthusiasm for all things new and exciting rubbed off on all of us, and inspired us to become ever more inventive in meeting her challenges. She joined us swimming, and went along on early Puget Sound and British Columbia cycle tours, conquering occasional long hills with our pushes from behind when gears were inadequate or non-existent. Not only that, she even did some downhill skiing, using ski poles that we fitted with forearm braces and tiny short skis on the pole ends. In our eighties and nineties now, Susan and I still get together each year with families on San Juan Island, her home roost, and that of her husband Jim and daughter Jenny.

Susan Meredith is a good storyteller in her own right, and in a 1976 retrospective issue of the Washington Kayak Club's member magazine, she recounted one of her favorite Bauer foldboating stories for the membership. An accompanying cartoon shows a woman with a camera perched precariously on a stout tree branch, stretching out over a roiling river. The woman depicted is Harriet Bauer, the best sport in the world. Susan wrote in the article:[58]

ONE OF THE EVENTS THAT SPURRED HARRIET to seek to enlarge the [fledgling kayaking] group occurred during an afternoon wait at the junction of the Tolt and Snoqualmie Rivers. Harriet was the shuttle driver in those days quite frequently, as she was the mother of two small boys. After situating the boys in a safe place, she had crawled out on a log that extended over the river, and she was lying there on her stomach, camera focused on some hydraulics, all set to get some good pictures when Wolf came through. However, instead of flashing blades and Wolf's yodel, the first thing she saw was a broken paddle drifting through the waves, this closely followed by a longeron and then a cross frame, all of which she recovered. After a short wait to ensure that no more parts or bodies were floating down, she packed up the boys and drove back upstream, fearing the worst until she saw Wolf and his bow man packing their boat into its bags.

Wolf and a friend had been in a double, and when Wolf's paddle broke, the boat had wrapped itself around a rock in midstream. Unable to free it against the pressure of the current, Wolf had climbed on the rock and dismantled his boat piece by piece, tossing each one to his partner, who had made it to shore. The pieces Harriet had seen and retrieved were a couple that got away.

Those were the days of hearty outdoorsmen.

—◦◦◦—

ON EASTER MORNING IN 2008, in a cabin at Mosquito Pass on San Juan Island, the egg-hiding women were in a furtive huddle. Personalized eggs were to be concealed all over the Sound-front property, and cunning would be required of bunnies and hunters alike. "Don't put Wolf's egg where he can easily find it," one warned. "It insulted him last year when we put it at eye level."

"Make it a challenge this time!" Wolf admonished from the other room, eavesdropping on the strategists.

"But don't put it twenty feet up in a tree like the year before *either*," one whispered more quietly.

"He didn't have any trouble getting it, did he?"

"No, but he was only ninety-four then. And it made everyone else terribly nervous to watch him. We need to think of them, too."

Susan and Jim Meredith bought the lot on the beach near Roche Harbor after years of annual kayaker gatherings at Wolf Bauer's adjacent property, near his old lime plant job. The place of the Bauers' golden, Eden-like honeymoon years, retained as a vacation home, enjoyed a new life as "the Bauery." When Wolf and Harriet's fledgling Washington Foldboat Club first began outings and classes in 1950, Susan and Jim were amongst the first to sign up, individually. Their kayaker wedding near a river put-in soon followed. A committed and extended kayaking family developed, creating a social kinship that is perhaps impossible to reproduce in the twenty-first century. This group spent *decades* together, touring rivers and saltwater reaches throughout Washington, British Columbia, Idaho and beyond, and have, as a long-standing tradition, met annually to celebrate Thanksgiving and Easter in the San Juan Islands. The Bauers sold their property in the 1980s, but the tradition moved next door to the Merediths. At this particular assembly, the paddlers were celebrating the sixtieth anniversary of the club. There were fewer kayaks on the car racks than in years past, but the surviving stalwarts came with casseroles and desserts, enthusiasm and stories-told-a-hundred-times, like winter tales around the fire in a Salish longhouse.

Of particular amusement to the clan was the story of the power boat that became stranded on a sandbar right off shore during one of their gatherings, sending Wolf out in the only double-seater foldboat to rescue its passengers one at a time. The very first evacuee was a smartly but inappropriately dressed woman wearing spike high heels, with which she promptly punctured the neoprene hull. All the others had to wait until Wolf patched his boat to be rescued from the yacht, its list becoming more and more pronounced as the tide retreated. After fifty years, the tale still has the club in stitches.

Wolf finds his egg, after a lengthy search in a place chosen to elicit the hunter's keen powers of observation rather than derring-do. To celebrate finding the egg in the eaves of a shed, he leads a historical walk to locate old plant sites of the Roche Harbor Lime Company. We have not gone far before he squints and studies an opening in the brush. "Let me see if that's the right path to Quarry 9," he advises, and bolts like a colt, running ahead to save us walking up the wrong path. He doesn't totter, hobble, shamble, or shuffle. He *runs*—there and back—posture ramrod straight, fluid as an antelope. "Yes, this is it," he announces with no sign of breathlessness, and we turn off through the trees. He points out a concrete pad, cracked and covered with moss—a ruin of a former compressor pad for the machinery. It has not weathered the ages as well as our guide. In a moment, we are at the edge of the pool that was once Quarry Number 9, and rather than a scarred pit, we see a lush natural oasis embracing a high rock face in glistening verdure. The man-made escarpment is mined nearly clean of its limestone, but is aesthetically none the worse for the facelift. The clear water reveals every pebble and leaf at the bottom of the pool, and the expected image of a blighted landscape recedes into the memory of our imaginations. Wolf is not surprised. His faith in Nature is unwavering. It appears to be at least as resilient as he is.

PART V

Environmental Crusades

Homeland Treasures

From Rainier's steamy crater dome,
From Sound to Mount Olympus white,
There lies a land we call our home—
Woods, Lakes, and Rivers in our sight.

Refreshing raindrops in the air,
Our blue-green land restores in mist,
If you want green—it's everywhere,
And blue, when Sound by sun is kissed.

Mineral-marked streams guide salmon back,
Their juvenile hatch implanted, too,
While we such chemistry may lack,
Eye-recognition has to do!

Hidden wet ribbons dot our land
With streamway islands known to few,
Kayaks and paddles now on hand,
New vistas wait our quests anew.

That rocky-gravelly-sandy shore
Framing our lakes, the Sound and sea,
Has beauty, wildlife—use galore
And 'tidal-gifts' for you and me!

—WOLF BAUER

NINE

Allemansrecht

*"Nature has made neither the sun nor air nor
waves private property. They are public gifts."*
—OVID (displayed on Wolf's office wall)

B Y THE MID-1960S, Wolf had paddled most of the rivers in Western Washington, and this ongoing experience not only gave him tremendous pleasure, but also fired his curiosity and imagination as a naturalist. He needed to understand the processes that made stream banks and shorelines such changing and beautiful places. As the years passed, the destruction by human development of these beautiful places alarmed him. After decades as an engineering consultant, his passion for preservation and for what he would call "geo-hydraulics" began to grow. The term geo-hydraulics may have a decidedly intimidating technical ring to it, but what it really meant was that Wolf could watch the dance of water sculpting land all day long. Always one to find spiritual sustenance in the world he played in, Wolf heard the clarion call; he wanted to join in the dance, and to ensure that others always could, too. He had to be the messenger to alert the public to what was happening to all our waterways around Puget Sound. Ultimately, he would have to bring his engineering career to an end to accommodate this passion, and to tailor an entirely new field to satisfy its siren song.

Coming from Bavaria, perhaps Wolf's perspective on real estate development lacked a Lockean inevitability. Instead of faith in the sacred English rights of private property, Wolf subscribed to the Norwegian concept of "allemansrecht" (widely known today as "allemansrätten") or "every man's right"—the idea that everyone has the right to walk freely through nature on both public and private property. In Wolf's case, this meant shorelines in particular. (In England and Canada, tidal shores are "Crown land" up to a certain upper tide level. In the United States, only a few states concur with this idea, among them California and Hawaii, where one can find beach signs posted that proclaim: "This is your beach—Enjoy yourselves.") What Wolf could see becoming increasingly characteristic of stream banks and shorelines was that, plot by plot, development was negating the natural system that created and maintained its beauty and value. It was closing off public access to the enjoyment of Nature, converting the shores to private property, to the extreme detriment both of the public good and of the ecosystem.

Because of the British-American sacred cow of private land ownership, the management of the shores of the rivers, lakes, estuaries, and sound-waters of our country evolved as a legal and political issue rather than one of natural reality. The issue in land management thus becomes a question of a landowner's right to "improve," or degrade his land any way he sees fit, rather than the larger consideration of whether the ecosystem can recover from the degradation, or whether the damage will spill over to infringe upon the quality of life of other property owners, or of the greater public.

In the natural world, it has always been necessary for life forms to adapt to geologic processes, not the other way around. Yet in our culture, man has never been willing to admit that Mother Nature is the boss, and in spite of temporary victories over the obstacles she poses, she has a way of imposing long-term paybacks. We have long felt that as long as that payback is the next generation's problem, it is worth the sacrifice. Coming from outside that mentality, Wolf could see the error in this. "It is an overdue time," he wrote in 1978, "for drawing realistic boundaries between resource and real estate."[59]

Wolf came to understand that a shoreline is simply the terminus of a water system that begins in the highest Alpine lake, and that the system needs to be understood as a whole. He lamented the narrow thinking of land-use planners dealing with geographical landscapes. Planners overlay the land with artificial grids of use and ownership that pay scant attention to the natural processes of the land, water, and air converging there. A shoreline is a system of natural processes, not a static landform; one may always find water, sand, and gravel at a point on the grid, but it is ever-moving water, sand, and gravel. Just as one can never step in the same river twice, one can never step on the same beach twice. All is in perpetual motion, water and wind acting on the land to cause erosion and move the sediment, and, in the case of many Puget Sound beaches, accretion or build-up of eroded materials elsewhere. Surveyors' lines do not recognize or accommodate this fluidity of landscape. And the fluid landscape does not recognize surveyors' lines. "The boundaries of such imposed management zones obviously have little relationship to the boundaries of integrated shore-process systems," Wolf wrote in 1978.[60] The test of wills between Man and Nature takes a heavy toll on both parties.

The plant and animal life of the shore area evolves to reach a balance in harmony with these shoreline processes. But when man intervenes with land movement or artificial and arbitrary structural boundaries (bulkheads, jetties and riprap), the interference with those geologic processes wreaks havoc with the adapted ecosystems. Beaches are washed away and wildlife leaves. Sometimes the damage is so extreme that the aesthetic value that attracted the development in the first place is ruined, a bitter irony that does not bother the long-departed developer one bit.

So, as far back as the late 1950s, in his spare time, Wolf began studying the interaction of water and wind and land as a personal academic hobby. He and Harriet took scuba diving lessons so he could observe the hydraulics at work below the water line of rivers. Unfortunately, his first exploration in scuba gear into the mountain rivers prompted him to abandon the technique immediately. When the current banged the oxygen tanks against the rocks, the noise was deafening, and the portent of disaster presented itself aurally. From then on, he was a confirmed man of the snorkel.

Over the years, Wolf not only studied Washington rivers this way, but also spent a month in England and Scotland studying shoreline systems. He explored the beaches along the east coast of the North Sea and the coasts of the western Atlantic and the English Channel—all part of matriculation in his own private university. He learned about erosion and the complex physics of eddies at stream banks and around boulders and fallen snags. He also learned about fish spawning and farming run-off and the loss of plant buffers to logging—all disciplines he had first encountered during the summer jobs of his college years in the 1930s. He saw that everywhere engineers had tried to straighten or concrete a river channel into submission, it became lifeless, not just where the interference had taken place, but downstream, at the estuaries at the rivers' mouths. Certainly fish runs are shattered from loss of habitat. But in addition, the balance of the estuary ecosystem requires the nutrients and sediment deposits the river should have eroded. Estuaries starve where men "improve" rivers. As habitat for most of the Northwest's commercial fish catch, as water-purifying systems, and as recreational areas, the benefits of estuaries are incalculable. Devoid of all three of these characteristics, Seattle and Tacoma, Washington both sit on virtually dead estuaries.

Along streams, wherever humans build directly on the river banks, they begin a never-ending battle with a river that is required by the laws of physics to continuously move its bends downstream, to continuously alter the profile of its banks within its "meander belt" (the valley corridor within which the river's course remains relatively consistent even while its bends move). It is a battle in which engineering solutions offer only temporary victories, and in doing so, the beauty and value of the natural systems that invited the human settlement are compromised, if not altogether lost. When man bulkheads a naturally eroding riverbank property in a meandering stream, it upsets the downstream meander sequence, creating fishery problems in the estuary. Real estate tradition offers few solutions for wildlife and those humans who suffer the results.

Wolf ultimately moved his studies downstream to Puget Sound, where he found different geologic forces at work and different man-made problems. By building on fragile beaches, engineers and developers were actually altering natural geo-hydraulic processes in a way that would ultimately accelerate the erosion that would undermine the development. Nature seems to rise up to reject development, like a horse flicking a fly with its tail. The only question is the length of geologic time before the flick is complete.

In Puget Sound, the typical shoreline works in a series of systems that Wolf would name "drift sectors"—sections of shoreline where wind and water sculpt the land independently of adjacent shores— bordered on each end by landforms, such as rock promontories, hooks, spits, rivers, etc., that prevent all but the finest material from drifting out of it. For example, a typical Puget Sound sand and gravel bluff is eroded away by wave action. Because of wind and water currents, waves usually hit the beach at an angle, so that the eroded material is carried laterally up the beach, until reaching a spot where the topography forces the wave to drop its sediment. At this point we find an "accretion beach," a term coined by Wolf to describe a place where the nature of the drift sector causes a beach to build rather than erode. Spits and hooks typify the growing (and ever migrating) beaches created by this process in Puget Sound. Often they extend to close in bays and lagoons, which gives rise to rich new pocket ecological systems.

Typically, developers attempt to bully the beach into the particular vision of a private landowner. But breakwaters and groynes block the path of sand and gravel en route to build beaches. Bulkheading and riprapping along the shoreline may appear to control the way water impacts someone's beach, but ultimately they *increase* erosion. Wolf explains: "Every time you build a bulkhead, the shore in front of that bulkhead erodes faster, because the wave-swash current is driven vertically up against the wall and straight down again, scouring out the bottom."[61] "By defending ourselves, we made an enemy of the very forces that created the environment that brought us there in the first place. We killed the goose that laid the golden egg."[62]

In addition to this, Wolf learned that the secret to accretion beaches is porosity. A porous beach can absorb wave energy, which allows the wave to leave empty-handed. But as soon as the surface becomes impermeable—with buildings, rock, concrete, or asphalt— it provides resistance and the waves work against it. Before long, the beach is eroding and the structures are undermined. Once again, Nature wins the test of wills.

Wolf began to lay the blame for the "single-purpose approach" of land management at the doors of two culprits: profit-motivated developers and cost-cutting engineering agencies. In his pamphlet *A Time for Understanding*, published in 1970 by The Mountaineers, he wrote:

INCREASING EVIDENCE is accumulating of the economic losses that communities sustain when they allow 'ecologically illiterate exploiters' to shape the landscape in a vacuum of outmoded zoning.... We are living in a generation that was not schooled in the basic and lasting values of recreational, esthetic, and ecological land usage. A realistic and honest appraisal of the changes that have insidiously crept into our lives and surroundings leaves us shocked and apprehensive. What was once abundant is now limited and disappearing. What was once convenient or inconsequential has now become dangerous and of major concern. What were once luxuries have now become necessities, and what was once taken for granted now becomes precious and priceless.... What remains is all we will ever have, for we cannot buy, restore, or legislate what has been lost back into existence.[63]

This publication came out the same year as the nation celebrated its first Earth Day. Wolf was caught up in and became an agent of the rising tide of Environmentalism.

Obviously, not everyone who enjoys Nature becomes its champion. How did Wolf make the transition from an engineer who liked to play in the mountains to a force for environmental advocacy? Wolf's efforts to champion the cause of halting waterfront devastation took two separate but parallel courses: political and scientific. In the 1950s, as the situation was becoming alarmingly apparent to him, he was still a consulting mineral engineer, developing mountain rescue and teaching foldboating, as well as launching his two adolescent sons into the world. He was noticing the changes to the land, but he was only beginning his study of the geology and physics of the changes. It required a catalyst to galvanize his thoughts, turn his energies to conservation, and change the direction of his life.

That catalyst was Tacoma City Light's[64] plan in the 1950s to dam the Cowlitz River in southwestern Washington in two locations, building powerhouses that ultimately would produce two billion kilowatt hours of energy annually. To this end, Tacoma would inundate one of Wolf's favorite river runs through the Dunn and Mayfield Canyons. These canyons are a geologic rarity in Washington State, cut by the lowland Cowlitz River through solid rock, rather than the ubiquitous glacial till found elsewhere throughout the state. These exquisite canyons were a paddler's paradise, and when construction on the dams began in 1955, it was a true wake-up call for the community.

Wolf invited his friends, the renowned photographers Bob and Ira Spring, to come along on a paddle through the threatened canyonland in 1958. The result was a gorgeous *Seattle Times* Sunday edition full-color rotogravure pictorial section on July 13, 1958. Ostensibly drumming up interest in foldboating, it included remarkable photographs of paddlers floating, camping, and running whitewater through the Dunn and Mayfield Canyons, at the bottom of eighty-foot cliff walls and under abandoned railroad bridges. A stunning photo of Harriet Bauer assaulting rapids in cool shades carries the headline "She's Awash!" and though no doubt wet, she is clearly in absolute control—and having a blast. At the end of the enticing article we see kayaker Hubert Schwartz paddling forlornly at the dead end of the line: a Tacoma City Light cofferdam, built in preparation for the powerhouse. A subtle postscript understates the sentimental nature of the journey down the river, as the waterscape depicted would soon be gone.

But recreationists had found this wonderland too late. Tacoma City Light had been working on the project since 1946 and had a good, though contentious, head start. Lawsuits delayed construction until 1955, and it was again halted as soon as it started. Public support for preservation was high, and fishing interests had made a successful bid to the State to protect the Cowlitz as a fish sanctuary. To circumvent the state protection, Tacoma appealed directly to the Federal Power Commission, which considered the power facility instrumental to national security, and issued the license to build in 1951. Despite valiant litigation by fishery groups and recreationists that lasted more than a decade and went all the way to the U.S. Supreme Court, Tacoma City Light eventually prevailed; the courts

ultimately determined that the State of Washington could not prevent the Federal Power Commission from licensing a project on a
navigable waterway. Construction on the Mayfield Dam resumed in
1959, to be finished in 1962. The Mossy Rock Dam downstream was
completed in 1969.

Seattle historian David Wilma remarked that at the end of World
War II in the Northwest, building hydroelectric dams was seen as little less than a patriotic act, especially since post-war power shortages were a pressing problem.[65] But thanks to the emergence of
environmental activists such as Rachel Carson, the times began to
change; the last great hurrah of Manifest Destiny was expending
itself. The national myth of fulfilling God's will by devouring the
continent was beginning to lose its unassailable orthodoxy. In 1968,
Congress would pass the Wild and Scenic Rivers Act[66] which would
eventually be a useful tool in protecting other valuable rivers like
the Cowlitz from similar fates. But in the early 1960s, this major legislative achievement still lay in the seemingly distant future, too
late for the Dunn and Mayfield Canyons.

Involvement in the battle over the Cowlitz started Wolf's career
in environmental advocacy. Informed by his ongoing research and
observations, he began authoring pamphlets and newspaper articles
to inform the public and government agencies about the growing
problems caused by human impact on the land. Population in the
region was growing exponentially, and recreation would no doubt
become an ever-larger part of everyone's lifestyle, as well as a major
economic force. He can be forgiven for not imagining Microsoft and
Starbucks when he predicted that the Puget Sound's recreation
industry would be top economic dog in the region by the turn of
the twenty-first century.

His writings, such as the pamphlet *Concept of River Wildness*,
published by the North Cascades Conservation Council's *The Wild
Cascades* journal in 1964, reveal a growing philosophical reflective-
ness about the rivers. He calls the public to political action, but first
he charges the public with defining "wilderness," suggesting that
"the state of mind may be as much a part of the experience of
wilderness as is the natural topography and wildlife therein." He
writes of solitude as a necessary ingredient for the solace of wilder-

ness, and that "a tiny virgin oasis in the depth of a canyon or on the hump of a wooded hill may be protected in a primeval state; but if it is overrun by people, one of the most precious assets will be lost."[67] Though these early writings were motivated primarily by the interest in recreation, he was formulating ideas that would ultimately express his understanding that we must find our own small natural places of sanctuary all around us, not just "out there" in the "wilderness." It was the beginning of his consciousness of the importance of the availability of and accessibility to Nature for all— on a daily basis. Wilderness space would continue to diminish with man's encroachment, and we would need to welcome Nature back into our communities and integrate it into our lifestyles and our politics. This led him downstream, closer to home, and his writings began to focus equally on preserving the inland sea—Puget Sound.

That pamphlet was also the first that spoke of his concerns about the Green River Gorge southeast of Seattle in King County, a spectacular twelve-mile long stretch of the Green River between what are now Kanaskat-Palmer and Flaming Geyser State Parks. Carving its way through rock only nineteen "eagle-miles" from Seattle, forming a gorge that is three hundred feet deep in places, the river is a twisting watercourse of Class III and IV whitewater rapids alternating with glassy vernal pools. This makes the Gorge the only river-cut rock canyon in western Washington not currently inundated by utility company dams. Its steep cliffs and overhangs reveal fossils of an ancient sub-tropical landscape, petrified wood and even native petroglyphs. Once the neighborhood of the productive coal mining town of Franklin, the geologically rich area was also a source of clay and cinnabar, from which mercury is obtained. (The "flaming geyser" that the State Park is named for is a methane vent opened from a coal seam in 1911 by a test tap. A bit of a hyperbolic misnomer these days, the "geyser" flame, which once reached several feet in the air, today has the impressive projection of a birthday cake candle and needs to be re-lit regularly.)

Determined not to lose yet another canyon to development, Wolf began a tireless crusade to obtain state protection for the Green River Gorge. He took his proposal for its preservation to the Nature Conservancy, and in February of 1965, they requested that the Washington State Parks and Recreation Commission continue earlier investigations (begun in 1962) to study the whole twelve-mile length of the corridor for designation as a Conservation Area. Washington State Parks enthusiastically agreed, and in collaboration with King County Parks and Recreation, began the research, which would ultimately get the legislature behind the plan. To raise awareness for the campaign, Wolf wrote a highly influential piece titled "A Ribbon of Wilderness in Our Midst,", first published in *The Seattle Times* on November 13, 1966 and in the October/November 1965 issue of *The Wild Cascades*.[68] Excerpts from the piece made their way into the State Parks' official Conservation Proposal for the Gorge, issued in1968.

Working with such agencies as the Washington State Department of Game (now Fish and Wildlife), the Washington State Department of Natural Resources, the Puget Sound Governmental Conference, and The Nature Conservancy, Wolf and his devoted allies in Washington State Parks, such as Director Charles Odegaard, produced a plan that would include aggressive land acquisition and development of Flaming Geyser and Kanaskat-Palmer State Parks at each end of the Gorge. The state legislature established the Green River Gorge Conservation Area in 1969, outlining the acquisition of 1,500 acres for recreational development and the further protection of 1,100 adjacent buffering acres, through acquisition of easements for development, timber cutting and trails. In the current era, much of this has been accomplished, yet much remains. (Sadly, the goals set by Washington State Parks have never been fully realized, due to lack of funding. More than thirty-five parcels of rim land have been purchased since 1969, yet the quest continues to "lock up" more Gorge rim lands from development. And the long-standing dream of developed trails and an interpretive center on the rim continue to need more support.)

Much of Wolf's passion for this project can be seen in his writings about it. He considers his work done there his greatest environmental legacy. As it is one of his finest pieces of environmental writing, we include an abridged version of his article, "A Ribbon of Wilderness in Our Midst," a science lesson and political call to action all in one:

"A Ribbon of Wilderness in Our Midst"

THE SUNLIGHT OF SUMMER AFTERNOON had long lifted from the floor of the Green River Gorge as my wife and I beached our kayaks on the white gravel spit directly under Planter cliff, garlanded with lacy greens hanging from tiers of sandstone strata above us. The restless current of the Green River had slackened mirror-like around our spit in one of its frequent pools, and the tumbling rush of the riffles around the bend was now only a faint murmur.

We had meant to make camp earlier, but the temptation of a moss-lined swimming pool, an inviting siesta under the dancing shadow patterns of a huge maple and a fossil find near one of the coal seams had interrupted the leisurely drift-pattern of our float. Already we had paddled past familiar landmarks such as jutting Pulpit Rock, in the upper cathedral of the canyon, past Lost Island, alongside its hidden dry-channel, under massive Caveman's Ledge, and finally into the cavern of Otter Cave.

Even then, the highlight of the afternoon's exploration was the photographing of an otter-slide, which, like a miniature ski jumping hill, sported a grassy in-run groove, a take-off lip, a clay-slick landing slope, and a splash pool out-run—all complete with a whimsical staircase of tiny paw prints heading back up along its edge. We waited at the judges' stand until a long awkward silence convinced us that we evidently did not qualify as a proper audience.

Now, in the gathering dusk, as the flicker of the little cooking fire danced over the gravel spit, we began to feel, even more than before, the isolation and mystique of this ancient river bed. How difficult to believe, in such sight and sound isolation, that we were within commuting distance of a million people!

There are, of course, many criteria for evaluating a natural area represented by an unspoiled and free-flowing river. Many such streams in the state of Washington will need protective classification to prevent drowning by last-gasp dams or colonizing by tract development, if future generations will have access to anything of our original riverscape heritage, and benefit from the unusual recreational and aesthetic values these fragile ribbons of wilderness bring to the cluttered backyard of modern man.

Unusualness and rarity are not sufficient in themselves to qualify an area as one of broad public value and interest. This Green River Gorge is, in reality, a fantastic corridor of natural history into which curious man can descend to browse among the open shelves of geological displays. Here, the Green River has cut through the Eocene sediments of the Puget Group of rocks, exposing some nine thousand feet of tilted strata to uncover one of the most complete stratigraphic sections to be found in the region.

Since many of these shales and sandstones were laid down millions of years ago during tropical climates, the most casual visitor will be particularly intrigued to see first-hand imbedded fossils and fossil imprints of shells and vegetation, as well as carbon remains and coal seams. How much more dramatic to touch and see these evidences and features in place than under museum glass.

The student, scientist and observant visitor can view the present dynamic forces of stream erosion, where, through caves, smooth channels and hollowed ledges, the water continues to carve through the earth's crust.

In its flora and fauna also, the Gorge has retained its original beauty and ecological balance, its topographic character serving to maintain it as a sanctuary for a variety of wildlife. Down its cliffs and gentler draws remain untouched first growth stands of evergreens above mossy and fern-covered grottos, with myriads of tiny waterfalls seeping down the canyon walls. Freshness and moisture permeate the floor in its shadowy twilight to nurture rain forest type vegetation. Placid pools, like miniature chain lakes, create an occasional corridor of silence, only seldom disturbed by the croak of a heron or rattle of kingfishers.

Thus, as a self-sustaining botanical and zoological garden, the Gorge represents an ecological entity, which owes its close-in existence and character entirely to its protective canyon walls rising up to three hundred feet above the river bed. As such, it supports a biologic community in a living laboratory that can sustain itself indefinitely into the future without man's help. It probably can do this better here than in any other instance and site in the area.

Native Washingtonians always seem to have taken the presence of the Gorge for granted. That it was there, unmarred and primeval, hidden and mysterious but available—this has been a basic satisfaction in itself, whether one visited the Gorge often or not. In a region of extreme and varied topography, climate, life zones, and waterways, a short stretch of natural canyon may be little to get excited about. However, it is obviously difficult to set aside a spot of special beauty in a land of general beauty, or to point to future needs in a land of present abundance.

This, then, is the core of the conservation problem in the Puget Sound country today. Many unconcerned citizens still parrot the legend of our endless miles of stream and saltwater shoreline, even while we are witnessing an unrelenting "lock-up" of remaining accessible waterfront by private real estate developments. Like many of the present generations, who deeply feel the limitations imposed by developments in the past, so will our future "natives" critically lament the loss of former accustomed access to the state's shorelines and waterways, with all that this implies recreationally and aesthetically.

The limited and rare junction of land and water that we call shoreline comprises but a tiny fraction of our living area. It is not only the borderline between familiar and relatively unknown worlds, but an interdependent littoral life zone. To man, it also is the threshold to wider horizons, where currents and wave action, or mirrored calm, await his view or participation.

What, after all, is a waterway without approachable shoreline from either land or water direction? How will the rare and special quality of the natural river bank and seashore be evaluated in the needs of tomorrow's crowded life? Can we yet find the political courage on the local levels to declare a moratorium on the haphazard, unchecked shoreline colonization gathering ominous momentum without regional design and buffer-zone provisions?

It may be hoped that county officials of vision and caliber will emerge to organize themselves with state and professional guidance for a concerted effort to protect what remains of our heritage of accessible beauty in this water wonderland of the "blue-green" state of Washington.

Forty years later, his work on this particular mission long ago completed, Wolf reflects on what the Green River Gorge meant to him personally, still with passion and inspiration:

RECALLING THE HIGH POINTS IN ONE'S LIFE becomes a growing pleasure with age. There are those that you cherish, and those that others have recognized. Of those I own, the Green River Gorge experience overshadows all the others. In a long-term future, a preserved Gorge will be a legacy that my generation will, indelibly, have left behind. A treasured thought.

The impact of the Gorge on my psyche remains undiminished. What was it about those first exploratory paddles into that hidden museum of

Nature? Was it its unbelievable isolation in the midst of a million people? Was it the antiquity of its ancient walls, hinting at massive faulting and erosion over millennia? Was it the sculptured images and fossilized imprints of ancient life forms from both above and below the seas? I think it was the realization that there are "cathedrals of Nature" that inspire awe and humility, far beyond any man-invented religious symbols and beliefs.

This fervency of belief explains how one of Wolf's professional detractors once said about him and shoreline conservation, "He believes in [this program] more than anything else in the world. It's a religion to him."[69] And it was, to a large extent, Wolf's crusade. In 1967, after a well-organized but unsuccessful effort to pass a Wild and Scenic Rivers law in Washington State, he and other conservationists came together to create a consortium of environmental interests that could lobby more effectively in Olympia. Thus Wolf was a contributing founder of the Washington Environmental Council,[70] which was dubbed "Mother Nature's lobbyist." This highly effective organization still works wonders today, more than forty years later, employing grassroots organizing, policy development, media communication and legal action to promote a healthy and protected landscape and populace.

At the same time as he was working with the Washington Environmental Council to propose legislation, he wrote a booklet titled *A Time for Understanding,* published by The Mountaineers in 1970. In it he outlined for the public many of his basic tenets, now focusing equally on Puget Sound and on the area's rivers: that the natural resources of Western Washington were invaluable for their recreation value and aesthetic value as well as their economic value, and that an informed citizenry *must* take responsibility for the stewardship of those natural assets. With no patience for complacency on the part of the public, his concluding appeal speaks to everyone:

WE REPRESENT THE LAST GENERATION that not only had unlimited and free access to these heritage-held marine and riverscapes, but also enjoyed, even though mistakenly, the freedom of ready resource exploitation with few ecologic considerations or guidelines. The days of environmental manipulations and alterations based solely on personal profit or engineering economics are hopefully numbered. This is an overdue time for learning what makes our landscape tick. This is the time for all citizens, both here and throughout the country, to assert their right to experience the astonishing legacy nature left in this region. It is a time to dedicate ourselves to maintaining and enhancing this special quality of our land. This is also a time for local and state government to exercise its responsibility in stewardship over these heritage resources, and to courageously test basic land-use philosophies in the light of highest public values and benefits. The time is now, for in the poignant fatality of [Nez Perce] Chief Joseph's manner of speech, we will have no more, forever.[71]

Among the first victories of the Washington Environmental Council was pushing the Shoreline Management Act through the State Legislature in 1971, a piece of legislation that was in large part influenced by Wolf Bauer's policy crafting. The Council presented Wolf's Initiative 43 to the voters, which competed with the legislature's alternative version, Initiative 43-B.[72] The latter passed. But part of Wolf's framework of values survived the revision—namely that public access to shorelines "shall be preserved to the greatest extent feasible" and that increased access and recreation should be actively sought.

Bringing his "religion" about the spiritual need of man to access Nature into legislation, Wolf leaves his pagan mark on Washington Shorelines. Though not comfortable with all the compromises and methodology of the Act, Wolf can still take pride in his contributions to a piece of landmark legislation, one that permanently altered the political culture of land use in his home state. He may consider the saving of the Green River Gorge his greatest accomplishment, but posterity has other nominees to judge from. Regardless, evolving from recreationist to conservation apostle, by 1971 Wolf had entered a new sphere of public-professional life.

TEN

Spreading the
Good Word

B Y THE EARLY 1970S, Wolf's transition from mineral engineer to
shore resource consultant was fully underway. His public writings and efforts to affect legislation had, up until this point, been a hobby. But this would change for the last two decades of his public life, as his avocation became his vocation. In accordance with his desire to reach just a few more acolytes, following is his primer for students of Puget Sound: Beaches 101.

Shore Resource Consulting

AFTER SOME TWENTY-FIVE YEARS EXPERIENCING, firsthand from kayaks, the extreme effects of currents and waves on both river banks and saltwater shores, it dawned on me that neither the public nor government reacted with understanding to Nature's erosion and accretion systems. Influencing and anchoring my thinking as well was my University Geology studies, especially Glacial Geology that, with my Engineering background, gave me professional standing with involved governmental entities. By 1965, it was time to change course, and create an environmental engineering field as a Shore Resource Consultant. It would be my last labor of love. Instead of working for some business client, I would now work for the public good. I would try to lean on the public's common sense through educational slide lectures, and provide involved state and county agencies with the field data and philosophy needed for a workable Shoreline Management Act that respected the natural system. Environmental consciousness also, by that time, had seen progress, as public initiative pressure at the ballot box created the Washington State Department of Ecology, and the Coastal Zone Management Act of 1972.

Director John Biggs of the Department of Game became the first Head of the new Department of Ecology. I thought he was a good choice. Several years earlier, he had encouraged me to lead the opposition to drowning the Cowlitz River Canyons with power dams for the City of Tacoma. During his first year of organizing and heading his new Department, I met with him to discuss what I had learned and developed as a realistic concept of shore systems and their management. He suggested that I address his new staff on the science of management issues, which I did. Some of these people were educated in environmental management issues, but not in hydraulics and geology. To them, my guidelines and terminology were too radical and new, making them turn down both concepts and methods. Director Biggs then said to me, "Wolf, I'm impressed by what you've learned and proposed, but I've got to live with my new staff!" The old German saying "Aller Anfang ist schwer"—"All beginnings are difficult"—reminded me to bide my time.

While all this sounds presumptive, the following five years proved a political education in how governments work. There seemed to be an obvious lack of communication, if not teamwork, between "competing" departments, concerning environmental issues. To gain access and respect, it was important to provide many technical facts and findings without taking credit personally. My satisfaction would come from the eventual adoption and use of suggested policies, methods and new terminology. Eventually, it garnered substantive field work to further test and prove more natural ways of preserving or enhancing beaches and streamways.

Much of what Wolf would bring to the legislative process was an understanding that few other geologists, let alone politicians, possessed about the natural shore processes of Puget Sound. Perhaps the greatest factor in this was Wolf's willingness in the 1970s to hire a former kayaking student and pilot, George Yount, to fly him over every mile of Puget Sound coastline at five hundred feet, so he could photograph landforms and current action. Both pilot and passenger were adventurous sorts, so safety regulations were not well observed. Though Wolf encouraged George to fly into places he had no business flying, George was a bit of a daredevil anyway, taking off short cliffs with a gas tank on empty, and buzzing freighter smokestacks kamikaze-style for laughs. The Plexiglas windows of the plane created a glare, so Wolf had to lean out open windows to get his shots, but the result was a voluminous collection of some two thousand color slides, and a perspective that brought the workings of the "drift sectors" mentioned earlier into high relief. Walking and kayaking the beaches was illuminating, but flying them made it possible to see both the forest *and* the trees. "It didn't take very long," Wolf explained, "to make sense out of nature's long-established shore erosion-accretion system, after my first viewing of the 2,500 miles of Washington's shores from the air."

Furthermore, Wolf had always been willing to go out and make his photographic observations when other geologists were off the clock—in severe storm weather at high tides—when all the most destructive processes were in full swing. So while academic coastal geologists were often inclined to discredit his lack of a pedigree (University of Washington minor in Geology notwithstanding), Wolf proved to be a gifted amateur with decades of field experience that the professionals couldn't begin to approach. (And growing up with Professor Hubert Bauer, the first man to chart the world's ocean tides, had to count for something.)

Based on this understanding, Wolf went on to devise a full personal curriculum on Puget Sound beaches that would be useful in proselytizing his gospel to the public and government. His interests were not in publishing academic works for other professionals to read; he only wanted to enlighten the public for their own good. The price that he paid for his "lack of credibility" was one he balanced with the reality of his years. As he was in his seventies and eighties during this time, pursuing another degree held little appeal. As he said, "when you are in your seventies, you like to goof off once in a while."[73]

Wolf developed his own terminology for these shore process systems, which were not always recognized by academics and professional coastal geologists. He was often criticized for this, with claims that new, non-academic terminology only made communication and understanding more difficult. But Wolf stood firm. "I'm simplifying a difficult subject, and I want to make a terminology that the biologist, the engineer, the planner and the politician can all understand.... If only one discipline were involved here—say biology, without politics or planning—then we could use the jargon of that discipline. But we can't do that, because the biologist can't understand the engineer and the engineer can't understand the geologist."[74] His terms like "feeder bluff" (for the cliff walls that provide the sand and gravel for beaches), or "accretion beach" (for the hooks, spits, and beaches that are then created), are still in widespread use in government circles around Puget Sound.

Yet the terms are not widely in use outside Washington. This is partly because they are specific to Puget Sound geology, but also because Wolf never sought to publish his theories. He spread his gospel at town meetings, conventions, seminars, and in classrooms, with slide shows of photographs and illustrative diagrams. "A picture is worth a thousand words," he would say, and his own talents and charm as a speaker won him many converts. But by failing to incorporate his ideas into a transportable medium, such as books, he both limited the dissemination of those ideas, and failed to garner the kind of academic validation that might have lent his opinions more political punch. But as Wolf has always maintained, his efforts were all motivated not by a desire for personal glory, but by a desire to do something for the good of the public.

And he did enjoy political punch, nonetheless.

Here he has given a short synopsis of his presentations.

The Enigma of Earth-Water Boundaries

WHETHER WE'RE TALKING OF FLOWING STREAM CURRENTS or pulsating shore currents in either rock-hard or earth-soft interface, we are dealing with both instant and long-term changes to our inherited landscapes. As an invasive species, we would normally adapt to the operating landscape, as life has always done in the past.

In the Puget Sound Country, our immediate predecessors lived within the limits of nature's food supply by hunting and fishing. In joining them, we added agriculture for both meat and grain. But in so doing, we've now ended up with levees and dikes that critically reduce the flood plain recharge of the soil, the very system that created and maintains this food basket. Every once in a while, the "weather gods" try to show us who's in charge, by inundating or sluicing houses, people or cattle down valleys. In our coastal environments as well, angry high-tide storm waves teach us how the system works.

Our lifestyle and land-use philosophies are beginning to change as we become aware of nature's reactions. It has taken me many years of aerial and shore-based photography to document the shortsightedness of ignoring these geo-hydraulic systems that have given us such unique and important land- and seascapes. There are still options for living environmentally, with flooding rivers and eroding shores. It's payback time for this immigrant. Let me try.

The Puget Sound Beach System

THANKS TO GLACIERS OF THE LAST ICE AGE—continental ones from Canada and local ones from the Olympics and Cascades—the Puget Sound basin and its shores have been left with an abundant supply of sand and gravel. In a wet climate, the stage is set for an amazing display of what the force of gravity can do with wind and water, even without an extra shove from the moon's sneaky pulls. Without getting into the many variables of fluid-dynamics, let me paint a simplistic picture that any layman can surely relate to.

After some underwater river-eddy studies in the early fifties, I soon became interested in the geo-hydraulics of coastal breaker waves. As I did on rivers, I dove into Hawaiian surf with face mask and snorkel, and later into Puget Sound, trying to learn the mechanics of beach accretion and erosion. So let's ignore complicated formulas and hydrology speak. We'll go down to a typical Puget Sound sand and gravel beach on a windy day, and watch the antics of surf. What happens there every few seconds is an amazing interplay of fluid dynamics with gravity.

The Surf Phenomenon

WHEN WAVES APPROACH THE FORESHORE SHALLOWS, they change from oscillating waves to flowing surf. This transformation begins when the water depth is less than one and a half times the wave height. It is then that bottom friction causes the now faster wave top to collapse forward into a moving waterfall, called "surf" when it hits the beach. (A somewhat stronger phenomenon occurs when strong offshore winds churn a deep-water surface into shallow breakers called whitecaps.) This surf, or breaker wave, finally collapses into the "swash" current as it flows up the beach. When it drains back, over and through the foreshore, its original dynamic and static energies are finally expended.

On a porous gravel beach, much of the returning swash-current is absorbed, leaving insufficient surface water to carry material seaward, resulting in beach accretion. On a sandy foreshore, by contrast, the denser and less porous beach surface restricts swash absorption, thus more material is washed seaward, resulting in beach erosion. Wind and waves, of course, most often hit a stretch of beach at an angle, moving material up the beach along the wind direction, while gravity pulls it more directly back down. In this way, successive waves create a zigzag path of material movement along the beach corridor. It should be obvious that the same regional wind affects the many involved beaches differently, depending on their sand and gravel composition (the materials in the "feeder bluff"), foreshore slope, beach orientation, local wind direction, and "fetch" (the length of open water over which wind can generate and push waves).

Storm-tide Surf: Beach Builder and Destroyer

AT A TIME OF HIGH TIDES AND STORM WAVES, a typical Puget Sound bluff-beach can undergo a number of transformations, depending on its composition. If, for example, the bluff is made up of sand and gravel without a cementing clay binder, its face is subject to frequent cave-ins and slides. Under those conditions, the high surf-breakers simply sweep the toe-gravel along the shore, while gravity pulls more material in its place. Such feeder bluff erosion, in turn, supplies accretion material for important down-drift "points," "spits," and "hooks," with their gravel and berm-protected lagoons and marshes. A good example of this process is the different drift sectors along Whidbey Island's west coast. It should be obvious that thwarting that process by feeder bluff bulkheading directly affects the long-established biologic and new-found recreational values of such beach environment.

In order to create an easily understood discipline of beach-shore dynamics, I designed simple sketches showing the roles that glacial beach material, wave fetch, and beach orientation play on the stability and intrinsic value of each segment. This, in turn, led to a simplified, non-technical beach designation based on whether the beach was undergoing erosion or accretion.

Wolf's traveling slide show presentations explored three different classes of Puget Sound beaches, categorized by their accretion and erosion characteristics. They are

Class 1: The Accretion Beach. This highly valued beach is best for recreation. It has a growing, dry backshore, which stays dry even during high tide. Wolf estimated in the 1980s that less than 5 percent of Puget Sound beaches could still be classified Class 1.

Class 2: The Erosion Beach, which is probably feeding a spit somewhere else. This beach has a narrow backshore that can *usually* be traversed at high tide, "But if you're going to camp there, you'd better bring your tide tables."

Class 3: This Erosion Beach has no dry backshore at high tide. Drift logs will generally not collect here.

—⟨⟨⟨⟨⟩⟩⟩⟩—

WHEN DEPARTMENT OF ECOLOGY DIRECTOR JOHN BIGGS began bringing him in to convert his staff, Wolf's clientele grew through word of mouth. The applications for his theories were two-fold: helping agencies regulate new shoreline construction, and helping landowners restore or redesign failing shoreline systems. With winter storms assaulting beachfront property in a veritable Northwest tradition of slides and cave-ins, Wolf was sure to have plenty of work. His client base grew to include private citizens, community groups, native tribal organizations, and local and state governments in Washington, Oregon and British Columbia. His academic courses and seminars were taught in institutions such as the University of

Oregon and Oregon State University, as well as the University of British Columbia and Douglas College in Canada.

Wolf once remarked that "the Indians never needed a word for 'erosion.' They knew the gravel went from one place to another and back again, and they didn't try to stop it."[75] Yet he was extremely pragmatic and practical about modern-day human habitation. He understood the need to work with pre-existing structures on an owner's property. He was not the kind of extremist who could condone no development. He understood that people would come, and land would be developed. The best he could hope to achieve was the compromise of sustainable, ecologically friendly design in that development and to establish a legacy of public accessibility that did not yet exist. For existing landowners in trouble, he would try to reestablish the pre-existing natural system. But if that were impossible or impractical, due to permanent structures or changes to the "drift sector" in adjoining properties, then he would mimic a type of natural formation that would produce a sustainable result. His main strategy to combat erosion was a process of "beach nourishment." Though the solutions Wolf was formulating were beginning to be realized in other places in the world, too—namely Europe—they were completely new in the region. He was far ahead of academic thought in the Northwest at the time the ideas were coming to him.

Restoring a beach typically began with removing bulkheads and bringing in gravel—the most porous material for absorbing the force of wave water. The berm was oriented to wave and wind action, so that those forces could help hold the gravel in place, perhaps even build on them. He chose the size of the gravel based on the nature of the wave action at the site. The larger the waves, and the longer the fetches, the larger the gravel would have to be. In some cases he built "drift sills," underwater groynes built of rock, perpendicular to the shore, to create an artificial end to the drift sector and stop beach erosion. Over the decades, by trial and error, he honed his techniques to a highly predictable science.

Wolf's old friends at Washington State Parks launched his prominence as Washington's "strandmeister,"[76] or beach builder, when they approached him to work on some problems at the waterfront of Tolmie State Park on Nisqually Beach near Olympia. His successful demonstration of his ideas at this park was the first of dozens of "Bauer Beaches" (as the Department of Ecology still calls them) built for the public between Vancouver and Olympia. More than thirty of these waterfront parks comprise Wolf's legacy to the residents of Puget Sound. Wolf remembers some examples of his storm-resistant park beaches.

Tolmie State Park

WHEN I LEARNED THAT THE ERODING SPIT-BEACH at Tolmie State Park was to be "saved" by riprapping in 1974, I convinced the Department of Ecology and the State Parks Commission of a great opportunity to fight the growing "Riprap Syndrome" with the installation of a properly graded gravel-berm beach with a dune-grass backshore. This showcase beach became the forerunner of more than thirty installations I've designed for the public sector in the past twenty-five years.

West Point Beach

WHEN A NEW SEWAGE TREATMENT PLANT was built on the shores of Puget Sound, adjacent to Discovery Park, money was made available to make improvements to the park. In 1981, the City of Seattle was anxious to create a people-friendly dry beach near the West Point Lighthouse at Discovery Park. I was able to make the case for removal of a beach-starving wastewater lagoon (a leftover from the days when sewage was discharged directly into Puget Sound). As a result of its removal, the Fort Lawton Bluffs could resume the historical feeding of the starving West Point shore. This involved a bit of a battle convincing the U.S. Coast Guard, the U.S. Army Corps of Engineers, and particularly the Civil Engineering faculty of the University of Washington to substitute a Bauer berm beach for the suggested riprap revetment. The project, completed in 1983, was a success, and I have ever since been called "friend of the city."

Seattle was no doubt grateful for Wolf's work in Discovery Park, but the city already counted him as a friend: Wolf received the "First Citizen of Seattle Award" from Mayor Charles Royer in 1979.

Wolf ponders the removal of riprap from the eroding West Point beach in Seattle's Discovery Park in 1989. The success of Wolf's plan for restoration of the beach is obvious today to all park-goers who have enjoyed the natural beach there.   PHOTO BY ROD MAR, *THE SEATTLE TIMES*

Golden Gardens Park

IN ORDER TO UPGRADE GOLDEN GARDENS PARK, I was able to establish a new pocket-beach with a dune-grass berm system, including a hidden gravel storage area for future maintenance. Bridged wild duck ponds, maintained by hillside bluff drainage across the railroad track, were added later. The pièce de résistance, however, turned out to be the removal of a buried hillside runoff pipe that had channeled a natural stream to Puget Sound underground. This "daylighting" liberated the meandering creek, which once again crosses the park and flows unrestricted over the beach foreshore. To the huge delight of children, they can now mess with it, and dam it with rocks to make ponds, and nightly tides take care of free clean-ups for the next day's fun.

What Wolf forgets to mention is his prior history with Golden Gardens Park in the Ballard neighborhood of Seattle. In 1971, the Seattle City Council approved a measure to build the new Seattle

Aquarium on the beach at Golden Gardens, a move championed by marine biologist and future Governor Dixy Lee Ray. A group of concerned citizens, led by Ballard resident Wolf Bauer, fought back. Golden Gardens was in desperate need of an overhaul, but Wolf's vision for its restoration was already taking shape in a very different direction—that of restoring the beach's ecology. In these early days of his public advocacy, Wolf held a neighborhood meeting at Ballard High School to sound the alarm to the community, and then oversaw the launching of a citizen initiative to prevent the construction. Teaming with then-Mayor Wes Uhlman, Wolf and his crew were ultimately successful in their battle with the formidable Dixy Lee, culminating in the City Council's reversal of its original decision. The ultimate site of the Aquarium at Piers 60 and 61 was set in July of 1972.

Environmental Education

A GROWING CROP OF IDEALISTIC ENVIRONMENTALISTS were starting to step on the toes of entrenched government agencies, bringing the two groups into conflict. I soon realized that more could be accomplished by providing the agencies in Washington State with knowledge of basic geo-hydraulic science so that they could test my concepts in the field, and then take professional credit for them. Soon, neighboring governments in Oregon and British Columbia asked for educational sessions, as well as the University of Oregon, Oregon State University, The University of British Columbia and Douglas College in British Columbia—some providing course credits for classes in which I detailed the environments of rivers, inland seashores, estuaries and open coast.

Not all of Wolf's memories of his environmental work are about the battles. He prefers to remember the humorous parts of his career.

A Damn Yankee in British Columbia

ONE OF THE MORE PRESTIGIOUS CONVENTIONS I've attended took place in Vancouver, British Columbia, a meeting of "Ministers of Environment" from all the Canadian Provinces. By that time, my several coastal installations in British Columbia had proved successful, and I was invited to be the lead-off speaker, setting the technical stage, so to speak, for the two-day program.

The meeting started with the Convention Chairman, an Easterner, explaining what the programs were all about. Perhaps with a slight chip on his shoulder, he hinted, among other things, that this meeting was truly Canadian, and not dependent on any advice form "our friends across the border." He evidently hadn't realized that an American engineer was the lead-off speaker. I had just minutes to think of a reply. As I got up, looking in his direction, I told the audience that this "Damn Yankee" had learned all he knew about river and beach systems from British Columbia sand and gravel that the Canadian glacier had dumped unceremoniously over Washington State lands, without permit, and that Canada is welcome to take it back anytime. That, to my relief, brought the house down, and I noticed that even the somewhat chastised Minister applauded at the con-clusion of my slide-lecture, probably because it was expected etiquette. In retrospect, my more than twenty-five years of environmental activities for British Columbia were some of the most cherished in my career.

The Nudist Factor

THE UNIVERSITY OF BRITISH COLUMBIA CAMPUS is located on top of a glacial moraine sea-bluff that was eroding back from wave attack at an average of three to five feet annually. Their recently built five million dollar Museum of Anthropolgy had been located about a hundred yards from the edge of the high bluff. To stop or slow down this erosion, a berm of sand was dumped against the foot of the cliff. However, it washed away with the first high-tide storms. When University maintenance engineers proposed to protect the bluff-toe with a skirting riprap roadway, beach users were immediately up in arms. At that point, I received a desperate phone call from a young lady who said she was secretary of the Vancouver Nudist Society, which had, for some years, laid claim to that eroding section of the University beach. "Mr. Bauer, you're our last resort for stopping this dreadful road and riprap scheme that would permanently wipe out our excuse for being!" she lamented. How did I ever get into this squabble? I assured her that, in any case, I would visit with both sides and see if a mutually acceptable solution were possible.

Unexpectedly, I found that mutual respect and cooperation existed between the school and the Society. The nudists had taken over the beach section farthest from public beach parking and use, marking their portion with a simple sign stating "Clothing Optional" (certainly respectful and democratic). Not only that, but they kept their beach section cleaned of all debris after each day's use. No wonder the University called them good neighbors. However, campus integrity and safety must obviously come first.

Here, I soon realized, was a great opportunity to demonstrate to the University's Geology and Engineering faculties that, under certain conditions, a properly designed natural beach system could not only be more economical than bulkheads, but far superior in terms of recreational and esthetic amenities. After the inspection of some of my Washington installations, such a protective beach system was finally installed, to the delight of not only students and the public, but, you guessed it, my skinny-dipping friends, who made me an honorary member of their "clothing optional" society! The last I heard from them was a New Year's card, with a photo of more than a hundred naked and kneeling rear-ends—an homage to the newly protected bluff, visible in the background.

Hierarchical Dilemma

ON VANCOUVER ISLAND, I was asked to provide technical judgment on the proper location of a proposed tribal marina. The young, university-educated native planner showed me a logical site near the highway, one for which he had made an economic case study. But there, on the eroding beach within the proposed site, teetered an old shack of a cabin, already tilting partly into high-tide water. Unfortunately, the owner and occupant was an old tribal elder who insisted on his right to live out his life where he was born, on that very spot. No cajoling or generous offers of a new and modern habitat nearby could persuade him to change his mind. The frustrated planner was wondering whether his education had been a waste of tribal money.

It was a frustrating situation, and one that has played out many times, where traditions take precedence over both logic and the common good. I could not find an economically viable alternate site, at the time, but on closer examination, we concluded that the elder's abode had no more than a couple of years before he would have to be rescued from the surf. We agreed that tradition does not always get the last word.

Fishery Equations

IN BRITISH COLUMBIA, where the lumber industry is "top dog" in relation to farming and fishing, the basic functions of estuaries have often been ignored or down-played. River deltas have been used for excessive log storage that not only introduces decaying bark acids and photosynthesis-robbing shade, but usurps juvenile salmon space and nutrients so critical to the Provincial fishery. Agriculture, in some instances, has also made critical inroads into fisheries by removing fish-rearing space through diking. The ignominy lies in the fact that while lumbering and farming can, in many instances, find other suitable space, wild salmon fisheries cannot. Native people, especially, have been negatively affected by this situation, both in Canada and in the United States.

On the lighter side, I recall a humorous incident on the Skokomish River delta, where I was helping tribe members with methods of reclaiming original estuarine areas from diked farmland. We had with us a white county official who kept looking at his watch as the noon hour approached. Despite our assurance that we could finish our inspections in less than an hour, he decided, nevertheless, to go for lunch at a nearby restaurant. This brought to my mind a humorous cartoon fitting the situation where a native observed (in admittedly offensive pidgin English) that "Indian eats when hungry; white man looks at watch to see if hungry." I wasn't sure how my tribal official would take that, but it bowled him over, and he said he couldn't wait to retell the story to our county friend when we could catch up to him. When we did, the county official listened to that philosophic Indian observation without comment, except to say that he needed to get back to his office now. 'Nough said! I long ago stopped wondering whether people of different colors are different underneath.

BECAUSE OF MY WORK WITH STREAMWAY MANAGEMENT, I was asked by the Quinault Indians to help them with various fisheries problems. One problem at the time was to find a suitable set of channel features that would make it possible to design a juvenile salmon rearing pond into the natural system. I designed an installation at a river bend in the small Salmon River nearby. The pond was kept safe from flood damage by a current deflector, which also protected the pond intake control gates. That, and some other flood-relief work on the Quinault River, earned me a treasured and official Tribal Fisheries cap, one that I still wear for special occasions twenty-five years later.

Wouldn't That Get Your Goat?

IT WAS IN THE EARLY SIXTIES that I was environmentally involved in pointing out the many landscapes of value, other than Snoqualmie Falls, that needed recognition by both the town of North Bend and the state capitol in Olympia. Foremost among them were the Middle Fork of the Snoqualmie River and Mount Si. Derailing Army Corps of Engineers dam project proposals would save an unspoiled river and valley within commuting distance of a million people. And, when one day I noticed the beginning of clearcutting on the North Bend side of Mount Si, I realized there was no time to waste—I had to stop the disfigurement of the valley's landmark, so prominently visible from the freeway. I'm sure Uncle Si (pioneer Josiah Merritt, the mountain's namesake) would have turned in his grave, had we not convinced Olympia that a little timber "horse-trading" was urgently needed. Thus was saved the mountain's future image, with only a patchy scratch that continues to heal.

During this time of growing landscape appreciation, where the term "environment" had not yet become an issue-word (or so I thought), I was asked by the principal of North Bend Public School to give the kids a slide show of their valley's "special places," a timely opportunity in many ways. To grab their imagination, I first showed what I told them was the famous "Monté See" in Italy, enshrined in storm clouds, showing only occasional vertical rock walls here and there with each slide. The kids seemed to be impressed and quiet, but soon I heard some whispering, and then one boy said, "It looks like Mount Si." Thus they were drawn in to the show, and I went on to display the different landscape features that would need their saving attention in the future, such as, for example, potential sites for parks, river access and trails, farmland and pasture protection, etc. Then suddenly, I heard some scuffling in the back of the hall, followed by loud door-slamming. After the program, I asked the principal, "What was that all about?" Reluctant at first, he eventually related that one or two men had come in and grabbed him, demanding, "Who gave you permission to have Wolf Bauer address our children?" They were local real estate developers. Luckily, the principal had the school board's backing. Such were the early days of the environmental movement.

While I was with my young audience, I shared a story with them of my experience on Mount Si the previous fall. I had climbed the peak with a camera and sleeping bag, to document what one can see and experience in a day and night on the mountain, especially sunset and sunrise. Having the peak all to myself, I chose a mossy overlook at the top, and fell asleep soon after nightfall. When I had to get up in the middle of the night (I remember sniggers from my young audience), I suddenly made out a light-colored shape some twenty-five feet from my sleeping bag. It was a large mountain goat nanny, and this was evidently her special place. As quietly as I could, I crawled back into my bag, making sure my camera was handy and ready for the "shot of a lifetime" at dawn. That picture would have highlighted this story, except that the nanny's breakfast schedule was well before sun-up, somewhere else. With thousands of visitors, I doubt this small herd of goats still claims the peak, but, for all I know, they may yet linger on adjacent Green Mountain.

Leavenworth

I CARRY WARM PERSONAL FEELINGS for the Leavenworth Valley, in that I was involved early on in its transformation from Scandinavian to Bavarian. Leavenworth originally was a lumber mill town that ran out of forest and income. To give it new life, the University of Washington College of Architecture was asked to come up with a new image to promote tourism. The choice was either to enhance its original Scandinavian character, or to create a new happy-go-lucky Bavarian-type mountain village. The latter won out.

In view of my Bavarian background, I made early contacts with the city fathers during its development. The town's backyard valley was a forgotten item. First, I made a color slide documentary of both sides of the valley during different seasons, with comparison slides of the Bavarian valley where I was raised. Then I gave a slide show to all the kids in the local school, and later in the evening to their parents in the Town Hall, where I made a case for preserving and enhancing the valleys as well, to complement the town façade.

When I learned that a contingent of local business people made visits to the Alps, and came back with all kinds of "great ideas," like an amusement park with a little railroad on the riverfront island, I showed them some of the river parks I had designed that would stand flooding and remain natural—to get them off their "Coney Island" mentality. With little cost, they could have a great nature park. I also advised them about my engineering solutions for flood control. They followed my advice.

Over the years, I've enjoyed biking on summer evenings through the valley, or having fun at the Rathskeller basement restaurant, where they would ask me to do a Schuhplattler Bavarian dance to their accordion music. I often celebrate with the many tapes of Bavarian and Austrian mountain music that I've bought there.

Legacy

When Wolf closed down his engineering consulting business in 1975, he was already sixty-three years old, and had certainly earned the right to retire. Yet, the benefit of remarkable genes and a wellspring of inexhaustible energy allowed him to continue in his new career throughout the 1990s, with slide show presentations still being given as late as 2004. He compiled a long list of accomplishments in shoreline restoration projects, and a bibliography of beachfront assessments on Puget Sound that includes more than 130 reports. He walked every mile of Whatcom County shoreline, and thereby converted the county government completely to his system. Seattle City Parks and Washington State Parks officials considered him the "go-to guy" for enhancing public recreation areas. The Washington State Department of Ecology was ultimately home to his protégés.

But Wolf wasn't universally loved everywhere he went. He had a direct, no-nonsense, German delivery of ideas that sometimes lacked the mollifying touch so useful in American-style negotiation. When he knew he was right, he might not have been the best listener, though when he knew he had made a mistake in a design, he was quick to own up to it first, perhaps before anyone else could use it against him. "There were people in King County and in the Corps of Engineers that didn't like me much," he ponders reflectively, remembering clashes over jurisdiction and pedigree. Some academics resented his uncredentialed presumptuousness. At times, the Washington State Department of Fisheries didn't care for him much, either; in a close battle of conflicting interests, he had an irritating tendency to put the needs of human recreation over the needs of fish. (These arguing twins of conservation and recreation access are a common feature of political life in the Pacific Northwest. Wolf always felt that using recreation to inspire conservation would ultimately save the fish—and a lot more.)

But he did underscore the need for government agencies to start working collaboratively rather than adversarially, and today the Department of Fisheries and the Department of Ecology have a much more successful and productive relationship than they had in Wolf's early days, largely as a result of his philosophy taking hold. As a living conduit of ideas and energy, Wolf created connections to enhance work for the public good—in any sphere of interest he engaged in. He *engineered* political acceptance.

Today, retired, Wolf is more of a legend in his professional circles than a participant. His core ideas, that bulkheading is a bad thing, and that damaging a public resource for personal gain is heretical, are alive and well throughout his field. It would be comforting to say that his vision of "allemansrecht" had gained a permanent foothold in Puget Sound planning, but his lasting legacy is rather in his shoreline restoration designs—a partial victory, with which Wolf will have to be content for now.

The glacially slow process of changing American beliefs about real estate ownership, if it is ever to take place, will bring fruit to a different generation than ours. But Wolf's enlightenment of the community to the public benefits of managing integrated shorelines, rather than rows of detached parcels of dead beach, helped create a revolution in public attitudes about land management. This revolution is still in process today.

Hugh Shipman, coastal geologist with the Washington State Department of Ecology and former student of Wolf Bauer, offered a testimonial regarding Wolf's legacy to the Northwest in a letter to a colleague:

As a coastal geologist, working for Washington's shoreline management program, it has been impossible for me not to encounter Wolf's ideas, his projects, or for that matter, Wolf himself.

Wolf recognized that in order to effect enlightened shoreline stewardship, planners, managers, and the general public had to understand coastal processes. He also recognized that the existing scientific community, through their academic caution and their language, had failed to do this. Wolf's extensive knowledge of local shoreline geology and his strong sense of the shore as a public resource led him to become an impassioned, but knowledgeable, advocate for coastal management. He developed his own lexicon for shoreline processes, for beach and river classification, and for coastal management. Terms like "feeder bluff," "accretion beach," "shore-process corridor," and "drift sill" are common terms in our region, and many are sprinkled through Washington's state and local shoreline regulations.

Wolf understood local beaches well from years of walking, kayaking, and observing. He also was a student of beaches in other parts of the world. This provided him the confidence to be creative in a field where most engineers adhere to a very limited range of solutions, almost all of which use the beach as little more than a foundation on which to build a wall or to pile rock....

The training of most coastal geologists and engineers is founded on principles and examples from sand-dominated systems and open ocean shorelines. This training turns out to be poor preparation for Puget Sound's mixed sand and gravel beaches, moderate exposure, and bluff-backed shoreline. What Bauer lacked in formal coastal training and "accepted" terminology, he has more than made up for in the quality of his understanding of the unique characteristics of beaches and rivers in this region....

Perhaps Bauer's greatest gift was as a teacher. His ability to explain the way things worked was tremendous. At any project or meeting we attended together, I always came away feeling I had learned something. His lasting legacy to us all is significant.[77]

Perhaps a personal anecdote of Shipman's leaves a fitting image with which to end this chapter of Wolf's story. In the 1990s, there was a movement to build a shoreline bulkhead at the base of Seattle's Magnolia Bluff, at the entrance to Salmon Bay. The City had mandated that they explore "soft" remedies first, and so Wolf was brought in to assess the bluff, which was, coincidentally, the view he had from his home and office window in Ballard. The small crew of Wolf and the Washington State Department of Ecology and Seattle city engineers approached the bluff from above until they reached the edge, all fronted by private homes. For government agents, trespassing on private property is something done with much anxiety and trepidation. But without those constraints, free-lance Wolf, only in his early eighties, wordlessly proceeded to disappear over the embankment and slide his way down the steep slope to the shore, nearly two hundred feet below. After all, isn't it presumptuous of any transient man to think he can "own" a landform birthed by the last ice age fifteen thousand years ago?

Disconcerted and oppressed by protocol, the engineers were all reluctant to follow, but with legitimate public access a matter of some time and distance away, they surreptitiously followed him. At the conclusion of their discussions, they were faced with the same problem of time and space in returning up the cliff to their vehicles. Scouting around for an expedient method, Wolf spotted a rope hanging down from a stump at the top of the bluff, no doubt left by some local children. Like a Bavarian ibex, wasting no time, Wolf charged up to the rope end and hoisted himself briskly up the face, hand over hand, feet barely touching the ground. The astounded men, each young enough to be his son, if not grandson, and rooted firmly in professional etiquette, stamped and stammered in the face of this octogenarian's dare. Slowly, one by one, glancing around nervously for witnesses, the group joined their leader at the top—two hundred feet above Puget Sound.

A better exemplification of Wolf challenging the pack can hardly be imagined.

EPILOGUE

FROM HIS DAYS AS A MASCOT in the Kaiser's Navy to the present, Wolf Bauer has led an extraordinary life. He is the son of two different homelands whose relations have run the gamut from vicious hostility to cordial alliance. He was imprinted in his youth with the values and perspectives of the Germany of a century ago, yet he is unmistakably an all-American boy. He calls himself an immigrant, but he's been walking our native streets since long before most of us were born. His pioneer family can trace its roots to Seattle nearly a century earlier than most of its current natives. He has lived his long life with a foot in two worldviews, to the benefit of all of us who call the Northwest home.

(Left to right) Lynn Hyde, Lisa Parsons of the Middle Green River Coalition, and Wolf Bauer at the newly named Wolf Bauer Lodge at Flaming Geyser State Park. PHOTO COURTESY OF LISA PARSONS.

In small communities of climbers, kayakers, skiers, and conservationists, the name Wolf Bauer is known and admired, but he remains largely unknown to the general public. Fortunately, in 2009, Washington State Parks and Recreation formally recognized Wolf's tremendous contributions in a way that will help rectify that. At a ceremony held on May 2, during the 24th Annual Green River Clean-Up,[78] the Lodge at Flaming Geyser State Park in the Green River Gorge was officially renamed the Wolf Bauer Lodge, finally granting him permanent recognition for what he considers to be his most important legacy.

As Wolf Bauer's biographer, I have gotten to know him well, learned tremendously from his insights, and derived great inspiration to participate in the battles that face our generation. Unlike so many elders, he remains unflappably curious and engaged with life on Planet Earth, always open to new possibilities, and always hopeful that mankind can rally to save itself from its own devastating power. Before allowing him to have the last word, I will pass on something he said in passing early in our work together in 2003 that I found singularly revelatory about his nature: "I wish I could live another twenty years.... There are so many interesting people I would like to know." I am glad I have the privilege of knowing you, Wolf Bauer. We are all in your debt.

Nature, Our Subtle Teacher

WHEN WE QUESTION SOMEONE'S STATEMENT OR STORY, but later find convincing proof of its accuracy, we must admit in all honesty that "seeing is believing." We've all learned, from early childhood on, how difficult that realization can be—think "Santa." Isn't it still, for example, a recurring thrill and proof-in-the-pudding illustration that our Earth is a sphere when we spy only the mast-tops of an approaching ship coming over the horizon? One can imagine how preposterous that contention must have seemed at one time. But seeing is believing. A later, but similarly surprising discovery of facts was made through Darwin's meticulous research, findings, and conclusions, all leading to an ever-expanding understanding of Earth's life-forms over vast time periods.

Suddenly, our globe's geologic "libraries" came into focus, with their miles of layered shelves. They are everywhere, with their open and closed stacks, often neatly arranged in periodic sequence for easy chronology. We catalogue layer upon layer of these history markers, with their preserved pages depicting Earth's geology and trapped paleontology in a world of climate changes. Even in the much shorter periods of glaciation cycles, we find trapped and preserved life forms. Children who have preserved leaves, flowers, or insects in their books can recognize that long time and pressure were involved in producing the result, even without knowing how calcium or silica can replace an organic body. Science has yet to determine the chemistry and physiology of fish adapted to the pressure and darkness of abyssal depths, or of the primitive, but specialized, plant life that grows over hot ocean bottom vents, sans oxygen. Will our inborn curiosity ever be allayed about life on this lonely planet? I hope not!

Thoughts for Tomorrow

OUR PHYSICAL LANDSCAPES are changing faster than our perceptions and reactions. Life-sustaining resources are shrinking. The basic laws of supply and demand have operated on our planet for eons, but opportunities to affect their deadly cycles came only recently, with the appearance of man. Our conservation efforts have been stymied, in part, by human-invented religious dogma that frowns on advocating world-wide birth control to ensure adequate space and food supply, so we "have it coming." The time has come for Mother Nature to give us a kick in the pants to get our attention—namely by showing that climate changes are not necessarily brought about by long-term natural cycles and causes, let alone by angry gods.

Living, so to speak, from hand-to-mouth on our little planet, we are a luck-trusting species that still has little knowledge of where and when the next uncomfortable or deadly natural event will strike. Our ecosphere, what the Greeks called "Gaia," or Mother Earth, is a constantly balancing system, both outside and within our earthly domain. Whether we are faced with meteors and meteorites, life-affecting cosmic rays, sunspots, or ozone belt changes ... whether we are faced with earthquakes, tsunamis, hurricanes, firestorms, floods, storm waves, mudflows and lava flows, or Earth-circling dust and chemical air pollution ... whether we are faced with climate changes or with melting ice and rising coastal water levels, we are all in this together! We have enough to keep us busy in a world-wide team effort, without being side-tracked by outmoded religious wars and edicts, international petty politics, and the lack of an Earth-community spirit. I ask myself, are there any possibilities or indications that we could change course?

Well, yes, I think there are! We are definitely approaching a period of world-wide Internet communications. It is a sudden and huge leap, especially in terms of interaction on the "common man" level, that provides us with a forum in which we can ignore the protocol demanded in international deliberations. Some of Germany's postwar youth were among the first in Europe to become politically active in joining the new Green Party, as an acceptable political alternative. With ever-widening travel and communication opportunities, an organized world youth could certainly breathe new life into fractured world politics.

All I can say is: It's your world. Never has there been such an opportunity. Good luck—you'll need it!

Sound Country Reflections

by Wolf Bauer

From homeland Alps, I came one day,
Wide-eyed, adventure-bound.
T'was in the merry month of May
That I first saw the Sound.

Tradition-wise we dipped, then licked
Our fingers at the beach,
A hands-on lesson, Father picked,
To prove the ocean's reach.

The "Inland Sea," so there it lay,
Twixt mountain ranges white,
Homesick no more, I, to this day,
Still marvel at the sight!

But since those years in travel made,
Through stormy height and seas,
With ice-axe, ski, or paddle blade,
My mind is not at ease.

The Sound has changed, some mountains, too,
At times have blown their top,
As though to warn, with no adieu,
It's time for us to stop.

And learn that runoffs need their space
When pouring snow-melt o'er the land,
And when to end the crowding pace
That threatens farm and food demand.

Sustain an agro-life, we can,
Both from the land and sea,
Provided that in man's lifespan
Some birth control there be!

World leadership—a vacuum still,
Religious strife—no end in sight,
To nature's warnings—where's our will?
Is over-crowding not our right?

So there I go, political,
Showing my real hand?
(No) Just hoping for poetical
Justice for our land!

ACKNOWLEDGMENTS

from Wolf

WHETHER THEY REALIZE IT OR NOT, friends and relatives, as well as some teachers, clients and writers, have all contributed to my life directly or indirectly. Family-wise, there is my sister Friedl Ney, who lives near me in Anacortes, my daughter-in-law Ingrid Fabianson and granddaughters Sara and Laura Bauer in Friday Harbor, my former wife Harriet Bauer, and sons Rocky and Larry Bauer in Seattle. Of the many friends still alive to whom I am indebted, there are climbers I have known for more than sixty years, like Jim and Lou Whittaker and later Lou's son, Peter, and wife, Ingrid, who, like myself, calls Munich her "Bavarian cradle." I share my lingering memories of the Mountain Rescue Council's Ome Daiber through his wife Matie and her daughters, and of Otto Trott through his wife Ruth and five daughters. Visits also continue with Dee Molenaar, author and illustrator of the classic volume *The Challenge of Rainier*, as well as his landform maps of Northwest coast mountain ranges. There are also the friends who are taken for granted, but whose lifestyle and philosophy reinforce and add to one's own. Lois and Ward Irwin of The Mountaineers and the Washington Kayak Club know of what I speak. Lucky me! I am lucky to have such supportive lifelines.

Last but not least, I wish to express my appreciation to the public at large for the governmental recognitions and public commentary regarding my efforts in advancing recreational and environmental causes in the American and Canadian Pacific Northwest. In British Columbia, especially, government ecologist Jonathan Secter became an enthusiastic proponent of my environmental approaches to the management of streamways and coastal shores.

In Washington State, coastal geologist Hugh Shipman, long associated with the Department of Ecology, became an early supporter of my shore-system philosophies and management solutions. As of this writing, both

Secter and Shipman continue to further the public dissemination of my ideas about shoreline ecology. Thank you for keeping my work alive.

I am also indebted to American Society of Landscape Architects member Bruce Dees of Tacoma for his efforts to have me considered for The LaGasse Medal.[79] The award has been a tremendous source of personal gratification for me at the end of a long career.

from Lynn

I would primarily like to thank Wolf for sharing his remarkable stories with me, and for entrusting them to a stranger from another generation. It has been a rare and invaluable lesson in the fading legacy of optimism and commitment to life and one's community —concepts that are sadly far too rare in the cynical and jaded 21st century.

I would also like to thank those who made my research possible: Wolf's family members—Friedl Ney, Harriet and Larry Bauer, Sara and Laura Bauer, and Ingrid Fabianson—for their insider stories and hospitality; Drs. Richard and Christiane May of Kreuth, Jim, Lou and Ingrid Whittaker, and Susan and Jim Meredith—again for insider stories and hospitality; the extraordinary historian Lowell "Skoogle" Skoog for his boundless patience and guidance; The Mountaineers Books publisher Helen Cherullo—for her editorial input and support; Peter Giese for sharing photos and stories of his father, Hans Otto, Wolf's fellow traveler through Northwest mountaineering history; Hugh Shipman and Jonathan Secter—for their clear assessments of Wolf's professional contributions and environmental legacy, as well as for their own efforts in the cause; Susan Taft and the indefatigable Tom O'Keefe of American Whitewater for enlightening me on the paddling history of the Northwest; Fran Troje, Queen of the Kayak—for bringing me and Wolf together for this project; and my son, Graham Mills, for allowing himself to be dragged through the Bavarian Alps in search of the well-spring of Wolf's vision, as ever, humoring his mother's flights of fancy with little complaint.

Lastly, I would like to thank all the uncounted and unnoticed ranks of Wolf's protégés and admirers who shared their insights: Lisa Parsons of the Middle Green River Coalition (who also deserves thanks for picking up Wolf's saber in the Gorge cause); kayaking alumnus Brock Evans, president of the Endangered Species Coalition; Tom Murdoch of the Adopt-a-Stream Foundation—all committed to carrying on the mission of preserving the natural world of the Northwest for the enjoyment and well-being of all.

It has been a wonderful journey, and my heartfelt gratitude goes out to all those I met along the way. Keep up the good fight!

NOTES

[1] The epic poem/song written by Julius Mosen in 1832 proclaims that Hofer's last words were "Ach, wie schießt ihr schlecht! Ade, mein Land Tirol!" or "Oh, how poorly you shoot! Goodbye, my land, Tyrol!" This can be found in the short biography published in German: *Andreas Hofer* by Hans Kramer, published by A. Weger's Buchhandlung, Brixen, 1963.

[2] *The Seattle Post-Intelligencer,* September 14, 1927.

[3] Hubert Anton Bauer's study of the way tides work on the shoreline was published in his article "A World Map of Tides." *Geographical Review* American Geographical Society, Vol. 23, No. 2 (Apr., 1933), pp. 259-270.

[4] David Thomas Murphy, *German Exploration of the Polar World: A History, 1870–1940* (Lincoln, Nebraska, and London: University of Nebraska Press, 2002), p. 210.

[5] A surviving Seattle cable car is on display in the Smithsonian Institution in Washington, D.C.

[6] Wolf Bauer, "Telemarks, Sitzmarks, and Other Early Impressions," *Mountaineer Annual*, 1963 (Seattle: The Mountaineers), pp. 9-10.

[7] Skijoring is a ski sport that entails being pulled like a water skier behind a dog, horse or vehicle.

[8] Greg Johnston. "Silver Mettle: Hell-bent Memories Still Fresh After 60 Years." *Seattle Post-Intelligencer*, April 18, 1994.

[9] ibid.

[10] Bauer, "Telemarks, Sitzmarks, and Other Early Impressions," pp. 14-15.

[11] Wolf had crafted home-made metal edges for his skis, and the metal held the broken wood together.

[12] This would be the unhappy Hans Otto Giese, who Wolf claims never fully forgave him.

[13] Though Wolf participated in the 1935 Olympic Trials for both downhill and slalom, he was not selected.

[14] "Mountaineers' Marathon Ski Racers All Set", *The Seattle Times,* March 14, 1936

[15] The winning time was 4:37:23.

[16] Andy Anderson, "Skiing in Retrospect," *Mountaineer Annual*, 1936, p. 19.

[17] For more information on the history of skiing in the Pacific Northwest, visit Lowell Skoog's excellent Alpenglow Ski Mountaineering History Project at www.alpenglow.org.

[18] Wolf Bauer, "The North Face of Mount Rainier," *Mountaineer Annual*, 1934 (Seattle: The Mountaineers), pp. 3-5.

[19] A bergschrund is a gap or crevasse that forms at the edge of a glacier, where moving ice separates from stationary ice on the mountain. Wolf defined "schrunds" as "the melted back gaps on the sides of a glacier."

[20] Jim Kjeldsen, *The Mountaineers: A History.* (Seattle: The Mountaineers Books, 1998), p. 53.

[21] Kjeldsen, p. 53.

[22] Harry Majors. Recorded interview of Wolf Bauer. August 27, 1974. University of Washington Special Collections, Accession 1669-2, Tape 182.

[23] The original Cowen Park Bridge, replaced in 1936 by the current concrete bridge, was a wooden trestle bridge, and the ravine, prior to absorbing Interstate 5 construction fill in the 1960s, was much deeper than it is today. The Ravenna Creek was still running above ground in 1935.

[24] Majors interview.

[25] Kjeldsen, p. 54.

[26] Unknown author, "Climbers," *Mountaineer Annual*, 1968 (Seattle: The Mountaineers) p.50.

[27] Wolf Bauer, "The Final Conquest," *Mountaineer Annual*, 1935 (Seattle: The Mountaineers).

[28] Majors interview.

[29] "Climbers."

[30] Majors interview.

[31] Malcolm S. Bates, *Cascade Voices: Conversations with Washington Mountaineers,* (Seattle: The Mountaineers Books, 1998), p. 32.

[32] George MacGowan. "Goode Conquest." *Mountaineer Annual*, 1936 (Seattle: The Mountaineers), p. 14.

[33] Majors interview.

[34] Bates, p. 12.

[35] Harry Majors. Internet posting September 19, 2003. See: http://cascadeclimbers.com/forum/ubbthreads.php/topics/218286/Re_Mox_Peaks_Twin_Spires#Post218286

[36] Bauer, "Final Conquest," pp. 5-6

[37] Kjeldsen, p. 62.

[38] Lowell Skoog, "Wolf Bauer: Eighty Years on the Sharp End," *Northwest Mountaineering Journal,* Summer 2005, issue 2. http://www.mountaineers.org/nwmj/05/issue2.html.

[39] A skyhook is the crane system on freighters that can swing a cargo load over the side of a ship.

[40] This section on labor unrest is an excerpt from Wolf Bauer's "Life at Roche Harbor in the 'Roaring Thirties,'" *Island Scene: the Journal of the San Juan Islands,* January 15, 2003.

[41] For an exhaustive study of the treatment of German-Americans during World War II, see Arnold Krammer's *Undue Process: The Untold Story of America's German Alien Internees* (Boulder: Rowman and Littlefield Publishers, 1997).

[42] Peter Giese, son of Hans Otto Giese, personal communication, 8/7/2009.

[43] Harvey Manning is given credit for saying this about the early founders of Mountain Rescue. Manning writes about them in his book *REI: 50 Years of Climbing Together* (Seattle: REI, 1988), p. 63. However, in the book Manning places the remark in quotes, prefacing it with, "commentators have noted," with no concrete attribution made.

[44] Ben Groff, "Indomitable Ome Daiber," *The Seattle Times/Post-Intelligencer,* May 3, 1987.

[45] Harry Majors, "Mt. Index First Ascents," *Northwest Mountaineering Journal,* Summer 2004, issue 1. http://www.mountaineers.org/NWMJ/04/issue1.html.

[46] Ira Spring, *An Ice Axe, a Camera, and a Jar of Peanut Butter,* (Seattle: The Mountaineers Books, 1998), p. 102.

[47] This stump can now be found at the northbound Smokey Point rest stop on Interstate 5, milepost 207, 11 miles north of Everett, Washington.

[48] The friendly tug-of-war for credit for the Mountain Rescue logo has gone on between Wolf and Otto Trott for decades, and continues to this day in their dueling biographies. See *The Making of a Rescuer: the Inspiring Life of Otto T. Trott, MD* by Nicholas Campbell Corff. (Victoria, B.C.: Trafford Publishing, 2008). The 1953 Mountaineers pamphlet, "Can You Handle an Emergency?", written by Wolf Bauer, was reprinted from the club magazine *The Mountaineer.* Volume XLV, No. 13, 1952.

[49] To view Wolf's map, visit American Whitewater at the following web link: http://www.americanwhitewater.org/content/Document_view_documentid_578_

[50] Susan L. Taft, personal communication. For a thorough history of river paddling, see her book *The River Chasers: A History of American Whitewater Paddling.* (Mukilteo, WA: Flowing Water Press and Alpen Books Press, 2001).

[51] The mission of American Whitewater is "to conserve and restore America's whitewater resources and to enhance opportunities to enjoy them safely," which reflects their role as the primary advocates for whitewater resources in the United States. In addition to helping found American Whitewater, Wolf was one of the founders of the Adopt-a-Stream Foundation, a non-profit environmental education and habitat restoration organization. Their mission is to teach people to become stewards of their watersheds.

[52] Wolf Bauer, "Pioneering a New Sport: Early Club History," article written for Washington Kayak Club history.

[53] Matt Coco, "Das Faltboot," *The Mountaineer* (Seattle: The Mountaineers), Spring 2000, Interview of Susan Meredith by Matt Coco.

[54] Wolf Bauer, "1950 Foldboating Season," *Mountaineer Annual,*1950 (Seattle: The Mountaineers), pp. 48-49.

[55] Wolf Bauer, "Waterways Unlimited," *Northwest Boating World,* June, 1958.

[56] Wolf Bauer, "Paddle-Cruising Our Island Waterways," *Northwest Boating World,* April, 1959.

[57] Bill Holm is an acclaimed scholar on Northwest Coast Indian art, and his eight books on the subject have won him notoriety with both scholars and Northwest Coast native peoples. His 1965 seminal work, *Northwest Coast Indian Art: An Analysis of Form,* is currently in its seventeenth printing. In 2003, the Bill Holm Center for the Study of Northwest Coast Art was established at the University of Washington's Burke Museum in Seattle to ensure that his legacy in the field is continued.

[58] Susan Hull Meredith, "1948-1976.", *Washington Kayak Club.* January, 1976, vol. 12 no.1.

[59] Wolf Bauer, "The Geo-Hydraulic System as a Basis for Shoreline Management," professional paper delivered at the Shore Management Symposium of Canada in Victoria, British Columbia, October 4, 1978: 17.

[60] ibid. 20.

[61] Korte and Dee Brueckmann, "Wolf Bauer's Mission," *Oceans.* May, 1987, vol. 20 no. 2, pp.48-53.

[62] Gordy Holt, "Saving Our Dying Beaches," *Seattle Post-Intelligencer,* June 4, 1985.

[63] Wolf Bauer, *A Time for Understanding,* Our Heritage of Sound and Stream Series. (Seattle: The Mountaineers, 1970), pp. 3-6.

64 The Light Division of Tacoma's Department of Public Utilities now goes by the name of Tacoma Power, though in the 1950s it went by the name of Tacoma City Light, a name that is still commonly heard.

65 David Wilma, "Tacoma City Light's Mayfield Dam on the Cowlitz River Generates Electric on March 30, 1963," HistoryLink: The Free Online Encyclopedia of Washington State History, December 16, 2002. http://historylink.org/essays/output.cfm?file_id=5027.

66 The Congressional declaration of policy reads: "It is hereby declared to be the policy of the United States that certain selected rivers of the Nation which, with their immediate environments, possess outstandingly remarkable scenic, recreational, geologic, fish and wildlife, historic, cultural, or other similar values, shall be preserved in free-flowing condition, and that they and their immediate environments shall be protected for the benefit and enjoyment of present and future generations."

67 Wolf Bauer, "Concept of River Wildness," *The Wild Cascades*. North Cascades Conservation Council, October-November, 1964: p. 13.

68 Wolf Bauer. "A Ribbon of Wilderness in Our Midst," *The Seattle Times,* November 13, 1966: 10-11. Also in *The Wild Cascades*. North Cascades Conservation Council, October-November, 1965.

69 Brueckmann, p. 53.

70 The mission statement of WEC says it all: Washington Environmental Council protects what Washingtonians care about—our land and water, fish and wildlife, and our special way of life. We engage the public and decision makers to improve and enforce protections for the health and well-being of our communities. Our work ensures that we will all enjoy natural areas, clean air and clean water for generations to come.

71 Wolf Bauer, *A Time for Understanding*, (Seattle: The Mountaineers Books, 1970), back cover.

72 According to the Washington State Department of Ecology, Washington's Shoreline Management Act (SMA) was adopted by the public in a 1972 referendum "to prevent the inherent harm in an uncoordinated and piecemeal development of the state's shorelines." The SMA has three broad policies:

   1. Encourage water-dependent uses: "uses shall be preferred which are consistent with control of pollution and prevention of damage to the natural environment, or are unique to or dependent upon use of the states' shorelines…"

   2. Protect shoreline natural resources, including "…the land and its vegetation and wildlife, and the water of the state and their aquatic life…"

3. Promote public access: "the public's opportunity to enjoy the physical and aesthetic qualities of natural shorelines of the state shall be preserved to the greatest extent feasible consistent with the overall best interest of the state and the people generally."

Among the guidelines the State set forth are the priorities to:

- recognize and protect the state-wide interests over local interests
- preserve the natural character of the shoreline
- result in long-term over short-term benefit
- protect the resources and ecology of shorelines
- increase public access to publicly owned areas of the shorelines
- increase recreational opportunities for the public on shorelines

[73] Brueckmann, p. 53.

[74] ibid, p. 53.

[75] ibid, p. 50.

[76] Ibid, p. 48.

[77] Hugh Shipman (Washington State Department of Ecology), letter to Roy Metzgar (Everett Public Works, Everett, Wa.), Spring 1999.

[78] The Annual Green River Clean-Up is a stewardship festival held at the Green River Gorge each spring, sponsored in 2009 by the Washington Recreational River Runners, Friends of the Green, and the Washington Kayak Club. Information on the event and on preservation efforts can be made by visiting the Middle Green River Coalition website at: http://www.mgrc.org.

[79] The American Society of Landscape Architects offers this national award annually to no more than two recipients "to recognize individuals who have made notable contributions to the management and conservancy of natural resources and/or public landscapes." The award's namesake, Alfred B. LaGasse, spent his career as a proponent of "the proper management of the nation's public lands and the judicious use of the country's natural resources."

BIBLIOGRAPHY

Allen, E. John B. *The Culture and Sport of Skiing: From Antiquity to World War II.* Amherst: University of Massachusetts Press, 2007.

Anderson, Andy. "Skiing in Retrospect," *Mountaineer Annual*, 1936. Seattle: The Mountaineers.

Bates, Malcolm S. *Cascade Voices: Conversations with Washington Mountaineers.* Seattle: The Mountaineers Books, 1998.

Bauer, Hubert Anton. "A World Map of Tides." *Geographical Review.* American Geographical Society, April 1933, vol. 23, no. 2.

Bauer, Wolf. "1950 Foldboating Season," *Mountaineer Annual*, 1950. Seattle: The Mountaineers.

Bauer, Wolf. "A Ribbon of Wilderness in Our Midst," *The Seattle Times*, November 13, 1966.

Bauer, Wolf. "A Time for Understanding," Our Heritage of Sound and Stream Series. Seattle: The Mountaineers, 1970.

Bauer, Wolf. "Concept of River Wildness," *The Wild Cascades.* North Cascades Conservation Council, October-November, 1964.

Bauer, Wolf. Interview by Harry Majors, University of Washington Libraries, Special Collections, Accession 1669-2, Audio Tape 182. August 27, 1974.

Bauer, Wolf. "Life at Roche Harbor in the 'Roaring Thirties.'" *Island Scene: Journal of the San Juan Islands.* January 15, 2003.

Bauer, Wolf. "Pioneering a New Sport: Early Club History." Written for Washington Kayak Club history.

Bauer, Wolf. "Telemarks, Sitzmarks, and Other Early Impressions," *Mountaineer Annual*, 1963. Seattle: The Mountaineers.

Bauer, Wolf. "The Geo-Hydraulic System as a Basis for Shoreline Management." Professional paper delivered at the Shore Management Symposium of Canada in Victoria, British Columbia, October 4, 1978.

Bauer, Wolf. "The Final Conquest." *Mountaineer Annual*, 1935. Seattle: The Mountaineers.

Bauer, Wolf. "The North Face of Mount Rainier." *Mountaineer Annual*, 1934.

Seattle: The Mountaineers.

Bauer, Wolf. "Paddle-Cruising Our Island Waterways." *Northwest Boating World,* April, 1959.

Bauer, Wolf. "Waterways Unlimited." *Northwest Boating World.* June, 1958.

Brueckmann, Korte and Dee, "Wolf Bauer's Mission," *Oceans.* May, 1987, vol. 20, no. 2.

Coco, Matt. "Das Faltboot." *The Mountaineer.* Spring, 2000. Seattle: The Mountaineers.

Corff, Nicholas Campbell. *The Making of a Rescuer: the Inspiring Life of Otto T. Trott, MD.* Victoria, BC: Trafford Publishing, 2008.

Groff, Ben. "Indomitable Ome Daiber." *The Seattle Times/Post-Intelligencer,* May 3, 1987.

Holm, Bill. *Northwest Coast Indian Art: An Analysis of Form.* Seattle: University of Washington Press, 1965.

Holt, Gordy. "Saving Our Dying Beaches." *Seattle Post-Intelligencer.* June 4, 1985.

Johnson, Greg. "Silver Mettle: Hell-bent Memories Still Fresh After 60 Years." *Seattle Post-Intelligencer,* April 18, 1994.

Kjeldsen, Jim. *The Mountaineers: A History.* Seattle: The Mountaineers Books, 1998.

Kramer, Hans. *Andreas Hofer.* Brixen: A. Weger's Buchhandlung, 1963.

Krammer, Arnold. *Undue Process: The Untold Story of America's German Alien Internees.* Boulder: Rowman and Littlefield Publishers, 1997.

MacGowan, George. "Goode Conquest," *Mountaineer Annual,* 1936. Seattle: The Mountaineers.

Majors, Harry. Recorded interview of Wolf Bauer. August 27, 1974. University of Washington Special Collections, Accession 1669-2, Tape 182.

Majors, Harry. "Mt. Index First Ascents." *Northwest Mountaineering Journal,* Summer 2004, issue 1. http://www.mountaineers.org/NWMJ/04/issue1.html.

Manning, Harvey. *REI: 50 Years of Climbing Together.* Seattle: REI, 1988.

Meredith, Susan Hull. "1948-1976," *Washington Kayak Club.* January, 1976, vol. 12 no.1.

Murphy, David Thomas. *German Exploration of the Polar World: A History, 1870-1940.* Lincoln, Nebraska, and London: University of Nebraska Press, 2002.

Skoog, Lowell. "Wolf Bauer: Eighty Years on the Sharp End." *Northwest Mountaineering Journal*, Summer 2005, issue 2. http://www.mountaineers.org/nwmj/05/issue2.html.

Spring, Ira. *An Ice Axe, a Camera, and a Jar of Peanut Butter.* Seattle: The Mountaineers Books, 1998.

Taft, Susan. *The River Chasers: A History of American Whitewater Paddling.* Mukilteo, WA: Flowing Water Press and Alpen Books Press, 2001.

Unknown author. "Climbers." *Mountaineer Annual*, 1968. Seattle: The Mountaineers.

Unknown author. "Mountaineers' Marathon Ski Racers All Set," *The Seattle Times,* March 14, 1936.

INDEX